Praise for *The Female Playback in Bombay Cinema*

"Building on the author's wealth of research across the long history of the recorded female singing voice in Bombay cinema, this groundbreaking book sets the scene for a long-overdue shift of scholarly focus from the visual to the aural. Jhingan surveys her field with authority, care, and passion. The book itself sings."

—Rosie Thomas, author of *Bombay Before Bollywood*

"*The Female Playback in Bombay Cinema* shows how the sonic attributes and affective force of the female voice in Bombay cinema have been shaped by media assemblages, from the early days of playback to the televised reality shows and digital platforms of the 2020s. Jhingan's sensitive analysis of the shifting relationships between the visual and the aural, body and voice, makes an important contribution to cinema and sound studies within South Asia and beyond."

—Amanda Weidman, author of *Brought to Life by the Voice: Playback Singing and Cultural Politics in South India*

"Shikha Jhingan's book maps out the complex and contested destabilization and emergence of new norms for the female playback singing voice from the 1940s to the present, discussing changing relationships between voice, body, technology, and listening practices."

—Neepa Majumdar, director of graduate studies for the Film and Media Studies Program, University of Pittsburgh

"*The Female Playback in Bombay Cinema* maps a dazzling itinerary of the female voice from radio, gramophone, and playback through to audiocassette, television reality shows, and YouTube uploads. Shikha Jhingan pursues rigorous film, musical, and sound analysis with an alertness to the wider intermedial imprint of the voice. A landmark for the field."

—Ravi Vasudevan, codirector of Sarai, Centre for the Study of Developing Societies

The Female Playback in Bombay Cinema

Contemporary Approaches to Film and Media Series

A complete listing of the books in this series can be found online at wsupress.wayne.edu.

General Editor

Barry Keith Grant
Brock University

The Female Playback in Bombay Cinema

Voice, Body, Technology

Shikha Jhingan

WAYNE STATE UNIVERSITY PRESS
DETROIT

ISBN 9780814350942 (paperback)
ISBN 9780814350959 (hardcover)
ISBN 9780814350966 (ebook)

Library of Congress Control Number: 2025931229

Cover art © 123rf. Cover design by Tracy Cox.

Published with the assistance of a fund established by Thelma Gray James of Wayne State University for the publication of folklore and English studies.

Wayne State University Press rests on Waawiyaataanong, also referred to as Detroit, the ancestral and contemporary homeland of the Three Fires Confederacy. These sovereign lands were granted by the Ojibwe, Odawa, Potawatomi, and Wyandot Nations, in 1807, through the Treaty of Detroit. Wayne State University Press affirms Indigenous sovereignty and honors all tribes with a connection to Detroit. With our Native neighbors, the press works to advance educational equity and promote a better future for the earth and all people.

Wayne State University Press
Leonard N. Simons Building
4809 Woodward Avenue
Detroit, Michigan 48201-1309

Visit us online at wsupress.wayne.edu.

In gratitude to Daisaku Ikeda

Contents

Acknowledgments

The book is born out of many abiding experiences, practices, and sonic immersions. I grew up listening to my father's singing of film songs at social gatherings, surrounded by enthusiastic listeners. At family weddings, the stars were my aunts singing Punjabi songs describing the feelings of love and separation. I soaked in the tunes, the words, and the sensory response to these sessions. In the 1990s, when I was an independent filmmaker, two of my projects formed the kernel of this study. With Ranjani Mazumdar I codirected a twelve-part documentary series on Bombay cinema. The episode on the female vamps pushed me to think about the singing voice. Later, I started research for a documentary on the Mirasans in Punjab, who sing for their patrons at life-cycle rituals. I recorded the voices of women singers in various genres, watching them as they sang with gestures and hand movements, and listened to their stories about the songs and the spaces in which they were performed. This deepened my interest in female genres of music and how we listen to them in a particular social and political context, who sings and who listens.

There are many people I would like to thank for my first book. It has grown from my dissertation that I submitted at the School of Arts and Aesthetics, JNU. I had a great opportunity to work with my supervisor, Ira Bhaskar. I have benefited enormously from my extended discussions with her on Hindi film songs and their cinematic presentation that enriched this project. Over the years, Ira has been a wonderful colleague and an exceptional friend.

This book wouldn't have been completed without the support of my Mediastorm family in Delhi. First and foremost, my deepest gratitude to Ranjani Mazumdar for encouraging me at every step as a friend and fellow traveler. She pushed me into research and academics in a manner that was far ahead of my own imagined capacity. I want to thank Ranjani for her rigorous reading of all of the chapters and thoughtful comments at every stage, from conceiving the project, dissertation writing and final outcome as a book. With Shohini Ghosh and Sabeena Gadihoke, I share a love for popular cinema and Hindi film songs. I want to thank Sabeena for sharing ideas, books, and readings and taking such an avid interest in my project. I am grateful to her for pointing me toward print media archival resources such as photographs and advertisements befitting my project. Shohini has been a victim of my constant babble about the book, which always resulted in bouncing off ideas that she generously shared with me. I have benefitted enormously from her encyclopedic knowledge about film songs. I am immensely grateful to Sabeena Kidwai for constantly nourishing me with her warmth, positivity, and sustained friendship. Charu Gargi has always been a phone call away, readily offering me timely help during my research trips to Bombay.

I owe a lot to the three Ravis of CSDS. Ravi Vasudevan has been a great support for all of my academic endeavors. His infectious smile after paper presentations made academia a far less intimidating space for me. I am grateful to him for inviting me to publish my work in *BioScope: South Asian Screen Studies* and giving me his vote of confidence. Ravi Sundaram has provided enthusiastic encouragement to me, lending me his ears and suggestions on important thematic tracks like piracy and the shifts from analog to digital, and helping me track valuable e-resources and readings. To Ravikant, I am indebted for sharing his insights into Hindi film songs, especially their circulation on radio shows and print media. I am especially grateful to him for helping me translate songs, access magazine archives, and bounce ideas. I consider myself fortunate to be in the company of my cinema studies colleagues at the School of Arts and Aesthetics, who have helped me enormously in bringing a sound studies perspectives to my engagement with cinema. Vena Hariharan and Kaushik Bhaumik have been forthcoming when I asked for resources, books, and their time. I have received tremendous help and intellectual sustenance from my colleagues in SAA, including Vibhushan Subba, Ratheesh Radhakrishnan, Parul Dave Mukherjee, Shukla Sawant, Y.S. Alone, Naman Ahuja, Suryanandini Narain, Bishnupriya Dutt, Ameet

Prakash, Urmimala Sircar Munsi, Partho Datta, Brahma Prakash Singh, Rustam Bharucha, and the late Kavita Singh. At JNU, I have been fortunate to enjoy the support of my colleagues Lata Singh, Udaya Kumar, Surajit Mazumdar, Ayesha Kidwai, Sucharita Sen, Nivedita Menon, and Navaneetha Mokkil.

Neepa Majumdar's enthusiastic interest, encouragement, and scholarly inputs have been crucial for shaping this project. While presenting academic work at conferences, I have been fortunate to get generative comments that widened the intellectual arc of this book. I want to thank Neepa Majumdar, Priya Jaikumar, Madhuja Mukherjee, Nitin Govil, Jonathan Sterne, Peter Bloom, Rosie Thomas, Pavitra Sundar, Usha Iyer, Meheli Sen, Kiranmayi Indraganti, Amanda Weidman, Nasreen Munni Kabir, G. Arunima, Madan Gopal Singh, Madhava Prasad, Lalitha Gopalan, Vebhuti Duggal, Jeebesh Bagchi, Richard Allen, Moinak Biswas, Anna Morcom, Tejaswini Ganti, Shuddhabrata Sengupta, Aditya Nigam, and Stephen P. Hughes for their interest in my project, feedback, and stimulating conversations. In no small measure my conversations with film scholars, art practitioners, filmmakers, and sound designers have enriched this book. I want to thank Kartik Nair, Pallavi Paul, Shaunak Sen, Amala Popurri, Priyanka Chhabra, and Suvani Suri for sharing their ideas with me or alerting me to films and their sonic complexity.

I owe a debt of gratitude to my wonderful colleagues at Lady Shri Ram College in Delhi, where I started writing my PhD dissertation. My colleagues Meenakshi Gopinath, Bindu Menon, Pankaj Jha, Arti Minocha, Nayana Dasgupta, Krishna Menon, Sumangala Damodaran, Sharada Nair, Sunalini Kumar, Shivani Kapoor, Shipra Nigam, Pooja Satyogi, and Ambar Ahmed provided a vibrant space for conversations and intellectual rigor. I want to thank Krishna for giving her helpful comments on one of the chapters. My deep gratitude to Bindu Menon for reading two chapters and giving me useful and detailed feedback.

There are many people whom I wish to thank for sharing their knowledge and love for music with me. I am indebted to Urmila Bhirdikar for introducing me to the debates on music and modernity. Amlan Das Gupta has been a great source of encouragement, and I am indebted to him for giving me insightful comments on my proposal. Gregory Booth gave me valuable feedback at an early stage of my project. I want to thank Vidya Rao, who has always been accessible and generous in sharing with me her enormous knowledge and insights in areas related to gender, voice, and Hindustani music. I have gained enormously by following Saba Dewan's posts and comments on Facebook covering a range of discussions, and links to *thumris*, *kajaris*, *ghazals*, and film songs. Kalidas's provocative insights into Hindustani classical music have been extremely engaging. The late Saleem Kidwai was always generous with sharing his thoughts and his encyclopedic knowledge of the repertoire of the courtesans. With Partho Datta and Ashwini Deshpande I have enjoyed extended listening sessions and conversations on diverse hues of Indian music. I am indebted to Lakshmi Subramanian for her enthusiastic support and encouragement. I have benefited enormously through my extended discussions with her on classical music, film music, singing shows on television, gender and performance, and cultural nationalism. I thank the James Beveridge Media Resource Centre at the AJK School of Mass Communication, Jamia Millia Islamia, for granting me a Senior Research Fellowship, which helped me to carry out much of my research on this subject. I received a generous grant from FOKUS/IAWRT that helped me enormously in my fieldwork in Mumbai.

I am deeply indebted to Jaichandiram, the founder and director of IAWRT, who passed away in July 2013, for her encouraging support. Friends at IWART-India have always provided fun, warmth, and support. I want to thank Sameena Mishra, Subasri Krishnan, Padmaja Shaw, Nupur Basu, Reena Mohan, Nina Sabnani, Kiron Bansal, Aparna Sanyal, Anitha Balachandran, Gauri Chakravarty, Bina Paul, Paromita Vohra, Aaradhana Kohli, Jabeen Merchant, Anchal Kapur, Archana Kapoor, Deepika Sharma, Anjali Monteiro, and the late Chandita Mukherjee for our warm exchanges and comraderies. When prodded, Paromita Vohra has always come up with dazzling information on songs and star singers.

For my fieldwork in Mumbai, I got timely help from Joy Roy, Sanjeev Sharma, and Bhavdeep Jaipurwale. Gitanjali Murari helped me source an entire season of *Indian Idol* from Sony TV. Esther Dubey has shared with me valuable material from her husband, Vijay Krishna Dubey's, collection of archival material. Nasreen Munni Kabir was extremely generous by offering to help me meet singers and music directors in the industry. Prashant Pandey helped me get access to sound studios and watch recordings of contemporary film songs in progress. Anuradha Paudwal, Shilpa Rao, Richa Sharma, Ila Arun, Shreya Ghoshal, Sunidhi Chauhan, Bela Sulakhe, Shantanu Moitra, Daman Sood, Prajakta Shukre, and Ankita Mishra were extremely generous with their time. This project would have been impossible without the support and help that I received from Urmila Joshi at the NFAI library in Pune. I want to thank Lakshmi Iyer, Arti Karkhanis, and Kiran Dhiwar at NFAI for their generous support during my archival research.

I want to thank the staff at the Shanta Ram Library and the *Times of India* archive in Mumbai for their kind help. In Delhi, the staff at the Soochna Bhavan was extremely helpful in getting me access to the print archive. Thanks to Smita Banerjee, Arti Wani, Bindu Menon, and my fellow dissertation writers at the School of Arts and Aesthetics. Smita was the one I disturbed at odd hours for mundane inquiries on the phone. I am grateful to the late Mr. Ghulam Rasool at the SAA library for his valuable help. Many thanks to Diwan Ram ji, Vinayak, Savita, Harsh, Moveen, Allauddin, and Dilip for making SAA such a pleasant place.

Marie Sweetman at Wayne State University Press has been a constant support. Thank you for showing interest in this project, for your timely input, and for pushing me to make the revisions. Sandra Judd, thank you for your support and patience and for your meticulous reading during copyediting. I am grateful to Carrie Teefey, Emily Gauronskas, and Wayne State University's marketing team for their timely support and communication. I want to thank the two anonymous reviewers for providing their insightful comments.

Friends who have sustained me over the years have made no mean contribution to the making of this book. With Sumit Ray I have shared a vision for a better world. I can't thank him enough for his generosity and abiding friendship. I value my bond and sustained friendship with Ratna Mathur, Sumita Chatterjee, Nilanjana Ganguly, Rekha Natarajan, Awadhendra and Sheyphali Sharan, Saumya Gupta, Aditya Nigam, Payal Randhawa, Iffat Fathima, T. Jayashree, T. K Rajalakshmi, Rahul Roy, Saba Dewan, Pankaj Mehra, Himanshu Malhotra, Abhilasha, and Ras Bihari Das. Thank you, Seema Gulati, for your constant support and always being a phone call away. I cannot thank Ravi Singh and her husband, B.M., enough for hosting me in Patiala during my fieldwork for the Mirasan project.

My family has been a wonderful source of support during this entire period. My brother Shailendra and sister-in-law Shalini's warm hospitality made fieldwork in Mumbai a pleasant experience. Shalini always stepped up to help me negotiate the city so that I could plan my research trips with practical wisdom. I thank Shailendra, Shalini, Vrinda, and Ishaan for their abiding love and affection. My brother Somesh's and Savita's home in Delhi was a welcoming refuge whenever I needed food, sympathy, and entertainment. I thank Somesh, Savita, Nimish, and Samta for their cheerful presence, warmth, and support. I want to thank Sudarshan Sharma and Madan Mohan Sharma, my aunt and uncle in Pune, for their generous hospitality. My cousins in the Jhingan/Sharma/Pathak family have always been loving and supportive.

Sandeep, Vasundhara, and Niharika, thank you for your unconditional love and nourishment. Niharika and Vasundhara have been a great source of entertainment and fun. I have often coaxed Niharika to sing for me when I needed a break from writing. Sandeep has been endlessly patient and cheerful despite the stretch, and has always responded to my unreasonable demands of formatting the visuals at unearthly hours. He will be glad that this is finally coming to an end. To my mother, I owe the most. She is the one I have neglected the most while writing this book. Her uncomplaining nature and calm presence have been a source of tremendous strength. And finally, this book is dedicated to my father, who is no longer with us. It is the memory of his melodious voice, singing Lata and Hemant Kumar songs, that guided me at every stage of this project. Without his eternal presence this book could not have been written.

I'd like to acknowledge the following publications that published early versions of some of the material of this book:

Jhingan, S. 2013. "Lata Mangeshkar's Voice in the Age of Cassette Reproduction." *BioScope: South Asian Screen Studies* 4 (2): 97–114.

Jhingan, S. 2012. "Teenaged Girls and Global Television: Performing the New Hindi Film Song." In *Super Girls, Gangstas, Freeters, and Xenomaniacs: Gender and Modernity in Global Youth Culture*, edited by Susan Dewey and Karen J. Brison. Syracuse University Press.

Jhingan, S. 2016. "Sonic Ruptures: Music Mobility and the Media." In *Media and Utopia: History, Imagination, and Technology*, edited by Arvind Rajagopal and Anupama Rao. Routledge India.

Jhingan, S. 2022. "Volatile Scales, Contingent Bodies: The Many Voices of Asha Bhosle." In *Companion to Indian Cinema*, edited by Neepa Majumdar and Ranjani Mazumdar. Wiley Blackwell.

Introduction

The Sonic Force of the Female Voice

Consider a scene from the film *Mirch Masala* (Mehta, 1987) in which an arrogant revenue collector representing the colonial state arrives in a village and summons the village patriarchs. As they gather outside the revenue collector's tent to pay their obeisance, the subahdar, an officer, flaunts his prized possession: He hand-cranks his gramophone device and plays a 78 RPM record. The men are intrigued; they try to guess what this could all be about. The subahdar asks them to be quiet and pay attention. Following the initial hiss, a woman's sharp singing voice fades up, creating a thrilling effect. The camera pans toward the listening bodies, who respond with wonderment, pleasure, and devotion. The village headman leans toward the horned machine, staking his claim on the sonic object (figure I.1), while the subahdar twirls his mustache, amused by these reactions. A slow zoom out from the horn of the gramophone player nudges us to pay attention to the voice and the song's melodic setting. As the voice soars, we see birds taking flight in a pastoral setting. A high-angle shot frames the site of pleasure in the background, as we see women carrying water vessels on their heads in the foreground. The gestural, embodied response of the gathered audience creates a sensory effect, pointing toward the lure of the techno-material female voice as a commodity, available for private consumption. The marking of an acoustic territory by the woman's recorded voice gestures toward a *kotha*, an exclusive male space, where courtesans entertained men with their music.

Figure I.1. The village headman in *Mirch Masala* (Mehta, 1987). Screenshot by author.

The female singer's recorded voice on the gramophone in the early twentieth century was in many ways a precursor to the film songs that became an integral part of the Indian talkie film.[1] The temporal and ontological status of the film song was shaped by recording companies that had already created a market for *thumri*, *ghazal*, and devotional or light classical North-Indian musical genres, where women artists had a strong presence (Joshi 1980).[2] The radio network introduced in British India in the late 1920s became another platform for listeners to access this music. These industrial and intermedial networks were reanimated by sound cinema, leading to the widespread proliferation of film songs as pervasive aural objects. The acousmatic voice of the female singer created an aurophilia that helped build a wider market for gramophone records. Sound in Bombay cinema gave us film songs, endowing the voice with a body, the missing object in the described scene from *Mirch Masala*.[3] Though connected with the film text, songs get repackaged as independent objects to memorialize an era or the work of particular artists involved in their creation; for instance, the recollection of a film star is shaped in public memory through the voices of playback singers. Thus, the actress Meena Kumari's star persona is embedded in memorable songs sung by playback singer Lata Mangeshkar in *Pakeezah* (Amrohi, 1972), while playback singer Asha Bhosle's singing style remains critical to the excavation of memories of films like *Hare Rama Hare Krishna* (Anand, 1971) and *Umrao Jaan* (Ali, 1981).[4]

This book focuses on the recursive presence of the female playback voice in Bombay cinema until the 1990s, and its attenuation in the post-millennium period. The term "playback" gained currency because songs recorded by trained singers were replayed so that actors could perform them in front of the camera while moving their lips. I will explore the playback voice's spillage in the public domain through diverse media forms that created sensory regimes for the on-screen star's cinematic presentation. The female singer's voice is located at the interstices between material, technological, and industrial practices, and the cultural, musical, and cinematic environments that harnessed its sonic production. Encountering the voice as a sonic force involves an engagement with a range of stakeholders, such as actors who perform the song on-screen; auditors within the narrative community; the spectators; the critics; and the listeners at large, who consume film songs through various devices, including online fans, amateur singers, and YouTube celebrities.

The Female Playback traces the auditory charge of women's voices produced through the playback system that enabled a wider circulation of the film song of Bombay cinema, and its intermedial circuits.[5] My research is located in the period that begins at the end of the 1940s when the playback system became a stable norm in the industry and ends at the contemporary moment when digital software has completely transformed the way film songs are recorded and incorporated as background tracks in films.[6] Each chapter in this book will engage with the gendered force field of the voice within which material practices, moral debates, aesthetic choices, mimetic registers, affective alliances, performance codes, and listening practices have been staged across shifting consumption technologies. I focus particularly on those moments when the sonic trace of the voice exceeds the song's visual resonance, or when the play between the playback singer's voice and its embodiment forces us to question our notions of a stable female voice or a body. *The Female Playback*, therefore, follows a cross-disciplinary approach to situate sound studies in a productive relationship with cinema studies to demonstrate how the playback system as an aural, material, and industrial practice played a critical role in making the sonic, corporeal, and affective female body available in the public domain.

Conjuring the Female Body Through Playback

In the first few years of talkie cinema, sound was recorded along with the image track, making the filming process tedious. This was particularly difficult for song sequences where the musicians and singing actors had to perform before the camera while struggling to hold on to their notes. By 1935, studios started using the playback system to record songs in a far more controlled environment, greatly enhancing their musical value. The industry continued to work with actor-singers for another decade, even though they had moved to the playback system.[7] By the mid-1940s, music directors started looking for trained singers for song recordings who could sing with a live orchestra in Bombay's makeshift sound studios.[8] The "term *playback*," notes Gregory Booth (2008, 45), "became an adjective that was applied to the new breed of specialist singers" who could display their vocal abilities. By the late 1940s, Lata Mangeshkar had established herself as an accomplished singer, a star in her own right, who could record her voice for different on-screen stars.

A song sequence in *Aji Bas Shukriya* (Hussain, 1958) depicts the recording studio as a productive space, inviting the spectator to a heightened vision of cinema's assemblage form. It demonstrates the flow between singing and listening, or the star singer and the star body that is visually available on the screen. Geeta Bali plays the role of Geeta, a young woman who loves to dance and watch films. After losing her job in a theater company, she gets the heroine's role in an upcoming film. "Saari saari raat teri yaad sataye" (Tormented by your memories, I keep awake all night) depicts Geeta performing the song in a recording studio with a live orchestra.[9] The sequence opens with shots of a chaotic space where musicians are getting ready for the recording, while the producer is getting restless. The producer then asks for silence, and the sound recordist shouts "Start sound." As the diegetic music played by the orchestra becomes aurally intelligible, we encounter Geeta standing in front of the microphone with a piece of paper in her hand. Picking her musical cue, Geeta begins to sing, with her gestures and eye movements acknowledging the presence of the live orchestra in the adjacent room.

Though the sequence indexes an early phase of the playback era when actors sang their songs, the staging of the sequence along with Lata Mangeshkar's voice draws on spectators' knowledge about the playback system. This connects with Neepa Majumdar's (2010, 177) important argument that song sequences were constructed through a combination of the alluring body of the visual star with the familiar and identifiable voice of the aural star, "appealing simultaneously to two sets of pleasures." I want to consider the larger implications of the playback system in upholding the star body on-screen. In Mary Ann Doane's (1985, 568) theoretical interventions on voice in cinema, the "voice is not detachable from a body," especially when the body is that of a star.[10] Doane makes a distinction between synchronous sound and voice-off, where the former is deployed to mask the "material heterogeneity of [the] cinema" (571). In Bombay cinema, however, playback technology was deployed essentially to bring the aural star's voice in sync with the actor's body. As Majumdar emphasizes, the "cultural work" that produced knowledge of the playback singer served to "undermine the techno-psychic mechanisms of synchronicity" (192).

Indeed, central to the playback system was the technology of sound synchronization that enabled actors to lip-synch the voice of the playback singer while performing for the camera. Amanda Weidman (2021, 2) describes playback as a distinctive form of celebrity that engenders a difference and disjuncture between the "on-screen body and the singing voice." Drawing on Ervine Goffman's concept of animation, Weidman highlights the twin forces of performativity and voicing in playback, as the actor's body animates the song visually, while the singer's voice "animates the song's words and the melody" (10). My close analysis reveals several layers to the enactment of the body, involving listening, gesturing, dancing, and masquerading to flow with the song. This becomes particularly apparent in the phantasmatic song sequences where an alluring female body gets conjured on the screen with the voice of the aural star. The production of the playback voice involves engaging with the material practices of sound: an embodied practice of breath control and close listening to the musical arrangement and its durational form. More significantly, it requires an immersion in the song's lyrical, spatial, and sensory imaginaries, where the performance of a gender identity becomes critical.

Nina Sun Eidsheim's (2011, 136) critical discussion on the voice draws attention to the bodily engagement with the materials in which [it] sings and hears.[11] Focusing on Juliana Snapper's experiments with underwater singing, Eidsheim observes that music analysis cannot be bound by notation or tied to a representational framework. Instead, Snapper's vocal practice nudges us to think about the "physical and sensory properties of singer's and listener's bodies; and on the spaces and materials on which sound disperses" (134). In the song sequence from *Aji Bas Shukriya*, we are made privy to the material practices in the sound studio as we see the singer's body and vocality getting attuned to the process of sound's transduction through the air. First, we see Geeta moving away from the microphone for a split second to clear her throat and then she moves forward to pick up her vocal cue. Geeta's gestures point to an awareness of the need to control her respiration in front of the microphone and to coordinate her singing with the live orchestra.

As the song unfolds, a plain-faced Geeta dissolves to reveal an alluring Geeta repeating the same line in a dream-like space. The immobile body of the playback singer is transformed into that of an iconic visual star as Geeta enacts the song with enhanced facial expressions, combined with hand and torso movements. Freed from the constraints of the microphone, Geeta starts responding to the music in the interlude section of the song with fluid dancing movements: her sinuous costume, her hairdo, and the curved stance of her body emphasize her transformation and its productive role in engendering a sentient space. After this detour to an imaginary landscape, we return to the recording booth, to the mid-close-up of teary-eyed Geeta, followed by a point-of-view shot of the producer. The visual strategies draw attention to the singer's anguish, which flows into the sonic field. The sequence allows the spectator a peek into the recording studio—its spatial attributes, material practices, and sensory registers. By tracing the shift from the recording booth to a phantasmatic space, we can see how the aural and visual sources are yoked together through playback. The intimate connection between the playback singer and the female body foregrounds the song's "sensory and affective modalities," as the use of facial expressions, hand gestures, and dance movements becomes part of the "affect contagion"

(Gibbs 2010, 191). The sequence unmasks cinema as an assemblage form, where the playback system is deployed to establish an affective relationship between singing and listening bodies, creating a resonance beyond the film's immediate context.

Discourses Around the Female Voice

The female voice in Hindi film songs is considered distinct from the male voice, precisely because sound recording technology was imbricated in the postcolonial state's cultural nationalist project. Gramophone companies at the beginning of the twentieth century leveraged sound technologies to record the voices of the *tawaifs*, or courtesans, who were accomplished artists.[12] Despite facing stigma, several of these hereditary "singing ladies" joined the film industry as actors and later as singing actors with the emergence of sound cinema. The late 1940s was a transitional moment in many ways. With India's independence and the partition in the subcontinent, several singers of the industry moved to Pakistan. The industry needed new voices for playback singing at a time when the popularity of film songs was riding on the sale of gramophone records, and the expansion of the radio.[13] However, as Neepa Majumdar (2010, 304) has argued, the phonograph, gramophone, radio, and cinema also functioned in several ways to orient viewers/listeners in specific modes of listening and sound reception. This audio training, according to Majumdar, was directed toward

> protracted negotiations with two kinds of noise, one of which was the literal noise of the machine—by which I mean the noise of poor recording technologies and conditions. But at the same time, gramophone, radio and cinematic sound might also be understood as audio technologies that regulated and standardized a more broadly understood *cultural* "noise," specifically in the arena of music and voice: *in particular the timbre of the female singing voice*. (304–5)[14]

Majumdar's reference to the cultural noise is crucial, as it points us toward the female voice's enmeshment in intersecting techno-material practices that had a bearing on its circulation in the newly independent state in the 1950s. In its zeal to promote classical music, All India Radio (AIR) introduced new policies to reduce and later ban the broadcast of film music for a few years. This was concomitant with other directives that curtailed the performance of "women of the *kothas*" from AIR studios (Lelyveld 1994, 119).[15] But equally, what was at stake in cinema was the sonic performance of the playback voice and its material presence, aligned with the body of the female actor in song sequences. Several scholars have written about the timbre and tonality of Lata Mangeshkar's voice as playing a critical role in fashioning the modern Indian female identity, middle-class femininity, and the discourses of nationhood (Srivastava 2004; Majumdar 2010; Sundar 2017).[16] Sanjay Srivastava (2004, 2024) has argued that Lata's "forever adolescent voice" was used to offset the heroine's visible and threatening presence in public spaces. Lata, according to Srivastava, occupied a space at the conjunction of ideologies of masculinity, patriarchy, colonialism, and Indian nationalism (2026).[17]

In theorizing the audiovisual contract, Michel Chion (1994, 216) has emphasized that the "audio-visual relationship is not natural," rather, it is a "kind of a symbolic contract that the audio-viewer enters into," to accept that sound and image form a single entity. Pavitra Sundar (2023) revisits Chion's audiovisual contract to discuss its implications for the playback system in Bombay cinema. Sundar enumerates six clauses of the audiovisual contract to historically chart the shifting discourse on how "women were expected to look and sound" in popular cinema (27). Acknowledging that "the body has been a problem in discourses that idealize women as keepers of tradition, morality, [and] national identity," Sundar identifies the somatic clause as a key device that Bombay cinema used to give primacy to the voice over the body (40). Lata Mangeshkar's persistent voice monopoly is read as part of the somatic clause as the *voice* could alleviate the threat posed by the female body, regarded as a site of vice (40).[18] Recalling Weidman's (2006) ideas on the voice as the ground for locating the "true self" in Western modernity, Sundar (2023, 40) reads Lata's dominance in the playback system as symptomatic of the voice being treated "as a repository of the true self."

In *The Female Playback*, I step away from an overarching nationalist framework to examine the sonic and affective dispersal of the voice by tracking the material practices involved in producing, circulating, and consuming the voice. A focus on the production of voice through techniques of breath control, while singing in front of sensitive microphones, nudges us to consider how the sound apparatus was mobilized, in conjunction with the image, to uphold the phantasmatic female body on-screen. These transformations fashioned deep fissures between the performance style of the courtesans in *mehfils* and that of the playback singers who recorded "new" genres of female solo songs in Bombay's film studios. Roland Barthes's (1977) concept of the "grain" of the voice is extremely productive in discussing both the aural dimension of the voice and its productive presence in different regimes of listening. Through a textual analysis of song sequences, I discuss Lata's use of an "intimate" voice that helped her gain authorial dominance in the industry. The concept of "intimacy" inaugurates closeness, privacy, and proximity, thus opening the voice to its deep connections with technologies, acoustic spaces, and listening bodies. For instance, in duet songs like "Chod gaye balam" (I have been deserted) in *Barsaat* (Kapoor, 1949), Lata's voice was introduced in a soft alap (singing in aa vowels) layered over Mukesh's voice, to match with Nargis and Raj Kapoor's performance expressing the anguish of their separation in two discrete spaces.[19] Songs enabled lovers to create an intimate sonic universe across vast geographical spaces, through cinema's assemblage form. Female solo genres like *mujras* and party songs drew upon melodramatic registers to stage songs for listeners within the narrative domain while denying them the full import of the song's signifying impulses.[20] Though the narrative community was physically present in the auditory field, the voice was directed toward the listener spectators, beyond the diegetic sphere, creating an affective, sensory engagement. This shadowy play of concealment and revelation in women's songs produced the drama of the intimate voice, which spilled into the public domain through gramophone records and the radio.

By underlining the voice as sound that travels, marks a territory, and activates listening bodies, I enter a dense aural terrain to consider the female voice's enmeshment in bodies, technologies, and spaces. A materially driven approach is extremely productive to account for the ruptures and divergences in the female voice through shifting bodily practices of westernized vamps, courtesans, folk singers, and street entertainers as subaltern sonic bodies, affecting and affected by the corporeally driven performance of playback singers like Asha Bhosle, Lata Mangeshkar, Geeta Dutt, Shamshad Begum, and Ila Arun. This strategy allows me to take into account Lata Mangeshkar's erotic songs and cabaret numbers that highlight the way she molded her material voice to produce imaginaries for different kinds of bodies on-screen.

The sonic trace of the voice through these mimetic interactions is culled from star discourses, print media discussions, jacket covers of gramophone records, and radio countdown shows.[21] The arrival of inexpensive storage media like audiocassettes, and the unruly expansion of version recordings in the 1980s, unveiled covert practices of the music industry, such as relying on the fan labor of copy singers. I argue that the cassette revolution forged new auditory habits and embodied practices of the voice. The arrival of satellite television marks another important moment when a new generation of singers could perform in their "own style" while simultaneously paying homage to the older aural stars. The postdigital cinema posed a serious challenge to the playback voice, concomitant with the larger transformations in the media environment and sound practices of the Bollywood industry. With the advent of sync sound recording and the rise of the multiplex cinema, the Bollywood industry moved toward background songs without the lip-synched performance on-screen. In this mutated form of the film song, the auditory charge of the female voice was no longer tied to a shadowy dance with the "presence" and "absence" of the on-screen body.

Affective Listening

The Bombay film, according to Kaushik Bhaumik (2004, 3), was "predominantly built-in terms of its sonic structures," through a complex layering of dialogues, music, and songs.[22] Debashree Mukherjee (2020, 151) has drawn attention to the aural histories of the city of Bombay and its resonant structures. Radio, gramophone, and loudspeakers created a dense soundscape drawing listening bodies to acousmatic media and their sensory registers. Crucial to these debates is the object of listening, the recorded sound and the way it evokes a privatizing impulse. In several interviews, Lata has shared her experiences as a listener to her favorite musicians by accessing these technologies. In an interview with Ganesh Anantharaman, she describes her fascination with Noor Jahan's voice:

> Noorjehan [*sic*] is my favourite among the female singing stars. She was truly a great singer, with a style of singing that was original, and a beautiful voice. She used her voice very well having been trained in classical music. Also, she was without peer in getting the expression right, something crucial for film music. I fell in love with her voice right from her first song in the film *Khandaan* (1942). . . . Initially I used to sing like her because she was my idol. She was better than anyone else at that time. Listening to Noorjehan's songs helped me get my Urdu diction right. The way you articulate words in a song is critical to the overall effect of the song. (2008, 208)

Lata's account highlights her movement from a keen listener to a singer, a relay that involved affective alliances between singers, listeners, and the technologies that made this voice available to the public. In his philosophical insights into listening, Jean-Luc Nancy (2007, 7) shows how sound "resounds" in both external and internal space. For Nancy, a sonorous body not only emits sound but participates in a chamber of resonance (7). Michel Chion's theoretical insights on the relationship between sound and image and the voice in cinema have foregrounded the spectator's experience as a listener. I join scholars of Indian film studies who have started listening to cinema, engaging with the shifting modes of sound production and dispersal.[23] I trace the discussions, murmurs, and anxieties about the female playback, which, through its disbursal on the gramophone, the radio, and cassettes, seeped into print media. Film magazines carried photographs of playback stars in special articles by critics. For the music critic, who saw himself as a connoisseur, the female singer's voice became a cultural object of discernment and desire. In his biography on Lata Mangeshkar, Raju Bharatan (1995, 17–18) writes about his experience of listening to Lata's acousmatic voice on the telephone:

> What did I think when I first heard her voice over the phone? That I was in the seventh heaven! My, how hummingly sweet the queen bee sounded the first time I heard her velvety voice over the phone! Did the melody queen ever sing for me over the phone? Oh yes, she did. Pt. Husnlal passed away and I

> was cross checking with Lata, as the music critic for *Filmfare*, my selection of her songs to complete an obituary piece. "Please do remember to include Dil hi to hai," said Lata in that nerve tingling voice of hers. This was when Lata surpassingly sweetly hummed it out over the phone, something like an electric current passed through me as I savoured the tune of Husnlal's all-time greats for Lata in *Adhi Raat*.

What is distilled through Bharatan's account is an affective charge in Lata's telephonic voice, one of the audile technologies that Sterne has alerted us to.[24] Bharatan privileges the humming voice (over the speaking voice) evoked by the vocal intimacy of the telephone. This is meant to remind the reader about his *exclusive* access to the singer's "nerve-tingling" voice: the telephone instrument as an audile technology creating a space of intimacy.[25] Bharatan's response foregrounds two key aspects of my study: "affect" and "techno-materiality." Affect has been understood as synonymous with the "forces of encounter" that are experienced through the "troughs and sieves of sensation and sensibility" (Gregg and Seigworth 2010, 2). While there are several ways in which "affect" has been theorized, I would like to signpost affect as a sensate experience that brings together singers and listeners in a charged relationship.[26]

In her work on race, gender, and voice, Nina Sun Eidsheim (2019, 10) argues that voice is a "part of a continuous material field," rather than a distinct entity. The voice, adds Eidsheim, "does not arise solely from the vocalizer; it is created just as much within the process of listening" (11). Through a methodology that focuses on listening, Eidsheim critiques the way voices of African American singers were essentialized through the myth of an innate black vocal timbre. Central to Eidsheim's project is a critical engagement with how we respond to acousmatic sound. As she notes:

> In the context of the human voice, this assumption about the possibility of knowing sound in the first place extends to a second assumption: that it is possible to know a person. The acousmatic situation arises from the assumption that voice and sound are of an a priori stable nature and that we can identify degrees of fidelity to and divergence from

> this state. This position is grounded in a belief—and truth claims—about the voice as a cue to interiority, essence, and unmediated identity. (2)

Through intense scrutiny and speculation about their private lives as *truth claims*, the biographers and critics arrogated upon themselves a right to access an inner landscape of the lives of women singers. In biographical articles on Lata and Asha, the Mangeshkar sisters, there was a tendency to read into the melodic, lyrical, and emotional registers of their songs as an indication of their subjective state, while underlining their distinct personas.

Relevant is a discussion of the role of song sequences in exploring individual subjectivity and interiority in the Indian melodramatic form. Discussing the relationship of musical sequences to the narrational form, Ravi Vasudevan (2010, 125) has foregrounded Indian cinema's "fissiparous qualities," offered to the Indian spectator as a particular type of cinematic modernity. Through a detailed analysis of song sequences, Vasudevan has shown how the melodramatic mise-en-scène is crafted through the exploration of narrative blockages (43).[27] Noting its overt reliance on expressionist visual idioms, Ira Bhaskar (2018) has argued that the film song, presented through stylized amplification and exteriorization of emotions, needs to be seen as a critical aesthetic drive of Indian melodrama.[28] I intervene in this discussion by drawing attention to the acoustic properties of the female voice and its productive entanglement with multiple modes of listening. The print media became a productive site for evoking the melodramatic registers as journalists and music critics started writing accounts of *being spellbound* by the expressive qualities of singing. By highlighting the sonic performance of the voice in women's confessional songs, and its consumption on gramophone records and the radio, I consider how listeners were framed as key receptacles of exteriorized emotions.

By advancing an approach that highlights the sonic force of the voice, I query the term "song and dance" sequences, which lumps them together as part of Hindi cinema's visual culture. For instance, in comparing song and dance sequences of Hindi films with Hollywood musicals, Andrew Hassam recalls Jane Feuer's study of the musicals, particularly the distinction Feuer makes between the audience *in* the film and the audience *of* the film. The presence of the internal audience in Hollywood musicals works to "compensate the film audience for the loss of a live performance" (Hassam 2012, 261). Hassam examines the scholarship on the song and dance sequences of Bollywood films, in particular the role of the diegetic audience by focusing on three aspects: voyeurism in Indian cinema (Dwyer and Patel 2002), *darshan* (Lutgendorf 2006; Dwyer and Patel 2002), and frontality (Prasad 1998).[29] Hassam (2012, 263) suggests that the internal audience is generative of a "first person or a darshanic form of address" in song sequences of both Indian films and Hollywood musicals. However, this discussion does not consider the sonic dimension of songs and the presence of the internal audience as listeners.[30] By bringing a sound studies approach to reading song sequences, I query how spectatorship has been theorized in Indian film studies, by occluding "listening" as a key modality. Focusing on the dancing women of Hindi cinema, Usha Iyer (2020) has critiqued existing discourses around "song and dance" sequences, arguing for a need to reverse the image-sound hierarchy. Through her insightful analysis of the female star's corporeal performance, Iyer highlights how on-screen dancing bodies influence the "affective configurations of composed music" (28).[31] Music directors could scale up the musical sequences in the song in terms of rhythm and orchestration when they knew that a skilled dancer would perform it on-screen (Iyer 2020). Iyer's framing of the dancer as a "choreomusicking" body, engaging the spectator in a multisensory way, resonates with my theoretical framework of "listening" as a bodily-driven material practice.

Locating film songs as powerful auditory commodities, I demonstrate how they draw aural attention to the voices of playback singers. The relationship between singers and listeners is articulated through a mimetic bond between playback singers and on-screen actors/dancers. The close-up of the actor's face lip-synching the voice of the playback singer accentuates the song's auditory register, inviting the spectator to sonic alignment. The intimate style of singing underlining a confessional mode employed by women was made possible primarily by the arrival of sensitive microphones and other industrially driven material practices that separated the sound from the image. The sound of the voice in film songs became a force field for an affective alliance between singers and listeners, both within and beyond the narrative context of the film. Let me illustrate this through a song sequence from *Sujata* (Roy, 1959). The film follows the dilemma of an elite Brahmin Bengali family that has given shelter to an orphaned child from a "lower caste" family whose parents died in a natural disaster. The song that I refer to here is a soft lullaby sung by Geeta Dutt. The song fades in with an off-screen voice as the camera frames the sky with a moon from the window of a room. The woman's voice fades up with the lyrics "Nanhi kali sone chali, hawa dheere aana" (My little girl is sleeping, O wind sway gently).

In the next shot, the camera pans from the window to the other end of the room as we encounter a woman singing for her infant. The next shot frames another baby in a different location lying with her eyes open. The camera zooms into her, giving us a sense of her isolation. The woman's singing voice connects the two infants aurally, but we have still not been oriented to the spatial location of the second infant. We are made aware that, like us, this "other" baby is also listening to the lullaby. Suddenly the song is aurally intruded upon by the second baby's cries and, hearing this, the mother walks toward the window. The next shot frames the other infant from the mother's point of view as she begins to sing the second *antara* (see figure I.2). Even though the mother has shifted her position, the sound perspective of her voice remains unchanged. The song ends when the other baby falls asleep, responding to the surrogate mother's singing voice. Through a relay of singing and listening, we are invited into a sensate experience that is oral, aural, and ocular.[32] The mother is not only framed as the primary source of voice/sound but is also constructed as a listening body, responding to the cries of the other baby. "Listening and voicing are in a deep reciprocity," and this becomes a creative means of orientation—one that "tunes bodies to places and times through their sounding potential" (Feld 2003, 226).[33] Moreover, this sequence demonstrates the materiality of the mother's sonic voice

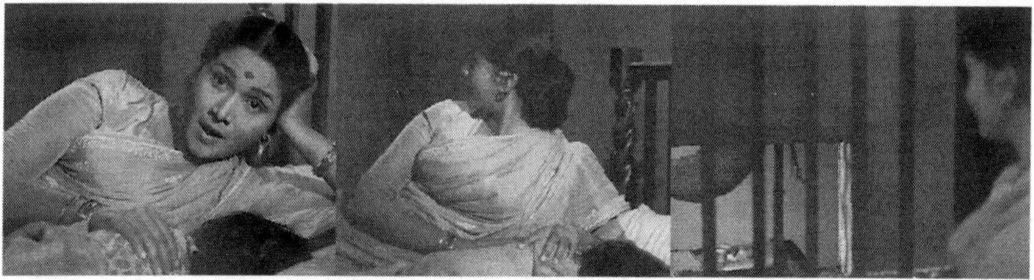

Figure I.2. The mother's song in *Sujata* (Roy, 1959). Screenshots by author.

in structuring aural and visual space. Our pleasure is heightened by the knowledge that the surrogate baby has also become part of this soundscape. Through this sensory experience, we are oriented to the affective dimensions of the voice relayed via on-screen listening bodies.

The playback voice, matched with a visible body on-screen, carries varying thresholds of habits, bodily practices, and accoutrements that gesture toward ethnic, caste, and class markers. In *mujras*, cabaret numbers, crooner's songs, or folk numbers performed by women, the embodied responses of on-screen listeners are foregrounded to create a layered aural field in cinema. Extending this notion of sight to the field of aurality, I engage with the acts of listening and singing that crisscross each other in the Hindi film song.

Media Assemblage

Discussions on the playback voice in film songs cannot bypass cinema's intermeshed relationship with other media, like gramophone records, the radio, the transistor, film magazines, song booklets, cassettes, discs, television, and the internet.[34] Affirming the premise of these interlinked media circuits, the overall aim of this book is to foreground the Hindi film song's female voice as a force engaging the listener as a key figure in the shifting forms of the media assemblage. The concept of the assemblage is useful in framing human and nonhuman agents, technologies, practices, bodies, devices, and objects and their material traces.[35] Playback technology is an assemblage, with deep implications for the auditory projections of the voice through an evocation of older media practices. Several cinematic presentations of song sequences have used inventive strategies to mimic the experience of listening to the radio without actually showing the auditory object.

The arrival of cassettes as an inexpensive delivery technology brought an unprecedented transformation that led to new imitative fan practices and mimetic alliances. In this context, the archive in its material form became an ever-expanding domain.[36] Audiocassettes, as rogue objects, pushed the demand for film music. A shadow economy driven by version songs led to the expansion of sonic textures as "copy singers" entered the networks of recorded music. Film music could not remain occluded or untouched by transformations in the aural domains as *ghazals*, regional music, and bawdy folk songs were now part of our listening habitats. Through their mobility and by creating feedback loops, cassettes introduced "deeper, heavier, huskier, grainier voices" of women, allowing local and regional music to proliferate widely (Jhingan 2016, 230).

Pursuing a media assemblage approach, I argue that transformations in the aural force of the voice played a significant role in the recalibration of the heroine's body. Television's infrastructural drive in the wake of structural changes in India's economy in the 1990s resulted in an intensified circulation of Hindi film songs.[37] The choreographing of gestures and body language in songs like "Choli ke peeche kya hai" (What's under your blouse) created a new visual language for women's sexuality in response to, and further animating the transformations in, the sonic landscape. The emergence of television as a hyperbolic sound-image media device in the postliberalization period finally allowed the singer to emerge from the shadows of playback singing. The use of wireless microphones, new modes of lighting, themed sets, glamorous attire, background dancers, and a live audience present in the television studio provided a new platform for aspiring singers. This resonates with Ranjani Mazumdar's (2007) reading of song sequences like "Sundara Sundara" in *Rakshak* (Honda, 1996), where the heroine's dance resembles the classic catwalk. This corporeal performance combined with a seductive look at the camera was similar to postmillennium singing contest shows on television that introduced us to fashionably dressed singers performing choreographed dance movements (Mazumdar 2007, 104). Through my analysis of music contest shows, I join Punathambekar and Mohan (2020) in questioning the scant attention given to television as sound media and the listening practices that get animated through its robust presence in our public culture. Reality TV shows like *Indian Idol* have thrown up questions about vocal training, pitch correction, fidelity to notes, and affective dimensions of the voice, foregrounding the sonic textuality of television (Hilmes 2008).[38] Playback singers and star actors as guest judges often respond to the performances of singers with moist eyes or "goose flesh" followed by their own "impromptu" performance that brings to life the memory of the original song.[39]

The postmillennium period ushered in a seismic shift in the production practices of film sound that had a distinct bearing on the recording, visual performance, and circulation of the voice. The intermittent use of the background song without the lip-synched performance on-screen created the conditions for the female voice's diminished status. Through an interrogation of studio practices after the arrival of digital media, *The Female Playback* highlights the destabilization of established connections between voice, body, and sound production technologies. This returns us to the "new" Bollywood song, its emplacement in film narratives, and its address to the sonic bodies. Thus, the voice as a material object, through shifting technologies, industrial practices, and media ecology, is a central concern of this book. The microphone, the magnetic tape, the Nagara machine, the sound mixing console, and the digital audio workstation draw our attention to the diverse technologies that have impacted the materiality of the voice.

Interpretative Strategies

This book embraces a media assemblage approach, to consider the shifts in the performances, practices, and circulation of the Hindi film song across multiple sites, technologies, and bodies. Moving away from an overarching framework of ideological readings and the symbolic terrain, I set up an inquiry that underscores the female playback voice as a sonic artifact, made available in the public domain through constantly shifting material practices. In engaging with a vast archive of film songs across various media, I have found Nina Sun Eidsheim's critical approach of "listening to listening" extremely productive in moving away from the essentialist reading of Lata Mangeshkar's voice within a nationalist framework. I draw upon Martin Daughtry's (2017, 56) method of layered listening to engage with the female singing voice as part of a "sonorous matrix," tied up with technologies, industrial practices, and listening bodies. Listening as a method and an embodied practice has allowed me to examine the way excessive presence of certain voices could "write over" other voices in the gendered soundscape of Bombay cinema. However, by excavating the trace of these "written over" voices, I have been able to signpost aberrant and inventive sound recording practices that could respond to the constant desire for the circulation of film songs across diverse media.

The Female Playback is a cross-disciplinary work that brings a sound studies perspective to film studies. In discussing song sequences, I invoke affective and intersensorial listening to highlight the charged relationship between the voice and the body on the screen through the cinematic assemblage. I draw on music analysis of song genres and their enmeshment in the gendered histories of Bombay cinema. In particular, I have traced the genealogy of female song genres like the *thumri*, which can be read as precursor texts to Hindi film songs. The intermaterial history of theater, the gramophone, cinema, and the radio has been critical in setting up my inquiry into the discourses of the female voice. The project has benefited from listening as a method across various contexts, enriched by my conversations with playback singers, recording engineers, music arrangers, composers, artist and repertory managers of music companies, dubbing artists, contestants of singing shows, and television producers. The print archive with its diverse material has emerged as a crucial site to examine how female playback singers were constantly negotiating a wider ecology of speculation, melodrama, and transformations in technologies and listening practices. By excavating the vast archive of singing shows on television, internet blogs, and the creative intervention of fans on YouTube, I have been able to map the shifting landscape of women's voices and the corporeal performance of film songs across media through diverse nodes of circulation. The emergence of an expanded definition of screen cultures requires us to revisit the domain of textual analysis. The convergence between the television and computer screen, ringtones, and ambient sound cultures demands new frameworks, questioning the established association between voice and human subjectivity.

Part 1 of the book focuses on the voice-image meld in cinematic sequences through an engagement with industrial practices, film form, star discourses, and the changing dynamics of bodies on-screen. In chapter 1, I discuss the significance of sensitive microphones and playback technology in Lata Mangeshkar's rise in the film music industry. The harnessing of technologies and material practices in this assemblage form allowed the lead playback singer to sharpen the existing divisions between the "open throated" style identified with the courtesan, gramophone singers, and theater actresses of the early twentieth century and a more intimate form of singing that became the norm in postindependence cinema. By focusing on four genres of solo songs, I argue that Lata's "intimate voice" became a key device in making intelligible the private selves of women on-screen. At the same time, the wider circulation of her voice through media devices such as the radio and the gramophone resulted in a "sonic excess" where the voice, now separated from the diegetic body, was free to move beyond the film's narrative drive.

In chapter 2, I examine the relationship between the voice, the body, and space to consider the sensory dimension of film songs. The phantasmatic body of the female star/actor (Doane 1980) is read through the auditory perception of the voice as a musicking body (Small 1998) embodying the voice as well as the space of the song's enactment. I consider the inconsistencies and asymmetries in the various thresholds of desire, intensities, technological mediations, and bodily mutations. While drawing attention to the nightclub as a three-dimensional acoustic space, the chapter notes a marked shift from the songs of the 1950s to the '60s, which signaled a cosmopolitan modernity, to the darker tonalities of the cabaret songs of the 1970s. Through a discussion of songs presented on a range of bodies like that of the star, and figures like the vamp, the courtesan, the classical singer, the crooner, the street singer, and the folk/ethnic dancer, the chapter traces the genealogy of the lived material body located at the interstices of both singing and listening. In the last section of the chapter, I focus on the rise of cassette technology twinned with the amplified presence of regional music that set the stage for the emergence of provincial/subaltern caste bodies, animated by the presence of folk singers in Bombay cinema. I argue that in the opening up of screen space for a hypersexualized image of the dancing heroine, the emergence of new auditory habits played a crucial role.

In part 2, I move away from cinematic representations of song sequences to unpack the intermedial footprints of the female voice involving a range of media technologies, listening bodies, and auditory practices. Chapter 3 mobilizes the writings of male music critics and journalists in popular film magazines focusing on the biographies of leading playback singers. While radio allowed listeners to have direct but limited access to Hindi film songs, the music critics of English language film magazines discussed gramophone recordings to self-consciously place themselves as arbiters of taste. By mobilizing articles, columns, and photographs of star singers like Lata Mangeshkar and Asha Bhosle, the chapter unpacks the way the voices of female singers (as opposed to the male playback singers) got entangled in debates on taste in music, moral binaries through melodramatic readings, and affective intensities. Pressured by star-driven industry discourses, the music critic often came across as both a "fan" and a "rational" figure involved in creating discourses about the female voice.

In chapter 4, I discuss the recirculation of Lata's voice through "copy artists" in the wake of the "cassette revolution." With the arrival of new delivery technologies, entrepreneurs and amateur singers could enter the circuits of production and distribution. The explosion of these imitative practices nudges us to confront the underbelly of the film-music industry: its hidden mining of cultural labor. The practice of "dubbing" and version recordings points us toward the modalities of imitation and intense listening so that amateur singers could enter the networks of the industry. However, this practice also pressured the relationship between star singers and fan devotees. The chapter also suggests that the "original" archive, threatened by "low-brow" and unruly sonic material, needed new inventories of cultural validation. Forced to confront the challenge posed by new music companies like T-Series, GCI reintroduced its own archive of music through marketing strategies highlighting their claim to Lata Mangeshkar as the "voice of the nation."[40]

In chapter 5, I focus on the corporeal performance of film songs through the combinatory force of transnational television and digital audio media. Music shows on television gave younger singers a chance to intervene in both the aural and visual domain, where imitation was combined with their own style. The explosion of Bollywood songs as sonic material was spearheaded by a convergence of the cinematic, the televisual, and the computer screen. This phenomenon inaugurated new practices involving major transformations in the techne, performance, and the dispersal of the voice. Mediated through software applications and plug-ins, the voice becomes data in an extended state of improvisation or erasure. I return to formal analysis of song sequences to highlight how the female body, sans the lip-synched performance, is deployed to disrupt the established voice-body relationship and to give us an experience of the present. Digital practices like the body in slow motion or subterranean layers of aural noise are discussed in connection with the transformations in the production and postproduction of sound in contemporary cinema that have softened the boundaries between songs and film soundtracks.

In the conclusion, I engage with the proliferation of cover versions of songs on YouTube and other internet platforms that nudge us to revisit the discourse around the attenuation of the female voice. The viral circulation of a new crop of singers on YouTube has created a new inventory of singers, listeners, and tastemakers, each in a constantly shifting terrain of flows and counterflows. I discuss the performative videos posted on social media, where we see both men and women lip-synching to the voices of erstwhile playback singers. On the other hand, androgynous voices of singers like the Nooran sisters have been used for background songs (see *Tiger Zinda Hai* [Zafar, 2017]), animating action sequences performed by the heroine while bringing in a disarticulated, spectral presence of queer and subaltern body in Bollywood. By focusing on the gestures, voices, and bodily practices of singers and actors on diverse screen media, including mobile phones, television, laptops, and cinema, I highlight the gaps as well as the accreting effects when the image and voice as data are joined together through digital technologies. This book, therefore, attempts to read the discourses as well as the affective dimensions of the voice, foregrounding a range of stakeholders/listeners and practices crucial for the circulation of the female voice in Hindi film songs.

Part I

THE MAGIC OF PLAYBACK

1

The Intimate Voice of Lata Mangeshkar

The earliest musical voice recorded in India was that of a courtesan. When Fred Gaisberg came to India in 1902, he found among the "nautch girls" a ready pool of talented singers who agreed to sing for his machines (Kinnear 1994).[1] The Gramophone Company soon realized the huge potential in marketing "Indian music" through these records. Unlike the photograph, marked by its indexicality, the "voice" circulating as a commodity had to be identified and marked. Gauhar Jaan, a *tawaif* from Calcutta who became a celebrity, would thus end a recording with, "My name is Gauhar Jaan," to inscribe her identity into the sonic format. An early history of gramophone recordings shows their predisposition for the individual musician. The constraining nature of sound technology ensured that only individual artists could be invited to the studio and asked to stand and sing loudly into a horn. While recording, the singer was asked to remain still and refrain from using any bodily gestures. Though the recording process was demanding and tiresome, the results were magical.[2] As Amy Lawrence (1988) has shown, gramophone technology privileged not only the individual performer but also the human voice over any other kind of sound reproduction.

In this chapter, I map the journey of the female voice from early sound media to talkie cinema, to finally focus on the playback system that played a key role in fashioning the normative singing voice for the heroine of Bombay cinema. Taking into account the shifting cultural and material practices that provided the labor and the repertoire of the film song, I argue that the shift from the actor-singer system to playback in the case of the female voice needs to be seen as distinct from the male voice, precisely because sound recording technology became imbricated with the moralizing overtones of the cultural nationalist project of the postcolonial state. I discuss five interconnected material practices that helped Lata Mangeshkar forge an intimate style of singing that paved the way for her unparalleled aural stardom. By singing in an effortless style that did not draw attention to her breath, Lata created a unique vocal style that set her apart from the image of the hereditary *tawaifs*. I argue that the aural force of Mangeshkar's star-driven voice was far in excess of the visual and the narrative domain. In the last section, I focus on the female solo song, with four distinct subgenres that became a key device for fashioning a confessional mode that rendered audible the "inner voice" of the heroine.

Music/Performance: A Contested Site for Women

The decline of the princely states led to a transformation in leisure economies: *kothas* became vibrant entertainment centers in cities like Lahore, Delhi, Lucknow, Benaras, Calcutta, Gaya, Patna, Agra, Amritsar, Allahabad, Bombay, and Kanpur. According to Anna Morcom (2016, 32), these shifts point us to the entry of the courtesans and dancers into "new forms of public culture" at the turn of the century. These salons were patronized by the new burgeoning class of merchants and traders. The mobility of women singers in search of new opportunities set the stage for a greater circulation of their disembodied voices through media technologies. The discourses around music recordings brought out by the gramophone industry foregrounded the intelligence, ingenuity, and skill of the individual artiste, as opposed to the *gharana* or the lineage that the artist represented.[3] The early history of music recordings shows how women artists used this technology to their advantage in marketing their music in the larger domain of reception. The semiclassical forms of vocal music like *ghazal*, *thumri*, *hori*, *kajari*, and *chaiti* performed by the courtesans formed the bulk of the recordings made between 1902 and 1908.[4] Urban theater was another important site that drew upon the resources of talented singers during the early twentieth century. The process of character "individuation" constructed through music was an important feature of modernity in the Marathi theater. Kathryn

Hansen's (1999, 127) work on Parsi theater in the late nineteenth and early twentieth centuries alerts us to the institution of female impersonation that played a critical role in the "construction of new norms of Indian womanhood." The representation of the woman with dress codes, bodily gestures, and stances by female impersonators was influenced by the postures of the companionate heroines celebrated in nineteenth-century reform discourses and fiction. For female impersonators to be able to play the role of a romantic heroine—an "embodiment of feminine perfection," a mellifluous voice was of great advantage (133).

In his well-known formulation of the "women's question," Partha Chatterjee argues that the discourse of nationalism supplied an ideological principle of selection between the material and spiritual and the inner and outer domain of culture. The appropriation of material life offered by the West had to be balanced by strengthening a "distinctive spiritual essence of the national culture" (Chatterjee 1993, 120). In this highly gendered discourse, the educated, modern woman had to carry the burden of demonstrating the nation's "inner spiritual self," its true identity.[5] The nationalists, according to Chatterjee, made a distinction between the new reformed, educated, and sophisticated women, and women from the lower class—maidservants, washerwomen, barbers, peddlers, procuresses, and prostitutes, considered to be part of an older and degenerate form of patriarchy that had been put under severe pressure by the "colonial interrogators" (127). Despite the complexities in the contours of the debate, one can argue that the nationalist reform project in the late nineteenth and early twentieth century, as shown by Chatterjee and Hansen, pushed women artists to negotiate the field of performance.

Along with theater and the gramophone industry, cinema, too, became a major site for courtesans to expand their networks, creating porous boundaries between music, technology, and sexuality. Debashree Mukherjee (2020, 146) has highlighted the way the arrival of sync sound recording in talkie films "enabled a new order of spectacular modernity" through sound media. The female body acquired a new auditory charge in cinema through the visual presence of the "voicing body" (146). However, this also meant that women who could sing and speak Urdu and Hindi fluently became the preferred artists, edging out in the process women from the Anglo-Indian and the Euro-Asian Jewish communities.[6] The arrival of sound cinema in 1931 turned several marginal performers into overnight stars. Several courtesans, in search of new sources of income, shared their repertoire with the film industry in exchange for signing lucrative contracts with gramophone and film companies (Y. Mishra 2009).[7]

In recent historiographic accounts music has also been identified as an extraordinary modernizing force that provided respectable middle-class women the opportunity to learn and perform in the public domain (Bakhle 2005, 225). Bakhle suggests that in order to open up the cultural space for women, cultural nationalists like D. V. Paluskar drew upon bhakti nationalism as a major force field for change. This meant that all "disreputable" links with the *kotha* had to be purged, and strict codes of respectability had to be maintained. In her work on the dynamics of gender and voice in Carnatik music, Amanda Weidman (2006) has shown the privileging of "sweetness" in women's voices as a marker of aesthetic value. The discourse around the female voice, according to Lakshmi Subramanian (2005), privileged the innocent, sublime, and evanescent quality of the female voice. By the early twentieth century, there was a move to allow women of middle-class families to learn music. But this was strictly meant for leisure within the domestic sphere. Only those women who were connected to *gharanas* of importance or considered disciples of well-respected *ustads* could get to perform on the concert stage.[8] One of them was Kesarbai Kerkar, who had to forge an identity of respectability through her strong association with the Jaipur Atrauli Gharana. To ensure a distinct and validating stature, and to maintain a distance from her devadasi or *kalavant* background, Kesarbai never sang for recording companies and made sure that no one secretly recorded her concerts.[9] In the context of Maharashtra, Urmila Bhirdikar (2007, 228) argues that the identification of women singers as *gharana* singers began in the 1930s with singers like Kerkar and Hirabai Barodekar making their appearance on the public stage as "classical khayal singers."[10] In the light of these negotiations that made possible the participation of women musicians in the wider public domain, it would be pertinent to turn to the discourses around the female voice particular to the practice of music in cinema.

Gendered Soundscape in Early Sound Cinema

Film actors/singers straddled the domains of celebrity culture as well as disrepute, positioned as they were as women of "easy virtue" (Gandhy and Thomas 1991, 109). Songs performed and sung by women in popular Hindi cinema from the 1930s, were drawn from musical and literary performance genres like the *thumri*, *dadra*, *kajari*, *jhoola*, *chaiti*, *biraha* and *ghazal* overwhelmingly associated with romantic themes. The collapsing of the voice of the narrator/ *nayika* within the song text and its performer/singer in cinema had powerful resonances, as the *thumri* and its allied forms had been intimately associated with the culture of the courtesans.[11] On the other hand, by the 1930s, the need for educated girls from "respectable" homes to act in cinema was articulated by the representatives of the film industry.[12]

It is important here to underscore material practices of sound recording in cinema that played a part in bringing about the transformations in the gendered soundscape. Since sound and picture were recorded simultaneously with a bulky and noisy camera and an immobile microphone, the songs were shot with few shot variations. To offset the noise of the camera and the lack of acoustically treated sound studios, singers had to adapt an open throated and loud style. This practice was not different from the style adopted in the theater before the advent of microphones. As Rajkumari (1983, 17) corroborates about her experience in theater, "we had to sing on top of our voice. The louder we sang, the louder the applause."[13]

This is how Naina Devi, a well-known *thumri* singer, laments the arrival of microphones in musical performance:

> Actually today's microphones have spoilt the real full throated voice and singers now sing in falsetto voices. . . . In olden days there were no microphones and they used to have—especially the professional musicians—female musicians in a *mehfil* without any microphones—and one could really hear them from here to the next house. . . . That was real music and real music voice production. Now we have this falsetto because the normal range of a woman's voice is not the same as a man. Now they have started singing in a man's range and because

> the voice does not suit, they have to sing with a falsetto voice. (2000, 54)[14]

Though Naina Devi is not talking about film songs, her insights give us a sense of the material practice of the voice required in large halls and live *mehfils*. In early talkie cinema, singing with a loud voice was an advantage, since it helped to drown out the noise of the camera and the nonmusical sounds of the studio. However, an amplified voice in front of the camera also requires producing a certain kind of sonic body with spatial and material attributes. A shift to playback technology resulted in the separation of the "processes of sound and image recording" (Booth 2008, 39). Though playback was introduced in 1935, for the next one and a half decades, the actors continued to sing and enact their songs (Booth 2008, 43).[15] In this intermittent phase, playback technology made song recordings less cumbersome: no longer bound by the position of the camera, singers were able to perform with ease near the musicians and the microphone.[16] Actor-singers like Noor Jahan and K. L. Saigal were some of the popular stars who recorded their songs and later lip-synched them in front of the camera.

Playback singers could perform in a more expressive, fluid style with the introduction of sensitive microphones and better studio facilities. The microphone narrowed the physical range of the performer, "serving as a kind of ballast for the singer," limiting her body movements (Weidman 2006, 126). Raghunath Seth (1980, 55) has emphasized the role of the microphone in creating a sharp distinction between the *mehfil* or theatrical style of singing among the first generation of singers and the less husky and more soothing style attributed to the later ones. According to Alison Arnold (1991, 110), the latter was a less dramatic, "smoother, yet more narrow style." This smoother sound was noted for being "more expressive and melodious, less nasal, less strident," adding only subtle embellishments and inflections in vocal performance. These discussions show that discourses around the voice shaped by the arrival of sensitive microphones created sharp divisions between "natural" and "unnatural" voices: in fact, it is through its mediation with technology that the "voice" could be characterized as "natural." Kajjan, Bibbo, Khursheed Zohrabai Ambalewali, and Amirbai Karnataki were known for their open-throated style of vocal performance, while Kanan

Devi, Uma Devi, Snehprabha, Shamshad Begum, Rajkumari, Suraiya, and Noor Jahan have been considered as representing the more melodious, nuanced, and expressive style of singing (Arnold 1991, 110).

With her wide vocal range and effortless style, Noor Jahan was often called the "queen of melody." Known for her unsurpassed vocal expression, she has often been referred to as a role model for Lata Mangeshkar. Noor Jahan stands out for her powerful on-screen performance, combining the emotional power of the lyrics with the musicality of her voice.[17] What made Noor Jahan stand out from the other singers was the embodied nature of her performance (figure 1.1). She retained the *mehfil* style in which the live presence of the singer was underscored by a heightened emotionality, clear enunciation of lyrics, and an intense investment in

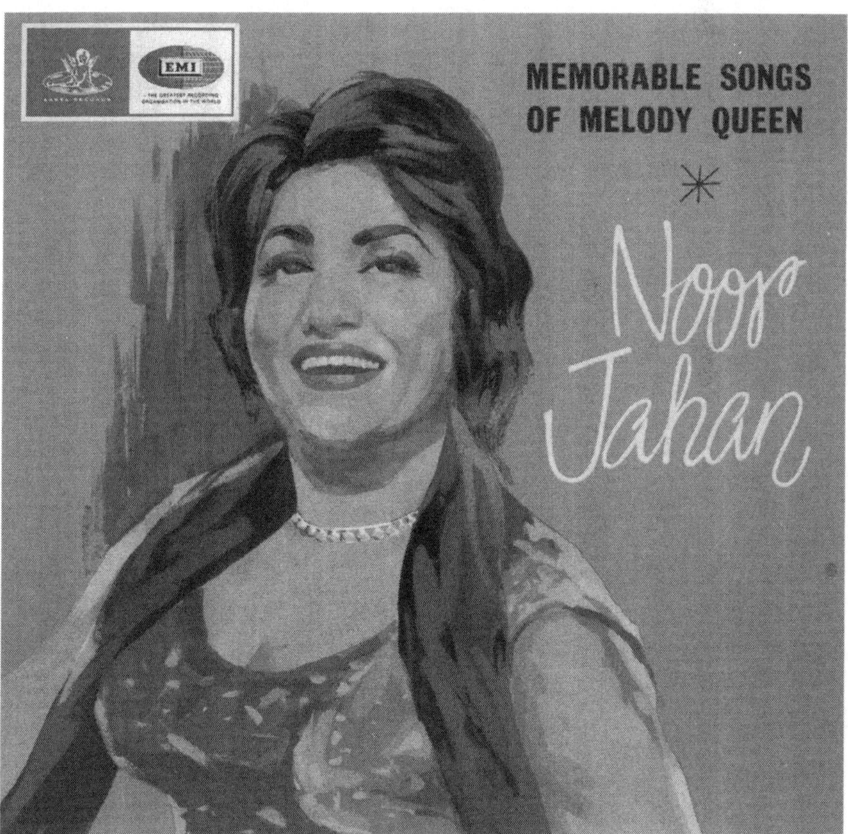

Figure 1.1. A jacket cover of Noor Jahan's album.

the expressive registers of the song. For instance, in "Jawan hai mohabbat" and "Awaaz de kahan hai" from *Anmol Ghadi* (Khan, 1946), Noor Jahan deployed an embodied style of performance; the mouth, lips, throat, neck area, and entire torso of the actor-singer were mobilized to match the embellished style of singing in front of the camera. As noted by Indu Bishnoi (1993, 49–50), "When Noor Jahan sang her entire body was involved. She fluttered her eye lashes, and embellished her tans with come hither looks, coy smiles and gestures."[18] This projection of corporeality can also be traced in off-screen discourses about her star persona.

The stardom that Noor Jahan achieved needs to be placed in the larger cultural and historical context of the decline of the studio system in the film industry. As Barnow and Krishnaswamy (1963) show, music and the star system became the driving force of the film industry in the 1940s, signaling the rise of the formula film. Playback technology was harnessed to create a separation between singing and acting, enabling the female star to concentrate more on her makeup and appearance, and not worry about the *sur*, or tone and pitch of the voice (Jhingan 2009). On the other hand, the playback singer could focus on the tune and lyrics of the song (Jhingan 2009). As songs started becoming more complex in their melodic content and structure, composers preferred to work with artists who were trained singers.[19] By the early 1940s, singers like Shamshad Begum, Zohrabai Ambalewali, and Amirbai Karnataki had established themselves as playback singers, and Noor Jahan, Khursheed, and Suraiya continued to straddle the world of singing and acting until Khursheed and Noor Jahan moved to Pakistan in 1947.

Lata Mangeshkar as a Playback Star

Transformations in the material, technological, and industrial practices, enabled by the playback system, offered women singers new opportunities.[20] By the end of 1949, with the release of *Mahal* (Amrohi), *Andaz* (Khan), and *Barsaat* (Kapoor), Lata Mangeshkar occupied the center stage in playback singing.[21] I will show that Lata's rise as the unparalleled star of the playback system involved complex mediations with objects, devices, bodies, and the material production of the voice. Taking a cue from Tim Gold's (2012, 428) work on materiality, I place the voice, the microphone, and the body not as stable objects but as fields of energy and circulation that draw on and respond to each other in an interrelationship. Drawing on industry discourses and the print archive of the 1950s and the '60s, I will map a dispersed terrain to invoke discussions on studio microphones, respiration, pitch and timbre, the act of enunciating the words, and practices of embodiment to demonstrate that these interconnected material practices formed the bedrock of Lata Mangeshkar's vocal style of an intimate voice, which set her apart from the singers of the actor-singer era. This expanded archive shows how the synaesthetic appeal of the film song was accentuated through constant and sometimes tense negotiations between these diverse nodes of production and their cultural and aesthetic moorings.

The Microphone

The microphone played a key role in transforming the relationship between the voice and the female body, ushering in the possibility of a more intimate production of voice and articulation of desire. In particular, the microphone paved the way for Lata Mangeshkar's aural stardom in the film industry. Its role in the projection of Lata's voice can be culled from an oft-repeated reference that her voice was almost inaudible without a microphone. In an article that appeared in *Filmfare*, Lata (Mangeshkar 1958, 42–43) shared her days of early struggle, when several producers rejected her voice due to its "thin" quality. Magazines often described her as a shy girl who was magically transformed into a confident singer the moment she was placed before the microphone. Raghunath Seth (1980, 55) notes that the microphone became a "musical instrument to be used creatively," which enabled Lata to bring out the "finest shade of expression."

In his analysis of the voice in popular music, Simon Frith (1998, 187) has shown that the microphone made it possible for singers to sing in "soft sounds, close sounds," which created an intimate relationship with the listener. In tracking Lata's trajectory, Punita Bhatt (1987, 27) argues that the composers who used Lata's voice in the early period need to be recognized for "their foresight and vision for they not only heard the frailty of her voice but also its potential." The microphone played an important role in effecting this transaction between the frailty of Lata's voice and its projection. The "frail" quality in her voice set her apart from her predecessors, who began their careers by singing in live *mehfils* or in the theater, which required a bolder projection of the voice. As a material object that remained close to the singer's body, while simultaneously amplifying the voice for its distant dispersal, the microphone's enmeshment in the gendered soundscape, as I will show, was aligned with the melodramatic registers of the film song.

The Breath

An important quality in Mangeshkar's voice, according to Ashok Ranade (2006, 410), was *Prasada*, a term that he borrows from the Indian medieval musicological literature to describe a voice that "enables listeners to receive the rendered music directly, immediately," and with "minimum distortion." Mangeshkar's voice was introduced in several songs as an extended alap/ prelude with the "a" syllable that showcased her control over her breath. Music directors noted her uncanny ability to control her breathing while recording her songs. This made her singing appear effortless, enabling her to foreground the emotional aspect of the song. Moreover, as I will show in the later sections of this chapter, this unmediated nonverbal prelude (alap) was used in cinematic sequences at key moments that alerted the listeners to the "grain" of her voice. Lata has acknowledged that Anil Biswas had advised her to pay close attention to her breathing.[22]

In his work on the materiality of music, Will Straw (2012, 229) has cited Phyllis Weliver's work on "air" (2005), and Jane Bennet's discussions on vibration (2009) to highlight the vital substances that form the "material basis of music and its dissemination." I hope to demonstrate that the microphone, the voice, and the singing body mutually implicate each other in "vibrating matter" (Straw 2012, 230). Moreover, this practice had deep implications for the way the performance of the actor, and the gestural vocabulary of her body, was read. In a series of articles on playback singers, Mukta Kodikal (1961a, 27) described Lata as "a songstress with a near-perfect larynx. [With] her ability to imbibe and synthesize the best in others: clarity of enunciation, unobtrusive breathing, voice, modulation, and getting a 'bol' to convey the maximum of feeling—all these from Anil Biswas and vocal expression from the veteran Noor Jahan."

The introduction of sensitive microphones thus created a demand for trained singers, who could sing with controlled respiration and bring clarity to the *bol*, or the lyrics. In writing about Mangeshkar biographers emphasized the "delicacy" of her voice, which was well aligned with the changes in recording practices. For instance, in his biography of Mangeshkar, Harish Bhimani (1995, 135) writes:

> But delicacy in rendering of musical notes is the soul of melody. If the first note hits the microphone with full force it sounds harsh. Anil Biswas taught Lata how to "fade in" every line while rendering a song, so that it glided unobtrusively, and then when the line ends, how to fade out with equal grace. The appeal of a song or its mellifluousness depends on how well this technique is employed. Although, undoubtedly, the gentleness and subtlety of rendering is, in essence, a reflection of the inner being of the singer.

Though Bhimani brings on board a discussion of Lata's vocal technique in relationship to the microphone, he quickly moves to another register about the "essence" and the "inner being" of the singer, thus demonstrating an anxiety to uphold a binary between the material and the immaterial (Miller 2005). A more pertinent point is the way Lata's style of performance, based on controlled breathing, spurred a demand from the heroines to bring in a form of "graceful femininity" (Kodikal, 1961a, 28). This quality in Lata's voice was seen as distinct from other playback singers, and especially from her sister, Asha Bhosle, whose "open" style of singing was seen as an extension of her outgoing personality. Songs performed as cabaret numbers or folk performances by Asha Bhosle were based on a corporeal style of singing involving obtrusive breathing and nonverbal vocal elements.

The Body

How did the pairing of Lata give voice to several actorly bodies on-screen? Discussions in magazines and biographies about the suitability of Lata's voice for the microphone, and her controlled breathing, helped create an image of aphysicality, a practice of singing film songs without involving the body.[23] However, this archive also points us toward greater scrutiny of female bodies on-screen, through the lens of moral binaries and the ossification of identities. Emphasis on the delicacy of Lata's voice in the print media was concomitant with the new set of demands on the physical body of the heroine.[24] Lata's rise to stardom was viewed as a sign of the eclipse of heavier or "rustic" female voices. In a series of articles on playback singers in *Filmfare*, Mukta Kodikal (1961a, 28) remarked, "sturdy of limb and voice, Shamshad is known to lend a rustic robustness to her presentations." Writing on Mangeshkar's early days of struggle, Girija Rajendran (1983, 42) describes what she was up against: "But, for an occasional solo or duet, Lata in the early 40s had to be satisfied with either being one of the crowd or being made to sing like the 'open voiced' Punjabi singers. . . . But by 1950, Lata had discovered her own individual identity."

In this highly gendered reading, we see a privileging of the playback voice that would match well with petite bodies. I recall here Pavitra Sundar's (2023, 26) important observation that "body is not just a visible entity, but an aural one."[25] The idea of a petite female body thus involved visual and aural imaginaries. Mangeshkar's voice was seen as the need of the time in a newly independent nation where the codes of femininity were being refashioned. This period of flux, marked by the departure of singers and actresses to Pakistan and the presence of "new talent" in the industry, brought to quick notice "aberrations" from the norm. For instance, the "heavy voiced 'ghosting' for a thin-voiced heroine" by Shamshad Begum singing for Madhubala in *Rail ka Dibba* (Arora, 1953), was termed unrealistic by Kodikal (1961b, 21).[26] These remarks point to a reworking of feminine codes, with a bias in favor of "petite" bodies on-screen, that would align well with Mangeshkar's intimate voice. This was particularly noticed in songs performed by actors like Nimmi, Kamini Kaushal, Nargis, Madhubala, Bina Rai, Nutan, and Vyjayanthimala during the latter half of the 1940s and the '50s. As Punita Bhatt (1987, 28) remarked, "Lata Mangeshkar's singing by the 1950s began to reflect upon the screen personas of the actresses, endowing *them* with femininity and softness of *her* voice."

However, as I demonstrate in the following chapters, Mangeshkar's vocal style could hardly be pinned down so easily to a single vocal style representing delicacy and aphysicality. Nor was her voice performed only by petite bodies on-screen. In several songs, Lata's embodied, vibrant singing enlivened the exuberant performance of the character and the actor on-screen, highlighting the intimate contact between the voice and the image, especially in songs performed in nightclubs, picnics, melas (fairs), and the like.[27] The discussion in the print archive of the first two decades of the postcolonial period hardly does justice to Mangeshkar's vast repertoire of songs demonstrated by the way her voice interacted with diverse kinds of bodies on-screen.

The Encounter with Language

The movement between the voice and the lyrics in film songs intersected with the sociality of music in the larger public domain. Ravikant (2021, 122) has shown how Bombay cinema was affected by the "hackneyed Hindi-Urdu-Hindustani debate" that was prevalent in the nineteenth century "print public sphere." Scholars have noted the role of film songs in providing listeners with a multilingual and an intermediated experience (Ravikant 2021; Duggal 2018). The categorization of playback voices being accessed by listeners became a subject of debate as the postcolonial state took charge of the airwaves of All India Radio.[28] The broadcasting code was linked to the acoustic properties of the voice, as a new system to audition artists for radio broadcasts was introduced to privilege professionally trained musicians over hereditary musicians. Although these transformations were not directly related to cinema, they had a bearing on the practices of the voice in film music. Both cinema and radio were involved in carefully regulating listening practices by eliminating the "cultural noise" associated with women singers from the courtesan establishments (Majumdar 2009, 319).[29] I argue that the anxiety around "cultural noise" in the aural public sphere also shaped the discussions on the question of language, accents, and vocal production of "Hindi" film songs. Ravikant's (2021, 121) assertion about Bombay cinema's "multitonal materiality" is useful in thinking about the conjunction between language, tonality, and gendered identity.

An emphasis on lyrics and their correct pronunciation in the Bombay music industry highlights Michel Chion's (1999) well-known argument that cinema privileges the voice over other sonic elements. Technically and aesthetically, song recording and mixing were calibrated to lionize the voice of the lead playback singer over other elements, such as the sound of musical instruments. This emphasis on vocality pressured playback artists to work on their accents by keeping in check regional markers or a shaky knowledge of the language. The repeated citing of Lata Mangeshkar's first encounter with Dilip Kumar on a local train during her period of struggle in the industry is useful here. When Anil Biswas introduced Lata to Dilip Kumar as an upcoming playback singer, he wondered how a Maharashtrian girl living on *dal-bhaat* would do justice to film songs with a liberal mix of Hindi and Urdu words.[30] Stung by these remarks, Lata took up the challenge and dedicated herself to taking lessons in Urdu. This anecdote has been repeatedly recalled in popular media to emphasize that Lata proved Dilip Kumar wrong by perfecting her pronunciation of Hindi and Urdu words.[31] The discussions in the popular press about Lata's decision to learn Urdu helped consolidate her image as an artist, willing to take on any challenge to excel in her art and meet the demands of the film industry. The forging of this style by Lata needs to be considered in the larger context of the 1950s, when the public nationalist discourse on language was in a tense relationship with the oral and acoustic practices of Bombay cinema. The discussions in film magazines about Lata's efforts in learning Urdu, a language that she embraced through hard work, helped her forge an identity that distanced her from her predecessors—hereditary women singers or courtesans who drew their lineage from the *kotha*. Many of these women were Muslim, proficient in performing the *ghazal*, with a deep understanding of the nuances of Urdu poetry.

In his work on music, image, and text, Roland Barthes (1977, 185) introduced the concept of the "grain" of the voice in music, which is "not merely its timbre." Borrowing from Julia Kristeva's distinction between the pheno-song and the geno-song, Barthes aligns the latter with the "grain" of the voice that foregrounds the "body as it sings," and provides the thrill to the individual listener (182). The geno-song for Barthes is the crucial site of the production of vocal music, an encounter between music and language, that is not tied to "communication" or "representation" (182). Lata's use of voice with a perfected breathing technique and her emphasis on the expressive quality of the text would ideally be categorized as the pheno-song in this formulation. However, I consider the discursive formation that highlighted Lata's approach to lyrics and pronunciation of words as a significant site for the "dual production of language in music." (Barthes 1977, 182). The grain of the voice, writes Barthes, is an "*encounter between language and a voice*" (181), a notion that I find productive for my analysis. In Lata's vocal style, a special and intended encounter with the Urdu language became another marker to distinguish her from hereditary singers. Moreover, it also helped her to be rid of the tag of a Marathi singer, allowing her techno-material voice to connect with cross-regional listeners of South Asia.

The Vocal Range

Journalists writing on Lata Mangeshkar in the early part of her career had noted the influence of Noor Jahan on her singing, with some even calling it an imitation (Dhurandhar 1976). Lata acknowledged her fascination for Noor Jahan but denied that she had ever tried to imitate her style.[32] Those defending Lata were quick to point out that in her early days she was forced to sing songs that had been composed to suit Noor Jahan's range.[33] Subsequently, she managed to cast off Noor Jahan's influence by raising the pitch of her voice in the early 1950s.[34] What followed was the formation of a template that edged out several playback singers, who were trying to adjust to the intermediate phase, when the industry was transitioning toward the playback system. Rajkumari, who acted and sang for the industry before moving to playback, has spoken about the shift in the industry when music directors started asking singers to sing "at a definite pitch," even if it meant they had to stretch their voice (1983, 19).[35] Raghunath Seth (1980, 55) was more specific when he wrote, "Now a woman singer who doesn't have a pitch similar to Lata is just not acceptable as a popular singer."

Even for a lay listener, a comparison of songs sung by Lata Mangeshkar in the late 1940s with those of the mid-1950s reveals a shift to a higher pitch.[36] This transformation in the industry discourse was often read as a symbol of the loftiness of Lata's music (figure 1.2).[37] But it also played a crucial role in establishing her hegemonic status in the industry.[38] Let us consider one of Lata's high-pitched singing performances that became a rage on radio countdown shows. In "Rasik balma," from the film *Chori Chori* (Thakur, 1956), the camera focuses on Nargis's facial expressions as she enacts the pain of separation described in the lyrics. However, with Lata's voice almost touching the third octave in the *antara* (verse), the song becomes a sonic object, exceeding the visual codes as Nargis's lip-synched performance, combined with her facial expressions, is unable to do justice to the high notes in the voice.[39] The affective charge of the sonic voice threatens to overpower the star's visual performance. Moreover, the popularity and the context of the song's dispersal show how

Figure 1.2. Lata Mangeshkar's star image in the print media carried an aura of respectability and devotion to her art. Source: *Illustrated Weekly of India*. Author's personal collection.

"Rasik balma" became an important star vehicle for Lata. Lata has shared that a seriously ailing Mehboob Khan called her from the United States, requesting her to sing "Rasik balma" over the telephone. This became a regular feature until he recovered completely (Mangeshkar cited in Kabir 2009). According to Raju Bharatan (1995), the song caused tensions between the singer and the music director duo, Shankar Jaikishan, when Lata refused to sing "Rasik balma" at the annual *Filmfare* awards in 1956. Lata was miffed that the composers had received the *Filmfare* award for "Rasik balma" in the "Best Song" category while the singer had not been acknowledged. As the story goes, this episode finally prompted *Filmfare* to introduce the "Best Playback Singer" category in the *Filmfare* awards.[40]

The vocal range of the playback singer's voice needs to be seen within a larger context of the song's cinematic presentation, to take into account how the voice was seen to uphold or diverge from the phantasmatic female body on-screen. This is where the assemblage of film, sound technology, voice, and the body, with all of its asymmetries, comes into full view. In a recent conversation with Yatindra Mishra (2016), Lata discussed her approach toward singing, which relied on paying close attention to the gestures and voices of female stars. She highlighted the difficulties she encountered when music directors asked her to sing at a scale higher than what she was comfortable with. She recalls recording a particular song for Shankar Jaikishan where they asked her to sing a *female version* of a song. "Ehsaan tera hoga mujh par," for the film *Junglee* (Mukherjee, 1961), was first recorded in Mohammed Rafi's voice for Shammi Kapoor. Lata notes that:

> Since the shooting of the song had to be wrapped up, they had decided to shoot the song with Saira Banu giving lip movements to M. Rafi's voice. Later, I was asked by Jaikishan to sing the song by looking at Saira Banu's lip movements on the screen. I found it a bit odd but decided to go ahead without saying anything. You won't believe this, since the song had been sung by M. Rafi, and because of his scale it was composed on a higher pitch, Saira Banu had lip synced the song accordingly, with her mouth being a bit too wide while doing her lip movements. This was quite natural since she was

> moving her lips according to a male scale. So, when I started singing in order to match Saira Banu's lip movements, I found the notes too high and therefore I had to almost shriek while singing. (Mishra 2016, 450–51, translation mine)

As Lata shares, the conventional process of recording the song, followed by its picturization, was reversed in this instance, making new demands on her as a singer. I recall Bill Brown's (2010, 60) observation that it is only during the "breakdown of [y]our habitual interactions with the world" that its materialities can be apprehended. An unusual production process brings into relief the negotiations singers had to make to respond to the flux in material practices.[41] While Saira Banu had to lip-synch the song while listening to Mohammed Rafi's voice, Lata was expected to sing while aligning her voice with Saira Banu's facial expressions and lip movements. This anecdote points to the limits of playback technology in holding up the phantasmatic body of the heroine, uncovering the gaps between the voice and the body caused by an overenthusiastic use of high-pitched singing.[42] The depiction of the female actor's mouth opened "too wide" to match the high-pitched singing conflicted with the intimate and confessional form that became a hallmark of Mangeshkar's style of performance in the first two decades of postcolonial Bombay cinema.

The Staging of the Solo Song

The five interconnected material elements in the playback system formed an important layer for staging the female self through song sequences. The solo song, in particular, became an important device to reveal the private self of the individual, articulating expressions of desire and longing. I examine four subgenres linked to four different situations, as conducive for the cinematic performance of the heroines' song that opened the space for Mangeshkar's intimate and confessional style. Carrying the sensory charge of women's experience of love, excitement, sexual desire, anguish, grief, and longing, the genre owes its antecedents to *viraha* (a condition and mood of love in separation), as a multigeneric form that, according to Kumkum Sangari (2011, 261), was tied to the representation of love. Sangari asserts that *viraha* has been tied to the "history of the female voice in both non-devotional and devotional compositions," registering many nuances of female desire, including the voice of the courtesan in love (271). The image of the *virahini*, or the woman suffering in separation from her lover, draws on several vernacular, literary, and cultural lineages across genres, languages, and religions (Knapczyk 2022, 84). In filmed sequences, these songs encapsulate an inner landscape through the use of close-ups that emphasize the poetic sensibilities and facial expressions, framed as point-of-view/audition shots for the narrative community. Ravi Vasudevan (2010) has drawn attention to the song's direct address and ability to disrupt the codes of continuity by giving the spectator a privileged position over the narrative community. This ties in with his larger argument about Indian melodrama as a public-fictional form that lays great emphasis on constructing a drama of the individual through a public form of address (2010, 10). In Vasudevan's formulation, however, there is room for the "aesthetic of the private," as song sequences enable individual characters to articulate their desires in public settings (151–52). Songs performed by female protagonists at social gatherings congeal a heightened melodramatic address in the presence of diegetic listeners. Ira Bhaskar (2012, 169) has argued that the song is central to the melodramatic *narrational* form (emphasis mine), in the specific historical and social context of Indian modernity.[43] The use of poetry, music, and gesture in film songs played a critical role in making intelligible the inner state of characters through the exteriorization of emotions.

An important aural motif in Lata's songs was the sudden intrusion of her voice with an alap, or musical elaboration through the sound of vowels. This was constitutive of the pull of the voice, drawing the narrative community toward the diegetic singer.[44] The affective state of listening bodies was foregrounded by surprised glances, gestures, or bodily movements. In the following section, I discuss four important subgenres of female solo songs that became intrinsically tied to the aesthetic staging of the female self. Through their aural and visual coding, these genres not only engaged the diegetic listeners in the film but also gained currency through their off-screen circulation. Further, as I will demonstrate, the discrepancies between the auditory and the visual fields created the ground for interesting cinematic possibilities.

Songs of Leisure, Mobility, and Desire

Panchi banoo udti chaloon
mast gagan mein
Aaj main azad hun
duniya ke chaman mein (Chori Chori, *1956)*

Like a bird I soar in the skies
Free to explore
These beautiful pastures
And the expanse that lies beyond

The songs depicting woman as nature were often deployed in films of the 1950s and '60s to introduce the heroine. The camera framed women running through pastoral landscapes, at river banks and in landscapes laced with trees. The intercutting between the women's bodies and the 360-degree pans of trees in low-angle shots framed against the sky heightened the aural power of the singer's voice, literally visualizing its expansive reach. I would like to recall here Ira Bhaskar's (2018, 264) useful assertion that the "individual and the environment, especially nature are brought into resonance via the voice" in the Indian film song. As I discuss below, the relationship between the voice and the landscape played a crucial role in the staging of the self in song sequences. The singing voice was used to map exterior spaces, symbolizing the woman's emerging sexuality, restlessness, an innocent past, and an anticipation of excitement and narrative development. My argument is that the strong physical presence of the female body is affected not just through her presence in the visual field but also by the voice that brings a layer of self-declaration. "Panchi banoo udti phiroon" (I am a bird in flight) from the film *Chori Chori* (Thakur, 1956), "Sapne suhane ladakpan ke" (My youthful dreams), from the film *Bees Saal Baad* (Nag, 1962), and "O Beqarar dil" (My restless heart), from the film *Kohraa* (Nag, 1964) used panoramic shots of seashores, river banks, valleys, and green fields, creating a dynamic between the singing voice and infinite spaces.

An interesting use of this genre is in the staging of "Kuch dil ne kaha" (Is my heart saying something?) in the film *Anupama* (Mukherjee, 1966), the only song performed by Sharmila Tagore in the film. Uma (Sharmila Tagore) is a sensitive and introverted young woman who loses her mother at the time of her birth. Her father, a wealthy businessman, turns away from his daughter, blaming her for his wife's death. The two live under the same roof completely alienated from each other. Shunned by her father, Uma takes refuge in solitude, spending most of her time amid nature. A chance encounter with Ashok, a young idealistic writer, infuses Uma with a fresh lease on life. "Kuch dil ne kaha" is performed by the heroine as she walks through an open landscape lined with tall trees and dense foliage at a hill station. The song describes in a subtle way the initial stirrings of desire. Uma sings:

Kuch dil ne kaha
kuch bhi nahin
Kuch dil ne suna
kuch bhi nahin
Kuch aisi bhi baaten hoti hai
aisi bhi baaten hoti hain

Did my heart say something
Nothing at all
Did my heart hear something
Nothing at all
Yet, there are things
Waiting to be told . . .

The song begins with Ashok (Dharmendra) enticed by Lata's rising voice on the soundtrack. Ashok looks for the source of the voice and locates Uma far below in the valley. The on-screen listener plays an important role in the acoustic relay of the song. The pleasure of this song is derived through the framing of the narrative that places emphasis on the heroine's reticence and self-effacement, driving our desire to unveil the dark recesses buried in her persona. The act of revealing the self, encoded within a soft, gentle voice and subtle lyrics, is commensurate with the enigma built around the heroine. The soliloquy is enabled through the presence of the hero, standing in for the spectator, simulating desire, curiosity, and aural pleasure offered by Bombay cinema.

"Kuch dil ne kaha" is a song with a deep subterranean register and articulates what Raymond Williams (1977, 132) has described as a "structure of feeling." In the first *antara*, Uma describes emergent feelings of desire and, a fear of the unknown future in this journey of love. This is a moment deeply embedded in the experience of the present. In the second *antara*, the singer shifts the terrain of the song from the realm of the phenomenological to the epistemological. The heroine subtly interrogates social and class distinctions that play an instrumental role in shackling private selves, forcing individuals to play along with "false" bourgeois morality. By the end of this *antara* we return to the personal, experiential realm. The affective registers of the song get mediated through the embodied presence of the diegetic listener, the hero, placed as a witness to a preemergent form, "active and pressing but not yet fully articulated" (Williams 1994, 608).

An interesting and important variant of this genre of songs is the deployment of a female chorus backing the voice of the lead singer. Here, the female voice is deployed to map an expansive aural space, much larger than the actor's physical body placed in the visual field. This tension between the voice and the body turns the song into a site of pleasure and female bonding. Sanjay Srivasatva has suggested that the encounter between the male hero and the woman in postcolonial Hindi cinema often took place on highways and the newly laid "bitumen roads." The Five-Year Plan (FYP) hero, representing modern scientific knowledge, became the "mark of post-colonised middle-class masculinity," while the woman, through Lata's soft voice, represented an innocent "provincial" sensibility (Srivastava 2006, 103).[45] This reading, however, overlooks the overwhelming depiction of modern girls in song sequences through both their visual and aural coding at picnic sites, highways, and other urban settings in the films of the 1950s and '60s. In these moments of leisure, multiple women's voices and bodies occupy exterior and non-domestic spaces, projecting fashion, style, and urban consumption. By focusing on the female protagonist, these songs delay the development of the plot and distract us from other important characters in the film. In "Ban ke Panchi gaye pyar ka tarana" (Birds in the forest are singing) from the film *Anari* (Mukherjee, 1959), Nutan leads a group of mobile and carefree young women on their bicycles, staking their claim on the highway. The lyrics express desire and longing for romantic love but somehow fall short of the exhilaration expressed in the sonic elements of the song. Each line of the verse section sung by Lata Mangeshkar is followed by the chorus extending it with the alap. The high-pitched female chorus, interlaced with Lata's voice and the orchestrated sound of the cycle bells, creates an intense aural effect, almost spilling out of the two-dimensional visual frame. "Sheesha-e-dil itna na uchalo" (Don't play with the fragile heart) from the film *Dil Apna Aur Preet Parai* (Sahu, 1960) is another notable song where a picnic at the beach becomes a productive site for female bonding and active leisure. In "Thandi hawa kali ghata" (Cold breeze and dark clouds) from the film *Mr. and Mrs. 55* (Dutt, 1955) we see the heroine reveling with her friends at a swimming pool in metropolitan Bombay. The presence of women in public spaces is buttressed by the use of the tracking camera and the female chorus that dominates this song.

The picnic songs underline women as autonomous bodies, articulating a spirit of romance not necessarily tied to heterosexual notions of love. For instance, the song "Main chali main chali dekho pyaar ki gali" (I am on my way to the street of love) from the film *Padosan* (Swaroop, 1968) becomes a fun excursion for a group of trendily clad modern women led by Bindu (Saira Banu) and her friends. Sung by Lata Mangeshkar, Asha Bhosle, and a female chorus, the song deploys a dense soundtrack with the inclusion of nonverbal vocal sections (la la la la la) and a heavy rhythmic arrangement by R. D. Burman. While the interlude and musical sections are framed through long shots of the landscape traversed by the girls on their bicycles, the sung portions are visually coded with low-angle mid shots of the girls, framed against the sky. Through a breezy conversational style, the sequence mobilizes an intense relay of singing and listening across multiple bodies, to create a sonic geography in which the voice becomes intense as well as ephemeral (Labelle 2010). The outpouring of desire is entwined with its limits through spaces signifying the boundaries of nature and culture. Yet, in terms of their effect, these songs capture the erotic registers of the female body in a playful dialogue with nature, expressing an exhilarating sense of mobility, leisure, and modern diversions. The first encounter with the hero, infused with comic banter, takes place at these landscaped tourist sites. What is significant is how these songs create a pact of knowledge between the heroine and the spectator, even before the male figure is introduced. This intimate pact paves the way for the popularity of the songs beyond the cinematic text. More importantly, I would like to signpost the aural dimensions of these songs and their recursive libertarian impulse as refracted through repeated listening.

Songs of Confession in a Public Setting

The gestures, facial expressions, and bodily dispositions of the on-screen actor play a crucial role in the exteriorization of emotions. Shohini Ghosh (2004, 56) has argued that song and dance sequences provide centrality to female protagonists that are denied to them in film narratives. Anna Morcom (2019, 136) has insightfully analyzed staged songs like "Pyaar Kiya to Darna Kya" from *Mughal-e-azam* (Asif, 1960) to underscore the dramatic potential of the live performance that allows Anarkali to hijack the situation and declare defiantly in the emperor's court that "love cannot be stopped or hidden." The diegetic audience remains witness to these dramatic sequences until the song comes to an end, giving room to the protagonist to articulate herself "fully," enabling a sense of both "completeness and catharsis" (2019, 136). The heroine's first confessions about love are often in the form of a direct address and/or mediated through the presence of a witness, symbolizing the spectator. There are scores of examples of such songs. For instance "Kissi ne mujhko bana ke apna, muskurana sikha diya" (My beloved has taught me how to smile) from the film *Patita* (Chakrabarty, 1953) is directly addressed to the spectator, while in "Tere mera pyar amar" (Our love is eternal) from the film *Asli Naqli* (Mukherjee, 1962), the address keeps shifting between the hero, the spectators, and the presence of the moon as a witness.

The more complicated versions of confessional songs, however, were staged in large gatherings. The drama was created by presenting the woman's private self through a selective form of address in a public setting. The presence of onlookers enacted the moral and authoritarian gaze of the society, turning the song into a productive space where familial, generational, and class conflicts could be played out. The party songs usually deployed a relay of point-of-view shots of key players, while the woman was allowed to articulate her love/loss of love for the hero in a veiled manner. This staging of the self in a confessional mode was dramatized through the presence of onlookers, unaware of the heroine's inner dilemma. Through selective focus, tracking movements, and point-of-view/audition shots, the camera foregrounded the singer and the addressees of the song within the narrative world. The spectators were invited to be part of this inner core through greater access to knowledge about the protagonist's inner self.

For instance, "Ajeeb dastan hai yeh" (This sure is a strange tale) from the film *Dil Apna Aur Preet Parai* (Sahu, 1960) follows the codes of a party song. Sushil Varma (Raj Kumar), a surgeon in a hospital in Shimla, and Karuna (Meena Kumari), a nurse, are drawn to each other but their attraction remains unexpressed. The narrative strategy deployed here is to make the spectator aware of existing psychic regimes. Sushil's marriage is arranged to Kusum (Nadira), whose father had paid for Sushil's medical education. The song is performed when the newlywed couple returns to the city. The setting is a boat bedecked with flowers. The center of attraction among Sushil's colleagues is Karuna, who begins to sing to mark this "happy" occasion while imbuing the song with a sense of loss and anguish. These subtle emotions alluded to through facial gestures, furtive glances, and eye movements are meant for only the camera, the hero, and one friend of Karuna's. All others in the visual field are excluded from this address. The song creates a dense aural field using the high-pitched voices of the chorus in Western chordal harmony. The chorus singing by the women on the boat forms an aural setting in which the personal is revealed by the solo voice of the singer.

The experience of desire, unfulfilled love, and dejection was also expressed through the use of doubling in party song sequences. These songs drew attention to women's silences through a split female subjectivity. "Ek bewafa se pyaar kiya" (I fell in love with a heartless man) in *Awaara* (Kapoor, 1951) at Rita's birthday party is performed by a dancing girl expressing Rita's feeling of despair and loss when she realizes that the man she fell in love with is a petty criminal.[46] The diegetic musical setting is complemented by a small band of musicians playing Western instruments. The song describes the unfaithfulness of the hero (Raj Kapoor as Raj), who has just left the party. Rita and Raghunath's point-of-view shots are intercut with shots of the doorway, marking a place of exit with the off-screen space symbolizing the space of the hero. Here, Lata Mangeshkar's voice is shared by two porous bodies, one who is dancing and miming the song while the other expresses an intense personal connection with the lyrics of the song. This rupture between the speaker and the utterance is dramatized through the use of Rita's close-up, framing her in the deep space of the hall with a score of onlookers attending the party. While the dancer sings and moves her body joyously, relaying a sense of exteriority, Rita remains motionless and silent, expressing a turbulent inner mental landscape. The disjunction between the voice and the body, between Rita's silence and the dancer's exuberance, turns the song into a "text of muteness" where a melodramatic message is formulated through "mute tableau and gesture" (Brooks 1995, 56). The intercutting between deep space and a selective focus on human faces is mapped by the voice of the singer. The staging of the song turns it into a porous entity; the song illuminates the inner state of the female protagonist through a selective play of camera and editing to highlight the drama between the dancer, Rita, and her surrogate father (figure 1.3). The song in some ways mimics and draws attention to the playback technology by separating the voice from the body.

The sense of an outer core with an inner, deeper voice is pushed further in "Kuch din pehle ek taal mein" "Not long ago on a lake" from the film *Lajwanti* (Suri, 1956). Kavita (Nargis) is separated from her husband and infant daughter after being accused of having an illicit relationship with her husband's friend. Humiliated, Kavita leaves Bombay and starts working as a schoolteacher in another town. The song is performed when the children in her classroom refuse to study and demand a story. At this moment Kavita begins to sing:

Kuch din pehle ek taal mein
Kamal kunj ke andar rehta tha

Figure 1.3. The party song in *Awaara* (Kapoor, 1951). Screenshots by author.

Ek hans ka joda
Ek hans ka joda

Not long ago on a lake,
In a lotus garden
There lived a pair of swans
A pair of swans

Kavita begins the song joyfully, interacting with the children as she sings. Using the story of the swans as a metaphor, the song describes the formation of a nuclear family upholding the reformist impulse of a companionate marriage.[47] But surprisingly, as the song unfolds, the narrative voice within the song and Kavita's own voice as a performer begin to collapse. This subtle shift in the address is played out dramatically in the mise-en-scène as Kavita moves away from the children to face the camera; it is at this moment that we see the subtle change of expressions on Nargis's face, matching the soft, intimate style of singing by Asha Bhosle.[48] With the shifting address, the song slowly becomes a story of Kavita's anguished life. This "becoming" resonates with Vidya Rao's notion of the *thumri* as an open feminine musical form that expands the space available to it in unique and unexpected ways. In an essay exploring the structure and form of the *thumri*, Vidya Rao (1990, WS-31) has cogently argued that women performers have enriched and expanded its limited space through creative interventions. Taking a cue from Rao, I suggest that female confessional songs stretch their limits through an inward expansion. The space within the song suddenly becomes much larger than what it sets itself out to do. As Kavita reaches the end of the second to last *antara*, she pauses briefly, lost in her inner world, until the children start singing the refrain ("Ek hans ka joda"). Awakened from her reverie, she concludes the song with tears rolling down her cheeks:

Phir ek din aisa toofan aaya
chali aisi hawa
Bechari hansi ud gayi
hoke sabse juda
Sagar sagar
Sagar sagar

Sagar sagar dhoondhe
ab ghoom ghoom ke

Then there came a terrible storm
The pen got torn away from them all
She wanders
across the sea
across the sea
In search of her family

In the last section of the song, Asha Bhosle's voice has an echo effect, leaving an extended aural trace on "saagar saagar," a word that is repeated six times in the *antara*. This sonic excess creates a sense of vast space, symbolizing the physical distance between the heroine and her lost family. The visceral effect of the voice's aural trace signposts the incompleteness of the narrative.

"Kuch din pehle" demonstrates how songs work as key artifacts of memory. Drawing on Henri Bergson's notion of perception, Laura Marks (2000, 147) has suggested that sense perceptions involve an engagement with individual and cultural memory. In this sequence, the narrator and the spectator, the singer and the listener, are involved in a sensate experience of remembrance. What is significant is the way the sequence draws upon the knowledge of spectators who occupy a privileged position. With each *antara* of the song, we are asked to delve deeper and deeper into Kavita's memories of her own life. Kavita takes charge of her own narrative by alluding to a story of the swans: the direct address functions here as a vehicle for the subject to assert ownership over a circuit of literary and imaginary conventions and draw attention to the vicissitudes of her own life. The affective force of the song is created by connecting it to Kavita's experience of a harsh and disciplinary experience of modernity.

The heroine's confessional songs are embedded in a potent relationship between the "real" and its affective flows. The sonic trace of the voice, the lyrics of the song, and the performance of the on-screen actor, with subtle facial expressions, evoke memories and the "truth claim" of the heroine. It is this "truth claim" that imports an emotional power to the song, making room for inflated expressions and melodramatic gestures. This melodramatic mode is also deployed quite effectively in films on *tawaifs*, as explored in the next section.

The Mujra *Song*

Songs performed by on-screen *tawaifs* have contributed significantly to the aural presence of the female voice far beyond the confines of cinema. Films based on the lives of courtesans (for example, *Benazir* [Khalil, 1964], *Sadhna* [Chopra, 1958] and *Adalat* [Kalidas, 1958]) have mapped transformations in the heroines' characters through *mujra* songs (Bhaskar and Allen 2009, 231).[49] Performed in the public space of the *kotha*, the *mujra* song was directly implicated in the moral and class identities of singers through the acoustical properties of their voices. *Mujras* were performed in the presence of the narrative community, men who patronized courtesans and looked at them as objects of desire. But in courtesan-based films, the cinematic narrative works to block the heroine's returned gaze, while slowly turning the space of the *mujra* into a private space. In *Devdas* (Roy, 1955), Chandramukhi (Vyjyanthimala) performs her first *mujra* in a live *mehfil*. The setting is grand for "Ab age teri marzi," with the mise-en-scène establishing the *tawaif* as a public woman and an entertainer par excellence. The framing of the musicians playing instruments like the harmonium, tabla, and sarangi, edited in rhythm with the song, further helps in creating the cultural milieu of the *kotha*. With each subsequent *mujra* in the film, the narrative voice becomes more personalized, and the space of the *mujra* shrinks, to exclude musicians and other listeners.[50] The voice of the singer is now presented in a softer register, matching the cadence of the musical instruments, to show that she is now in love with Devdas. "Jise tu qubool karle," the next song, is performed by Chandramukhi in her own room for the hero in a private, intimate setting.

Interestingly, all of the songs performed by Chandramukhi in *Devdas* are sung by Lata Mangeshkar. However, when Devdas leaves the *kotha* and moves into the bazaar, we hear snatches of a *ghazal* in Mubarak Bagum's voice. "Voh na aayenge palat kar, unhe laakh hum bulaye" (He will not show up again, despite my thousand pleas) is heard in the background, gesturing toward Chandramukhi's anguished state. Mubarak Begum's unfinished song is presented as a disembodied voice to recreate the milieu of the bazaar area, the (exterior) space, and to mark it as a distinctive voice of the stigmatized *tawaif.* Mubarak Begum has often been referred to as one of the victims of the "Mangeshkar monopoly," unable as she was to make it among the topmost singers in the industry (Bharatan, 1995).[51] Several of her songs were *mujra* numbers performed by lesser-known actors on the screen, and many of them were incorporated in films only as fragments or without distinctly identifying the on-screen actor who performed the song with lip sync.[52] The distinction Bombay cinema made between Mubarak Begum's and Lata Mangeshkar's voices, through on-screen and off-screen discourses, underscores the importance of acoustical properties for a reworking of the nationalist vision of modern femininity. Mujra songs on-screen staged the interiority of the female subject through a shift in the tonality of the voice. This aural strategy was further enhanced using the flashback to invoke the heroine's confessional self.

Let me cite the *mujra* songs from *Adalat* (Kalidas, 1958), a reformist narrative about an educated young woman who ends up in a *kotha* due to hostile circumstances. Nirmal's innocence and victimhood are underscored through a heightened performance of a tragic figure in the songs. The *mujra* songs of *Adalat*, composed as *ghazals* by Madan Mohan and sung by Mangeshkar, are considered a high point in Lata's partnership with Madan Mohan. In "Yun hastaton ke daag" (The scars of desire), Nirmal describes her anguish, sense of helplessness, and inability to articulate herself, while the lofty, high-pitched violins accompanying the voice underscore the nobility of her persona.

The second *mujra*, performed by Nirmal and another *tawaif* and presented through two distinctly different registers, engenders a split in the voice across two playback singers. In a rare departure from convention, "Ja ja re ja saajna, kahe sapnon mein aaye" (Leave me alone oh love, why do you keep appearing in my dreams) is performed by two courtesans in the *kotha*, not as a female duet but in two separate versions.[53] Seated at the center of the space of the *mehfil*, Nirmal begins to sing in a somber manner in a seated position, until Chandra starts performing at a faster tempo with robust dancing movements. Curiously, the two versions are set to different tunes.[54] Without making any eye contact with the guests at the *kotha*, Nirmal sings the sad, slow-paced composition expressing her longing for the hero, providing ample scope for Lata to show her virtuosity as a singer. The use of sustained notes and melody help to bring out the emotional intensity of the song, which is further relayed through the gestures of the diegetic listeners. However, to liven up the mood of the evening, a gregarious Chandra takes over the song, starting with the same opening lyrics but with energetic dancing movements. The tune of this version, aided by Asha Bhosle's style of singing, and Chandra's dancing suggest a self-conscious lowering of musical and aesthetic values.[55] This is commensurate with Asha Bhosle's own repeated remarks lamenting the "step motherly treatment" she received from an industry that denied her the opportunity to sing the best compositions of its music directors (Bhosle 1990, 52). Further, one must recall Anil Biswas's well-known remark in the industry that "Asha has body while Lata has soul," which was quoted to sharpen the distinction between the two sisters.[56] This hierarchy is further underscored by that fact that Chandra's role is played by Roop Mala, a relatively lesser-known actor, creating an easy slippage between indifferent, impersonal singing and ambivalent morality.[57]

The distinction this sequence makes between the triad of Chandra/Roop Mala/Asha Bhosle, on the one hand, and Nirmal/Nargis/Lata Mangeshkar, on the other, is quite crucial. The song performed by Nirmal and sung by Mangeshkar directly addresses the cinematic audience by unlocking the images of her past life. As Nirmal looks at the camera closing in on her face, we are introduced to images of her past with the hero. This flashback sequence grafted on the musical interlude works to articulate the inner life of the heroine, connecting us to her past. But it also functions crucially to disconnect her from the narrative listeners present in the *kotha*. As I have argued, "the *mehfil* form is muted through the denial of the returned look, thus arresting the flow of glances" (Jhingan 2022, 254). On the other hand, Chandra engages with the men in the *kotha* through eye contact and her body gestures. What is significant is the denial of a past to Chandra: bereft of a flashback sequence, encoded with private memories, Chandra's erotic performance acquires moral overtones.

"Unko yeh shikayat hai ki hum kuch nahin kehte" (He complains that I do not say anything), the third song performed by Nirmal in the *kotha*, highlights the woman's inability to express herself, foregrounding the film's melodramatic mode. The song encapsulates the drama of Nirmal's life by invoking her past. The spectators are privy to the same *ghazal* recited earlier by Nirmal in *tarannum* (verse intonation) style at a poetry competition at her college. In the early part of the film, we are introduced to Nirmal attending college despite financial difficulties. Rajen (Pradeep Kumar), a fellow student from a wealthy family, pursues her romantically and urges her to reveal her feelings. Nirmal remains shy and evasive. At the poetry competition, Rajen sits at the dais to judge the contest. Nirmal sets out to perform "Unko yeh shikayat hai ki hum kuch nahin kehte" (He complains that I do not say anything), a *ghazal* presented as a veiled address to Rajen, thus shifting the terrain of public performance to a personal register. Though the *ghazal* is performed in a *tarannum* style without any musical accompaniment, the emphasis is on Nirmal's musical rendition. This sequence once again constructs a potent relationship between the articulation of the personal self and higher musical values through the singer's voice.

Nirmal sings the same *ghazal* in the *kotha*, with a heightened emotional appeal, seated in the middle of the *mehfil*, with a motionless body. A much older Rajen, now a judge in the court of law, visits the neighborhood of the *tawaifs* before he makes a decision about whether to order its demolition. As Rajen is led toward the street, he is drawn to a familiar singing voice and words. Following the aural trace of "Unko yeh shikayat," Rajen moves toward the *kotha* and meets his long lost love. The song demonstrates that *tawaifs* can receive recognition as legitimate citizen-subjects only through an excavation of their private selves. While the other listeners in the *mehfil* represent archaic feudal subjects, the ideal listener is the modern subject, who now represents the court of law. The song thus becomes a force field to draw our attention to the *tawaif*'s private self through a melodramatic staging in the public domain.

The Haunting Song

The female haunting song gained currency in the films of the 1950s and the '60s, presented through ghostly figures. The genre stitched together the sonic dominance of the spectral female voice in both cinematic and extracinematic contexts. The haunting song first appeared in *Mahal* (Amrohi, 1949), where the spectral voice of a woman singing in an abandoned mansion was introduced. Sung by Lata Mangeshkar, "Aayega aanewala" (he, whose arrival is awaited, will surely come), keeps Hari

Shankar, the key auditor and protagonist of the film, on edge, since he is unable to locate a stable source of the voice as he walks into the mansion. The creation of an acoustic territory with a human voice but devoid of its embodiment in the visual field added to the enigmatic quality of the song.[58] Lata Mangeshkar's disembodied voice in "Aayega aanewala" played a crucial role in creating the song's sonic dominance over and above visual or the narrative context of the film (Majumdar 2009). The HMV record of the song credited Kamini, the character played by Madhubala in the film, for the song on its album. But the song's mounting popularity on the radio finally led to Mangeshkar's name being announced as the playback singer. The song marks a transition from "ghost voices" to the aural stardom of "playback singers," a transition "forced by fans" (2009, 189).

The haunting songs performed by malevolent figures, ghostly spirits, numbed sleepwalkers, or figures from a past life, tied to Mangeshkar's acousmatic voice, became an industrial form that powerfully spilled into other media. Michel Chion's well-known formulation about the acousmetre in cinema is important here. Acousmetre is a "special being" that manifests itself barely as a voice, not visible on-screen (Chion 1999, 21). By wandering around the "surface of the screen without entering it," the acousmetre generates a sense of "disequilibrium and tension" in mystery, gangster, and fantasy films (24). But once this voice becomes visually identified, the acousmetre loses its power, now rooted to a particular body and place (28). Chion identifies this process as de-acousmatization. In the haunting songs under discussion, the acousmetre creates an uncanny presence through the female singing voice as it seeps through unbounded territories, entering dark, eerie spaces of monuments, haunted mansions, or the rooftops of these abandoned structures. I contend that the listener becomes a key figure who is constantly being pulled by the acousmetre's powerful sonic trace. In *Bees Saal Baad* (Nag, 1962), Mangeshkar's voice works as an aural intrusion in the form of a *pukar*, or the use of the "o" vowel as a call for attention.[59] The heightened use of reverberation in a high-pitched voice and the reaction shots of the startled on-screen diegetic bodies add to the eerie quality of the song. After a moment of silence, the voice intrudes once again, this time much louder. Startled, the hero starts searching for the source of the voice and moves toward the balcony. As the voice becomes bolder with the refrain “Kahin deep jale kahin dil” (a lamp burns here, a heart singes there), we see the hero running out of the mansion. The source of the singing voice cannot be located firmly, evoking fears of displacement and placelessness and giving the voice an omniscient quality. The mise-en-scène demonstrates the limits of the camera, our vision, and its inability to establish a coherent female subject. Similarly, with “Aaja re pardesi” in *Madhumati* (Roy, 1958), a woman singing amid nature, including a flowing river, sloping hills, and a dense forest, entices teases the hero (Dilip Kumar). The thick mist rising from the river keeps the source of the voice elusive. While the singing voice remains a central component in the soundtrack, the physical female body eludes the visual field, denying the male protagonist a captive look. A recurring motif of Mangeshkar’s haunting songs is the denial of the close-up that had become a familiar strategy in the visual coding of women’s songs.

In her recent work on the supernatural in Hindi commercial cinema, Meheli Sen (2017, 27) has highlighted Lata’s singing voice as a key trope “through which the Gothic as a generic rubric gets consolidated in the post-colonial moment.” Sen challenges Sanjay Srivastava’s framing of Lata’s thin, childlike voice as a sign of woman’s infantilization in the public domain that helped shore up modern postcolonial masculinity. To recall Srivastava’s (2006) argument, the postcolonial Five Year Plan hero (FYP) was mobilized to deliver the Nehruvian vision of scientific development with a drive to work for the national good. Sen (2017, 28–29) argues that Lata’s dominant spectral voice in songs like “Aayega aanewala” “quite systematically ruptures the figure of the male citizen-subject.” Through her detailed textual analysis of the song sequences of *Mahal* (1949) and *Woh Kaun Thi?* (Khosla, 1964), Sen shows how Lata’s solo voice empowers the woman to “enthrall, seduce and render silent” the hero, rendering him incapacitated. It is important to emphasize here Sen’s larger point about the role of the Gothic and the repetitive use of the female ghostly voice in expressing an “anxiety about the rapid modernization and industrialization that national independence brought in its wake” (41). My interest is in elaborating on Lata’s haunting songs to underscore their ability to dislodge the narrative impulse of the film. Secondly, I want to demonstrate how the persistent dispersal of Lata’s ghostly voice through the radio and gramophone records becomes inscribed in the film text narratives, making it appear as a rogue sonic object. Lata's haunting songs perform the function of a synecdoche, foregrounding the powerful and rhizomatic presence of the feminine playback voice across various intermedial circuits.

Let us turn to *Kohraa* (Nag, 1964), where the key auditor who comes under the spell of Lata's ghostly voice is not the male figure but the female protagonist. Based on Daphne Du Maurier's *Rebecca* (1938), *Kohraa* builds an enigma around the supernatural force of the dead wife. Waheeda Rahman plays the role of Rajeshwari, who marries Amit, a wealthy widower (played by Biswajeet) and moves into Mayflower, his palatial mansion. It is interesting to compare *Kohraa* with Hitchcock's *Rebecca* (1940), since both films rely on the disembodied female voice. In the opening sequence of *Rebecca*, it is through the voice of the narrator (the unnamed second Mrs. De Winter) that we are introduced to Manderlay, the mansion occupied by the de Winter family, and the events that follow. *Kohraa*, on the other hand, introduces us to the first wife's voice. The film opens with a humming sound of a woman, as the image fades into the exterior space of Mayflower. The humming voice guides us into the interiors, revealing the fragmented shots of a woman humming to herself during a shower. The song that follows departs from the conventions of the female solo song with an emphasis on the physiognomy of the diegetic singer: the mise-en-scène is deployed to keep the woman's countenance away from the visual field, denying us the pleasure of the song in alignment with the on-screen performer's face. In Michel Chion's terms, this would be termed as half acousmetre. The song is introduced in Mangeshkar's voice with an alap as soon as Poonam starts descending the staircase. Over the first two *antaras* we see the enigmatic woman walking in the direction of the beach house, accosted by her lover, and drinking in his company. These acts of transgression are presented symbolically, through discontinuous editing and a distant camera, while the continuous presence of music and the singing voice fills the gaps created by elliptical editing and projection of deep shadows (figure 1.4).[60] The contradictory impulse of the film is revealed through the song, as the tonal inflections of Mangeshkar's soft and intimate voice offer a corrective to the moral overtones of the film depicting Poonam as a wanton character.[61] The use of the alap, the tune, and the lyrics of

Figure 1.4. The enigmatic woman in the haunting song of *Kohraa* (Nag, 1964). Screenshots by author.

the song are mobilized to offer a complicated text that expresses a woman's deep despair and unfulfilled desires. The *mukhda* and the first *antara* of the song are as follows:

Jhoom jhoom dhalti raat
Leke chali mujhe apne saath
Jhoom jhoom dhalti raat . . .

This swaying night
Hurtling and pulling me along
Oh, this swaying night

Jaane kahan le Jaaye
Dard bhara yeh dil
Jaise sada deti hai
Khoi hui manzil

Who knows where I am headed
With my aching heart
A voice pulling me
In search of that final crossing

The disembodied singing voice is assigned to Poonam's ghostly figure through reiteration. The accretion of the spectral quality of the voice can be attributed to the fact that neither is Poonam de-acousmatized nor is her face ever revealed in the film. After Poonam's death, the aura linked to her overwhelming presence permeates Mayflower and begins to threaten Rajeshwari (Waheeda Rahman), the new wife. Trapped in the intimidating space of the mansion and anguished by her husband's indifference, Rajeshwari tries to grapple with the presence of the past as we move into the narrative. The song of the earlier wife comes to life when Rajeshwari enters the dead woman's chambers. As the song reappears on the soundtrack, we see the ghostly figure of a woman dressed in white, haunting Rajeshwari with her intermittent presence in the visual field.[62] Marked by sonic dominance, the song sequence shows Rajeshwari obsessively following the trace of Mangeshkar's spectral voice. What is interesting about this sequence is the introduction of a new *antara* in the song. The ghostly figure sings:

Third Antara

Jisko koi samjhe naa,
Baat na vo dohraa
Mera tera jeevan kya,
Chaya hua kohraa
Mera tera jevan kya . . .
Kisne sunii kabhii dil kii baat
Jhoom jhoom dhalti raat . . .

Why repeat your woeful tales
Your life and mine
Will fade away in this enveloping haze
Your life and mine
Has anyone ever cared to hear us out

This swaying night
Hurtling along

This is the only moment in the film that we are given a sense of the deep despair of a woman trapped in an unhappy and restrictive marriage. Through the use of this third *antara*, the boundaries of the song expand from within. Marked by ambivalence and ellipsis, this particular narrative track never gets resolved in the film.[63] The recursive voice of the dead woman in the song performs a disjunctive function, drawing attention to the oppressive restrictiveness of the *haveli* and an indifferent male figure. While the pro-filmic event in the visual field shows Rajeshwari as a tormented woman, haunted by the voice of the ghostly figure, the aural track relays the anguish of the "tormentor," a rare articulation and one that remains completely unacknowledged by the narrative.[64] Further, the acousmatic voice in *Kohraa* at no time gets attached to the body, remaining dispersed and unanchored. The film's recurring use of the song works to challenge the narrative impulse of the film that implicates Poonam as wanton and irresponsible.

Kaja Silverman (1988, 45) has argued that classical Hollywood cinema makes the male voice both the vantage point of "textual origin" as well its authorial vision, which results in the male subject emerging as an enunciator. The female voice, according to Silverman, gets pushed into the interior of the narrative, thus denying the woman access to the primary site of textual production (56). In the context of popular Hindi film songs, Sanjay Srivastava (2006, 131) has suggested that Lata's adolescent-girl voice worked to "establish the authority of the written word over the recalcitrant possibilities of orality." Mangeshkar's voice is thus seen by Srivastava as performing the consolidation of textuality and literariness in the interest of patriarchal ideologies. A close reading of Lata's haunting songs, however, alerts us to the way her spectral voice spills out of textual and diegetic boundaries, challenging the notion of a female lack and the bracketing of the voice "within narrative recesses and closets," as discussed by Silverman (1988, 69) in the context of classical cinema. Let us consider an instance from *Mera Saaya* (Khosla, 1966), where we are presented with the recursive voice of a "dead" woman haunting the male protagonist. The film opens with a dramatic sequence of the death of Thakur Rakesh Singh's young wife, Geeta (Sadhana), following a brief illness. Devastated, the Thakur (Sunil Dutt) becomes a recluse and starts obsessively listening to his wife's recorded voice (the voice of Lata Mangeshkar) in the song "Tu jahan jahan chalega" (wherever you will be), being played on a spool tape player. The disembodied echoed voice of the dead wife is played several times in the film while the camera tracks the empty corridors and archways of old monuments of Rajasthan in search of the voice.

In a striking turn of events, Rakesh is then informed by the police that a woman caught in an encounter with a group of bandits has claimed that she is Geeta. Convinced that this mysterious woman, though bearing a close resemblance to his wife, is an imposter, Rakesh decides to challenge her in court. *Mera Saaya* makes a crucial distinction between memories that reveal intimate moments of the couple in the public sphere (the courtroom) through the "living wife's" testimony, and the husband's private remembrance of the songs, sung by his "dead" wife. The old system of morality and kinship networks is stretched to its limit to come under the purview of modern law. Lawrence Liang (2015, 100) has shown how *Mera Saaya* "moves between the public domain of evidence and proof" and the sensory domain of private memory. While anecdotal incidents linked to the couple's conjugal life are allowed to be revealed in the courtroom, the song "Tu jahan jahan chalega" remains sanctified as part of their intimate world, revealed to the spectators through selective address. This recalcitrant memory escapes both the disciplinary regimes of legal jurisprudence and psychoanalytic framing. The power of the "dead wife's" aural memory threatens her double—the living wife—thus destabilizing the couple's relationship.

In *Mera Saaya*, the woman's haunting voice upstages the narrative, challenging the relationship between the listener, who controls the technology of music consumption, and the singer, who demands to be heard. After spending a harrowing day in court, the restless husband sits down to play a gramophone record in his room. Geeta's framed black-and-white pictures on the gramophone player and her *mangalsutra* in her husband's hand are displayed prominently as objects of remembrance while we wait to listen to the sound of the gramophone player.[65] "Woh bhooli dastan" (That forgotten tale), a popular song sung by Lata Mangeshkar from *Sanjog* (Chakravorty, 1961), fades up, but as soon as we hear the opening line or the *mukhda*, another voice with an echo is introduced in the soundtrack.[66] Through the clutter of the two soundtracks we are now reoriented to hear "Tu jahan jahan chalega" as the shocked husband turns to look at the gramophone player at this moment of epiphany. The acousmetre, the singing voice of the dead wife, is activated on its own accord, taking control of the listening device against the will of the listener.[67] As Chion (1999, 24) notes, "The acousmetre is everywhere, its voice comes from an immaterial, non-localized body, and it seems that no obstacle can stop it." This sequence highlights Lata Mangeshkar's intractable playback voice, spilling out of diegetic boundaries, pointing to her unparalleled aural stardom in the industry. More importantly, it stages her position of dominance in the industry, which became a source of both devotion and anxiety.

Haunting songs continued to play a central role in Mangeshkar's oeuvre over the next two decades. Radio countdown shows, in particular, indexed the resilient and extradiegetic presence of these songs through cinema's intermedial routes. Therefore, it is not surprising that EMI, in partnership with HMV, released *Haunting Melodies of Lata Mangeshkar* (3AXE-5131).[68] What remains significant is the way the release of this special album in 1967 coincided with twenty-five years of Lata Mangeshkar in the film industry (figure 1.5). The album opens with "Aayega aanewala," once again reaffirming the unique status of this song in creating Lata Mangeshkar's stardom. This song, as noted by several scholars, allowed radio and gramophone listeners to directly connect with her voice, setting the stage for her aural stardom.[69] "Aaja re pardesi," from the film *Madhumati* (Roy, 1958) the next number in the album is equally important, as it is the first song that was selected to honor the "Best Playback Voice," by *Filmfare* in 1959. The album showcases the songs performed by Lata as a spectral figure, whose voice dominated the film soundtracks through its recurring presence. The heightened use of reverberation and the stretching of vowels in the opening line: "Aaja raeeeeee pardesi" (*Madhumati*) or the voice leaving a sonic trace at the end of the opening line, as in "Aayega aanewala, Aayega," became a recurring aural motif. The melodic setting of all of these songs expresses incompleteness, signifying the woman's unfulfilled yearnings.[70] The album described these songs as melodies that have "haunted and will continue to haunt the memories of discerning listeners for years to come. They are haunting in the literal sense too, all having been picturised in eerie

Figure 1.5. A special album of haunting songs. Author's personal collection.

and mysterious contexts. And they best illustrate what we have called voice of this angel known as Lata Mangeshkar."[71]

This text on the album jacket seamlessly tries to connect two aspects of Lata's stardom that sit uncomfortably with each other: the symbolic association of an angelic voice with that of the heroine, and the recursive presence of her uncanny voice, in excess of both narrative and cinematic boundaries. The female haunting songs operated as a source of narrative anxiety, as they gave voice to female characters whose authenticity and identity were deeply suspect. Yet, through their lyrics and tonal registers, they could articulate the innermost desires and sense of alienation of these spectral and disruptive figures. Mangeshkar's voice, considered soft, delicate, and melodious, was deployed to implode these songs, challenging the established notions of the sweetness of the voice as a marker of domesticated middle-class femininity. Further, several of these haunting songs were introduced into soundtracks repeatedly, while the identity of the on-screen woman who sings them remained deferred.

The four genres discussed above hardly do justice to the range of female songs that were performed by Lata Mangeshkar. However, by shifting my attention to the material practices of sound recording, I have tried to follow the dance between the aural and the ocular that corresponds with the way songs oscillate between their diegetic context and their extratextual circulation. This approach has been productive in contesting a dominant reading of Lata's voice within the framework of nationalist imaginaries. Through the circulation of film songs, Bombay cinema became a crucial medium for a corrective to the standardization and canonization of music followed by All India Radio and national public culture, thus making room for the articulation of the experiential, the sensuous, the personal, and the biographical of the female self. Lata Mangeshkar's haunting songs show how her voice on radio and gramophone records, in particular, seeped back into the film narratives, pointing toward its unruly counterflows.

2

Courtesans, Vamps, Crooners, and Street Singers

In the playback era, stars were expected to perform elaborate facial, hand, and bodily gestures in response to the song's tonal, rhythmic, and spatial setting. In this production ecology, film songs were heard repeatedly, so that actors could inhabit the lyrics, in sync with the song's aural registers. A song's successful aural and visual coding could result in repeat viewership and iteration in radio countdown shows. This voice-body relationship was further accentuated in the public domain in the 1970s, when song sequences became available on television through weekly shows like *Chitrahaar* and *Chayageet*. Helen, a dancing star of erotic songs and cabarets, lip-synching to the breathy voice of Asha Bhosle, or Waheeda Rahman's dance of freedom while performing to Lata's "Aaj phir jeene ki tamanna hai" (Today I renew my desire to live), were now available in our living rooms. In this chapter, I will engage with the visceral voice-body contact to examine how the female voice was mobilized to produce a phantasmatic and musicking body on-screen. The term "musicking," as developed by Christopher Small (1998, 9), introduces us to music as an activity that includes composing, singing, dancing, and listening, thus opening the field to discuss bodily engagements. Matthew Rahaim's (2012, 24) close attention to the gestural body while performing Indian music elaborates on the codification of bodies through the lens of gender and class while singing. A closer look at the auditory registers of the voice in songs filmed on characters such as courtesans, vamps, crooners, classical musicians, folk performers, and street singers helps us chart the body as a site of varying thresholds of desire enacted in contested terrains. Through a formal analysis of songs performed by diverse bodies in films, I will demonstrate how the voice gives us access to the lived experience of the body, its affordances, and its shifting dynamics as social and imaginary categories.

How did the on-screen diegetic body borrow and enfold the voice of the playback singer, when the body *itself* is not a stable category? As Elizabeth Grosz (1994, 190) has observed, bodies are not fixed or inert entities. Grosz's notion of embodied subjectivity accounts for a "lived body," with a range of gestures, postures, and movements, that interact with its psychical interiority (23). I draw on these ideas to discuss how the playback voice could powerfully evoke and simultaneously repress signs of labor, violence, morbidity, precarity, and social hierarchies. While highlighting the material practices involved in the creation of on-screen dance spectacles, Usha Iyer (2020, 5) signposts the involvement of "many bodies," including those of dancers, choreographers, playback singers, and musicians. Female playback singers have not only lent their voices to a range of bodies in different kinds of spaces; they have also performed discontinuous gender identities (Butler 1990, 17). These include new entrants into the industry, aging stars such as Meena Kumari, and narrative characters as diverse as prepubescent boys, mothers, vamps, crooners, courtesans, classical singers and dancers, men in drag, and working-class women singing and performing on the streets.[1]

In discussing the voice-body relationship, Mary Anne Doane alerts us to the spatiality of the voice. "Just as the voice must be anchored by a given body," writes Doane, "the body must be anchored in a given space" (1987, 568). I reframe this concept by demonstrating how the voice produces, extends, and defies space through the affective alliance between the playback star, actor, character, and spectator. I draw on Brandon LaBelle's (2010, xxii) assertion that that sound "opens up a field of interaction," to "carve out a micro-geography of the moment" (xxii). The spaces of the *mehfil*, rural fair, nightclub, sound studio, street, footpath, and urban landscape emerge as important sites for the manifold staging of the female musicking body through the singing voice.

This chapter positions the singing and dancing figure on-screen as a listening body, participating in the intermedial footprints of Bombay cinema's sonic ecology, taking into consideration the arrival of Polydor Records that played a significant role in bringing in the Western bass in the female voice and disco beats. A closer look at the new technologies of sound dispersal in the last section reveals how the voice-body contract in song sequences was increasingly shaped by the auditory charge of the cassette technology and later by the visual dynamics of television. I engage with these transformations to show how, in Bombay cinema, the listener-spectator is drawn into an audiovisual loop of divergent bodies and their attachment to changing technologies of sound dispersal.

An Unstable Star

Pakeezah (Amrohi, 1972) represents a classic courtesan film with several memorable songs and *mujra* sequences. The film is also an overlaid text with several behind-the-scenes stories, including the death of key members of its cast and crew during the making and exhibition of the film. Just a month after its release, Meena Kumari, a reigning star of the 1960s, who played the title role of *Pakeezah*, succumbed to her illness, which turned the film into an overnight cult classic. The film's rhizomatic journey across a cinematic and extracinematic landscape, and its larger-than-life textual form, lay out the auditory terrain for examination. The assemblage form is mobilized to mask the presence of an ailing, unstable body through an overt reliance on Mangeshkar's playback voice. However, the excess of Mangeshkar's voice in this affective and bodily alliance between the two stars also creates a ground for the erosion of other sonic bodies.

Pakeezah opens with the story of Nargis (Meena Kumari), a courtesan whose desire to escape from her profession remains unfulfilled as Shahabuddin (Ashok Kumar), with whom she elopes from the *kotha*, is unable to withstand the pressure from his feudal and patriarchal father, who refuses to accept this alliance. Feeling rejected, Nargis takes refuge in a graveyard where she ultimately dies after giving birth to her daughter. A letter that Nargis wrote to Shahabuddin about his daughter reaches him after seventeen years, prompting him to come to the bazaar to take his daughter away. But Saheb Jan has already been initiated to carry on with her mother's profession. *Bazaare-husn* is introduced to us as Shahabuddin's carriage enters the bazaar.[2] The entire exchange between Shahabuddin and Nawab Jan (Saheb Jan's aunt) is interspersed with aural tracks of female singers singing *dadra*, *ghazal* and *thumri*, giving a definite aural identity and authenticity to the bazaar.[3] The voices of these disembodied singers in the background fade in and out, framing the bitter exchange.[4] We hear only snatches of these voices, some less audible than others, providing us with a sense of the differential placement of each singer/courtesan in the sonic chain. This also helps in creating a sonic perspective for the voice tracks. We are denied a closer look at any of these singers. Yet, through the layering of these aural registers, we are presented with the courtesans' rich textual and musical repertoire performed for their patrons in live *mehfils*. Thus, it is not just the use of wide-angle lenses and the depth of field in the ocular that turns "bazaare-husn" into "deep space." Rather, a layered and dense soundtrack makes faintly audible a diverse set of genres, voices, bodies, and practices of singing, providing a spatial dimension to the cultural memory of *kotha* culture.[5]

The conversation between Shahabuddin and Nawab Jan ends with the rhythmic beats of the tabla, as the latter starts to climb the stairs to return to thc *kotha*. The next shot, with the opening line of "Inhi logon ne," frames Saheb Jan/Meena Kumari with her back to the camera as Lata's voice envelopes the soundtrack. We are introduced to Lata's familiar voice before we are visually introduced to Meena Kumari performing the song.[6] The use of Lata's playback voice in this sequence, according to Bhaskar and Allen (2009, 58), "enacts the process by which husky elaboration of the *thumri* performed in the kotha gave way to the sweet and melodious tenor of Lata's singing." I recall Martin Daughtry's (2017, 48) formulation of the "acoustic palimpsest," to draw attention to the calibrated use of sonorous objects or voices that engender a layered auditory experience. The acts of erasure in musical performances and recordings can be recovered only partially, but this requires "critical listening" and "leaps of imagination" (53). The palimpsest as a framework that accounts for both erasure and inscription is useful to understand the role of sound synchronization in shoring up the star body in conjunction with the playback voice, since this sets the stage for the erasure of all other sounds. What is erased by Lata's dominant voice in "Inhi logon ne" is not only the diverse voices of the courtesans and the varied genres in which they sing in the background but also all of the street sounds—the din of murmurs and arguments and the residual traces of tabla and sarangi.[7] The interlocking of Lata Mangeshkar's playback voice with the sound of the *dholak*, the tabla, and the ankle bells (*ghungroo*), in perfect sync with Meena Kumari's facial gestures, creates an embodied effect.[8] In contrast to the fragmented and disembodied voices we hear on the street, "Inhi logon ne" presents Lata's voice in perfect unity with Meena Kumari's phantasmatic body. The textures of voice and the repertoire of the women singing in the aural background carry the registers of a palimpsest waiting to be recovered and reappropriated. Sonic traces of these voices reemerge in another sequence in *Pakeezah* when Saheb Jan goes to visit her friend Bibban in a Lucknow bazaar. "Kaun gali gayo shyam," sung by Parveen Sultana, can be heard in the background as Saheb Jan enters her aunts' home/ *kotha*. Finally, when she gets to meet Bibban in the privacy of her room and confides to her about her restlessness, the sound of "Yeh dhuan kahan se uthta hai," a *ghazal* sung by Naseem Chopra, can be heard on the soundtrack and marks their exchange. Almost like a "print through," Chopra's voice becomes distinctly audible during the silences between the two friends. Unlike the *mujra* songs presented by Saheb Jan, both of these tracks in the background remain unanchored and detached from any listening body on-screen.

The making of *Pakeezah* was fraught with problems, causing delays at every stage of production. Though the filming began in 1958, the film was finally released in 1971. Kamal Amrohi is known to have initially shot a few reels of the film in black and white. Later, he switched to Eastman color, but abandoned the material after a few reels to move the film into CinemaScope. Well into its production, Amrohi separated from Meena Kumari, which delayed the film for many years. Joseph Wirsching, the cinematographer, and Ghulam Mohammed, the music director, died before the film could be completed. The shooting for the film was finally resumed in 1968 with much fanfare when Meena Kumari agreed to return to the set and complete the film despite her ill health.[9] *Pakeezah* became a text overlaid with circulating narratives about its production, as well as the changing dynamics in the private lives of its stakeholders. The release of the film, too, generated a lot of curiosity: journalists writing previews of the film did not fail to mention that though the film had undergone so many changes, including its hero, Kamal Amrohi had stuck to his decision to cast Meena Kumari as the heroine, even though she had started playing roles of older women on-screen. In an article in the *Illustrated Weekly of India*, Raju Bharatan (1972a, 52) wondered if the actor could carry off the show at that stage of her career. These remarks brought extracinematic information about her failing health into the public domain.

Pakeezah carries the figure of an unstable star with an illness on its surface. In several scenes, we see a much older Meena Kumari, followed by those where we see her bright and youthful persona.[10] Unlike the genre of the "rare disease films" of the 1970s, as discussed by Madhava Prasad (2013, 91), that focused on terminally ill characters, *Pakeezah* works hard through different strategies to cover up the lead star's afflicted body. In some key sequences, Amrohi is known to have relied on body doubles. For instance, in the romantic duet "Chalo dildar chalo," the camera avoids shots of Meena Kumari's face or frontal views of her body. Instead, the song is crafted through silhouette shots of a sailing boat going into the horizon, with Mohammed Rafi and Lata Mangeshkar's voices on the soundtrack. The film is thus marked by both Meena Kumari's presence and her absence, presenting Saheb Jan as a fractured figure who has to be recuperated by the spectator/listener.

Toward the film's end, Saheb Jan performs a *mujra* with a dramatic climax (figure 2.1). In "Aaj hum apni duaon ka asar dekhege" (Today I will see the outcome of my prayers), we see Padma Khanna performing as a body double for the ailing star.[11] Through the use of long shots, inventive camera angles, and a veil that covers Meena Kumari's face, Kamal Amrohi was able to shoot the frenzied dance movements, dancing on shards of glass, with Padma Khanna's body.[12] The playback singer's stable voice played a crucial role in upholding the aura of an aging star who was referred to as the "soul" of the film. The persistent presence of Lata Mangeshkar's voice for a contingent body helped in providing a sense of aura and cult status to Meena Kumari, as she passed away shortly after the release of *Pakeezah*.

The Middle-Class Girl

In the 1970s, Jaya Bhaduri (later Jaya Bachchan) emerged as a middle-class girl on-screen. In several of her early films, Jaya played roles that

Figure 2.1. The final *mujra* in *Pakeezah* (Amrohi, 1972). Source: National Film Archive of India.

focused on her transformation from a buoyant adolescent girl to a mellowed woman. In several films Jaya played the role of a trained classical singer. These films include *Parichay* (Gulzar, 1972), *Abhimaan* (Mukherjee, 1973), and *Bawarchi* (Mukherjee, 1972), in which she is shown to train herself in bharata natyam, a classical dance form. The narratives of these films underscored the middle-class woman's engagement with classical dance and music through a sharp projection of moral anxieties around women performing in the public domain. In the following section, I will discuss three films directed by Hrishikesh Mukherjee to demonstrate how Jaya created a template of gestures, bodily stances, and facial expressions by performing roles of women trained in classical arts. Jaya's screen roles, representing the aspirations of a middle-class artist, started intersecting with Lata's public persona. The songs she performed in these early films were crucial for these negotiations (figure 2.2).

Figure 2.2. Jaya Bhaduri on the cover of *Filmfare*. Source: National Film Archive of India.

For instance, in *Guddi* (Mukherjee, 1971), Jaya plays the role of Kusum, an adolescent schoolgirl with a talent for singing, which is revealed in the opening sequence of the film. We see Kusum rushing toward her school, while students have started with the morning prayer. The uneven singing is underlined by showing some discordant reactions from the schoolchildren. The close-ups show them sniggering and struggling to concentrate. As Kusum sneaks into the prayer hall, the headmistress gestures to her to come to the stage and lead the prayer. The mise-en-scène shows a marked change in the environment as Kusum starts leading the prayer, while the children repeat in chorus. The camera pans across the children's faces, now lost in the prayer, their eyes shut, in harmony with each other. Interestingly, the playback voice for the prayer song was provided by Vani Jairam, a new entrant into the industry who, according to popular press, "made as big a splash" as Jaya Bhaduri (Rajendran, 1973, 45). Journalists also opined that the songs in *Guddi* worked because a new voice was matched perfectly with the face of a new star (Jaya) (Bharatan 1971d, 43). The songs played an important role in staging the transformation of a naive, innocent girl to a middle-class homemaker. In *Guddi*, notes Madhava Prasad (1998, 170), the middle-class family is "threatened by the lure of cinema." Kusum loves going to the movies and is obsessed with Dharmendra, one of the current screen stars of the industry. Kusum's ability to sing well is cast within the framework of middle-class aspirations to provide training to young women in music in order to improve their marriage prospects. When Navin (Samit Bhanja), her prospective groom, takes Kusum out for the first time, they visit a nearby archaeological site of ancient caves with classically sculpted images. On Navin's request, Kusum reluctantly agrees to sing a classical song, "Bole re papih hara," lip-synching to Vani Jairam's voice. The intercutting between the sculpted images on the walls and shots of Kusum framed from Navin's point of view is offset by Kusum's coy demeanor. Kusum keeps tugging at her sari, conscious of Navin gazing at her.

In a dream sequence, Kusum envisions herself singing "Tujhe jivan ki dor se baandh liya hai" from *Asli Naqli* (Mukherjee, 1962), a romantic duet with Dharmendra. The dream sequence demonstrates a mimetic relationship with cinema—alluding to song sequences, in particular, as the site of sensuous knowledge and embodied memory that is steeped in the powerful force field of aurality. We see Kusum in a restless state, imagining a real-life encounter with Dharmendra. The voices playing on the track for this dream sequence are those of Mohammed Rafi and Lata Mangeshkar, as in the original song from *Asli Naqli*. The dream ends with a shot of Jaya dressed in bridal finery on her wedding night, facing the camera, while Dharmendra, dressed as a groom and framed in the background, sings to her. In performing this romantic duet (in Lata's voice) with a top male star, Jaya is established as a heroine. This transformation seems complete when, toward the end of the film, Kusum sings "Aaja re pardesi," recalling a song sung by Lata Mangeshkar in *Madhumati* (Roy, 1958). It is Kusum's birthday party and she is asked to sing a popular song for everyone. Having shed her adolescent infatuation for a film star (Dharmendra), Kusum is now in love with Navin. Anxiously waiting for Navin to turn up, Kusum sings "Aaja re pardesi," lip-synching to Lata's playback voice. This shift in the playback voice from Vani Jairam to Lata Mangeshkar is not unconnected to the off-screen discourses about Lata's monopolistic control over the industry. The effacement of Vani Jairam's voice in the film becomes more telling when we take into account the reports that "Hari bin kaise jioon ri," a third song that she had recorded for *Guddi*, was replaced by Lata Mangeshkar's "Aaja re pardesi" (Bharatan, 1971d).[13] The recall of Lata's voice singing "Aaja re pardesi" in *Guddi* thus symbolically represents the role played by the film industry in erasing Vani Jairam's voice.

I consider here a gendered discursive context within which the playback singer's voice got enmeshed with the body of a star. The interplay between off-screen and on-screen discourses can be traced through a series of recurrent tropes in Jaya's star persona. Jaya performed the role of a singer in several of her films, the most notable being *Parichay* (Gulzar, 1972) and *Abhimaan* (Mukherjee, 1973).[14] *Bawarchi* (Mukherjee, 1972) is another film that works hard to privilege the classical arts of music and dance as a distinct sacrosanct space for women within the realm of domesticity. Krishna (Jaya Bhaduri) is an orphan living with her paternal grandfather, uncles, and aunts as part of a joint family where she secretly harbors a deep fascination for dance. Krishna watches Nita (Manisha), her older cousin, learning kathak and practicing fervently for an upcoming dance competition. Nita's guru (Paintal) plays a *thumri* on a spooled tape and teaches Nita the basic steps to match the recorded music. The text of the *thumri*, "Kahe kanha karat barjori" (Kanha why do you harass me), sung by Lakshmi Shankar, describes a troubled *nayika* asking Kanha not to tease her, pleading with him to stop pulling at her light-skinned arms.[15] The *thumri* is interspersed with fast-paced rhythmic segments that allow Nita to display her skilled dance movements. During a practice session, Nita catches Krishna peeping into her room and humiliates her. Angered by this incident, and to teach Nita a lesson, Raghu starts training Krishna in classical dance. Raghu's crusading impulse to bring the bickering family into a mode of self-correction becomes aligned with a larger cultural project.[16] Counterimpulses are enacted at the dance competition in the college auditorium, as we see Nita's parents and the girls' grandfather (Harindra Nath Chattopadhyaya) prominently seated among the audience. A *lavani* dancer and a Rajasthani *ghoomar* are booed by the old man for displaying erotic body movements. Next, it is Nita's turn to perform the kathak piece that she had been practicing, which is followed by a boisterous bhangra dance. As soon as the bhangra dancer exits the stage, we see a marked shift in the audiovisual register: from the close-up of a sitar, we move to a silhouetted frame of Krishna (Jaya Bhaduri) in a bharata natyam posture as Lata Mangeshkar's familiar voice fades into the soundtrack.[17] The camera movement and editing style are mobilized to privilege the musicality of the performance, with shots of Krishna's dancing figure intercut with individual shots of different musicians seated on the stage, including Raghu on the flute. The song is loosely based on a *padam* that describes the lament of a slighted woman, waiting for her lover.[18] Jaya's facial expressions while lip-synching to Lata's voice display a range of emotions, detailing her longing for, and separation from, her beloved.[19] Jaya's performance draws its legitimacy from the aesthetic value of classical music, creating a hierarchy in which music is accorded a higher value than dance.[20] Lata's playback voice plays a significant role in making Jaya's dance acquire a sense of respectability and moral superiority. Moreover, the sequence demonstrates a careful reworking of the concert repertoire, so that women from middle-class families could perform in the public domain.

In the next scene, we learn that Krishna has won the dance contest while her cousin Nita has been ranked second. I wish to point out that in the film industry, Jaya Bahduri was considered a poor dancer, while the actor who played the role of Nita was a trained dancer who had learned kathak from Shambhu Maharaj. In the popular press, Jaya is herself known to have remarked about "being most uncomfortable [with dancing]" (Jhunjhunwala 2009, 17). Jaya's performance and subsequent victory in *Bawarchi* enacts a course correction commensurate with the nationalist reform project in the cultural sphere. This is staged through purging erotic elements from the song and infusing it instead with spiritual resonances. The familiar sad song of Hindi films perfected by Lata is reinscribed as a *padam*, in which the heroine is presented as a passive heroine who waits endlessly for her lover.

In *Abhimaan*, Jaya Bhaduri plays the role of a singer who has been well trained in music by her father (A. K. Hangal), a classical musician and a Sanskrit scholar. The film opens with a concert by Subir Kumar (Amitabh Bachchan), a pop singer with a huge female fan following. Subir is a successful singing star but often goes through bouts of loneliness and depression. During a visit to his aunt's place near Bangalore, Subir overhears devotional hymns sung by a woman at a temple. The next day, Subir follows the trail of the voice, to see Uma (Jaya Bhaduri) watering plants at a temple and absorbed in her singing. Drawn toward her talent and simplicity, Subir marries Uma and brings her to Bombay. Soon, on Subir's insistence, and with the enthusiastic backing of his business secretary, Chandru, Uma starts singing for the industry and becomes an "overnight star." Her meteoric rise in the film industry ultimately leads to a rift in the couple's relationship. Noticing Subir's increasing disenchantment and Uma's desire to quit, Chandru dramatically raises Uma's fee per song. To his surprise and Subir's envy, producers agree to pay the hiked fee. The narrative deploys several strategies to create a distinction between Subir and Uma as vocal stars. While Subir performs his songs by borrowing the voices of several playback singers, Lata's voice is deployed for all of the songs performed by Uma. This gives Uma's character a stable aural identity and points to the reiterative quality of Lata Mangeshkar's voice. Subir is denied any musical legacy and Uma's classical training gives her an edge over other singers. For Uma, music is deeply embedded in life itself, a natural extension of her being, while for Subir the connection between him and his music is shown as uneasy.

The 1970s marked an important phase in the film industry, with the rise of big stars and an excessive circulation of star discourses in film magazines. Since Jaya Bhaduri and Amitabh Bachchan had just gotten married a few weeks before the release of *Abhimaan*, film journalists noticed the close connection between reel and real life in the film. According to one review, "it required guts on the part of the lead pair to play what could become a reality in their life in three or four years" (*Star and Style* 1973). In my reading, however, *Abhimaan* makes several references to Lata Mangeshkar. The most significant similarity can be seen in Uma and Lata's inherited musical legacy. Lata's father, Dina Nath Mangeshkar, was a well-known classical musician, and her first guru. Moreover, in *Abhimaan*, Uma's quick rise to stardom with her growing number of fans and awards, and a prolific aural presence on radio, seems to encapsulate key fragments from Lata's life. The film draws on the industry discourses of the 1970s, when film producers were known to queue up to get recording dates from Lata. In an important song sequence in the film, Subir and Uma sing "Teri bindiya re" (Your adorned forehead) at their wedding reception. A senior and well-respected music enthusiast rates Uma as a far better singer than Subir and predicts that if Uma is allowed to sing for the industry, she may overshadow her husband. Interestingly, Mohammed Rafi sings "Teri bindiya re" for Subir, while Lata sings for Uma. One must recall that by the late 1960s, Lata had raised her fee significantly and demanded a share in the royalties. This resulted in a rift between Lata and Mohammed Rafi, as the latter refused to support her demand (Bharatan 1995, 107).[21] In the song "Ab to hai tum se har khushi apni" (Each happy moment of mine, I owe to you), Uma is shown recording the song in a studio with a glass separating her from the musicians. As the song unfolds, we see Subir listening with a grave expression. The song maps the transformation of a simple but talented singer into a rising star. As Uma mimes the song to Lata's voice, the camera stays focused on her, framing her in profile shots prominently behind a microphone. Through close-up shots we see subtle movements on Uma's face and eyes, underlining her emotional involvement in the song (figure 2.3).

Matt Rahaim's (2008) insightful work shows a close connection between gesture and vocalization in Indian vocal music. Rahaim (339) notes the development of gestural styles in the musical lineages in *khyal* singing. Taking a cue from Rahaim, I contend that in the context of performing a song for the camera, the gestural repertoire of the actorly body becomes significant, especially when it is the role of a singer. In preparing herself for Uma's role in *Abhimaan*, Jaya Bhaduri is known to have made several visits to recording studios to watch Lata sing. This

Figure 2.3. Jaya Bhaduri performs to Lata's voice in *Abhimaan* (Mukherjee, 1973).

provided a mimetic quality to her performance, enabling her to convey legible and external signs of Lata's star identity. Like Lata, Uma is shown wearing white saris with borders, using the end of the sari to cover her head, sporting small diamond studs in her ears, and maintaining a familiar posture with the microphone. As Jaya herself wrote, "When I played the role of a singer in *Abhimaan*, very consciously, I based my character on Lataji, I felt very close to her while working in the film" (Kabir 2009, 202). The visual codes in song sequences of *Abhimaan* highlight a porosity between the two stars, an accretion that leads to a doubling of affect (figure 2.4). Besides, the film provides us significant insights into the making of an aural star who emerged as the unsurpassed queen of film music. While the central narrative of *Abhimaan* creates an idealized image of Uma's purity and simplicity, at a subterranean level, the film displays an anxiety about how a singer's indispensable status could hold the film industry to ransom.

Jaya Bahduri's "girl next door" image became a template for the simple middle-class girl. As she remarked, "I have never had someone say I want to marry you—besides some crazy fans—but most often I heard women say, you are just like my daughter or, if only I had a daughter like you" (Jhunjhunwala 2009). The songs performed by Jaya with Lata's

a director," which probably means soon. Chopra's own [illegible] Tilak told us he is soon going to direct a film himself.

In another sense, Ravi had a bang-up engagement ceremony. It was Navy Day and its tubs were showing off at the waterfront, with criss-cross lights.

Rajendra Kumar and Raaj Kumar attended—stars from B. R. Films' vintage years. Sanjay wore glasses—he wears them in Chopra's current production "Dhund"—and thought the producer-director would be tickled. Financier Maganbhai Sawani told the story of a man who went to his occulist and was fitted with a pair of spectacles. "Can you read now?" the doctor asked. "No," said the patient, "I can't read or write anyway." Now where did Savani get the story—*The Illustrated Weekly*? Sanjay told two other stories, more interesing but unfortunately not printable.

Mukesh talked briefly of his performing tour abroad. He had sung in the U.K. and in Denmark and made brief visits to Switzerland and Paris. He had taken his wife with him this time. She is a strict vegetarian and this entailed some occasional discomfiture in finding the right hotels for her to eat in. Both husband and wife enjoyed a visit to the revolving restaurant atop London's Post Office Tower. Mukesh said "Gone with the Wind", now on the stage in London, was a fabulous show.

"I am one Nana Palsikar," said the twinkling old veteran, his way of saying one and only. Manmohan Krishna invited us to see his IPTA play "Shatranj ke Mohre". This energetic actor finds time for everything—films, plays, trade union work and trusteeship of the Filmfare Old Artistes Benevolent Fund. This last portfolio is not without its headaches — someone whose loan application wasn't passed came to his door shouting slogans.

The estrangement between the Chopra brothers seems to be settling down to a background thing. Pamela Yash Chopra came to Ravi's engagement ceremony. Yash himself was away location filming but attended on a subsequent day the party to celebrate the engagement of B.R.'s daughter Bina with Dilip, son of the late distributor K. K. Kapoor.

Continued on page 19

Star with her sound box: Jaya Bhaduri and Lata Mangeshkar. (Photo: Nath Gupta).

Figure 2.4. Jaya Bhaduri and Lata Mangeshkar. Author's personal collection.

playback voice played a crucial role in projecting this transformation in her fictional roles.[22] Jaya gained significantly from Lata's playback voice in projecting the persona of a middle-class girl. Conversely, Lata could reassert her successful status via the image of a simple girl. It would be instructive to add that by the early '70s, writers like Raju Bharatan had started questioning the hegemonic control of Lata Mangeshkar in playback singing. One of the stories doing the rounds in the industry was that music directors were being pressured by the star singers to block new singers like Vani Jayaram, whose voice had been appreciated by the industry in *Guddi* (Bharatan 1971d).[23] Given this context, I argue that by singing for Jaya's character as a "classical" singer in films like *Abhimaan* and *Bawarchi*, Lata could hold on to her image of a simple middle-class girl, devoted to her art. Mediated through Jaya's star persona, the songs in these films helped Lata offset some of the criticisms she received. This also ensured that her voice remained in circulation in a period otherwise marked by the "angry young man" image of Amitabh Bachchan or the erotic voice of Asha Bhosle.[24]

Singing, Whistling, and Clapping Bodies in the Nightclub

The modern girl of the 1920s and the '30s discussed in chapter one was a transnational phenomenon, fashioned through the intersection of colonial and national modernities. The overt visibilization of the modern girl was intrinsically connected to the expansion of markets, where women would play a key role as consumers. Priti Ramamurthy's (2008, 170) work on the modern girl has drawn our attention to the public appearances of "cheeky, cosmopolitan, and seductive sitara" in early Indian cinema.[25] Citing examples of movies where the modern girls played telephone operators, typists, actresses, teachers, or doctors, Ramamurthy highlights the "fluidity with which the sitara crossed religious and racial boundaries, and incorporated aesthetic and performance practices drawn from across the globe" (170). Ramamurthy challenges the assumption that the modern girl disappeared in the 1940s because the arrival of sound cinema edged out actresses who could not speak or sing. Instead, she attributes this eclipse to way the image of the modern girl became a source of anxiety to a "nationalism that sought to draw boundaries around proper Indian womanhood" (171). I draw on these ideas to foreground traces of the modern girl of the 1920s and the '30s in the westernized vamp presented as a nightclub dancer in the two decades of cinema after independence. The sonic registers of the cabaret song played a crucial role in constructing the modern girl's interracial body. The vocal textures of the playback voice interlaced with chorus voices and polyphonic sounds helped evoke a fluid racial and ethnic identity of the nightclub singer. I argue that this mode of representation changed in the 1970s, when the nightclub emerged as a much darker space with depictions of illicit sex and sexual violence. These were expressed through volatile scale shifts by singers like Asha Bhosle.

The nightclub in the 1950s and the '60s was often framed as a gangster's den with diegetic performances by dance bands with a sonically amplified performance by the lead singer, who made eye contact with the guests and danced with abandon. In *Baazi* (Dutt, 1951), the hero meets the guitar-playing Leena (Geeta Bali) singing "Tadbeer se bigdi hui tadbeer bana le." Sung by Geeta Dutt, the song begins with "he he he he he," a musical gesture that hails the noir hero to stay and try out his luck in the gambling den. In *Awaara* (Kapoor, 1951), "Ek do teen/123" frames Cuckoo singing and dancing in a smoke-filled den of gambling men as Raj and Jagga watch her performance (figure 2.5). Shamshad Begum's voice for Cuckoo competes for attention as we hear the men talking and laughing throughout the song.[26] This corporeal style of female vocality became an aural strategy that helped to invoke the nightclub as part of the city's underbelly. At the same time, the nightclub singer's voice was connected to an expanded sonic universe that included voices of chorus singers, rhythmic clapping of hands, foot-tapping sounds, and a bevy of musicians with an ensemble of Western instruments. This mélange of sound underscored the idea of a hybrid space of porous class and racial boundaries, where one encountered both illicit desire and violence.

Scholarship on the nightclub dancer of Bombay cinema has emphasized the binary between the vamp and the heroine on the axis of vice and virtue.[27] This framework, however, is not specific to the vamp presented in song sequences, particularly those enacted in the nightclub. Ranjani Mazumdar (2007, 89) signposts a more complicated landscape of the vamp's corporeal performance as "both fascinating and dangerous, embodying the dialectic that marks urban life." In her reflection on the Navketan films of the '50s, Mazumdar (2009, 17–18) draws a connection

Figure 2.5. Cuckoo in *Awaara* (Kapoor, 1951). Screenshot by author.

between Bombay's cosmopolitan vision and the depiction of free-spirited women like Sylvie in *Taxi Driver* (Anand, 1954) who occupy the space of the nightclub. Similarly, analyzing the nightclub songs in the city films of the 1950s, Aarti Wani (2016, 48) reads the image of the vamp/club singer/dancer as a sign of urban modernity, straddling neat moral binaries.[28]

Considering that music played such a defining role in the nightclub songs, hardly any attention has been paid to the vamp's sonic presence in the nightclub and its interaction with the spatial setting in the cabaret songs. The genealogy of the nightclub linked to the colonial history of the subcontinent has been traced by scholars like Naresh Fernandes and Bradley Shope to suggest that their presence in cities like Bombay, Karachi, and Calcutta from the 1930s enabled a heady encounter with the traveling jazz bands that revolutionized the soundscapes of Indian modernity. The city of Bombay in the late 1940s attracted Goan musicians who formed fluid connections between the film studios and the dance bands of its hotels and gymkhanas (Fernandes 2012). Several of these musicians became arrangers for the film music industry, introducing into film songs a hybrid amalgamation of sounds drawing on a range of sources that included Arabic influences, Latin American rhythms, and jazz.[29]

The musicking body of the nightclub dancer expanded the registers of female vocality carrying the sonic trace of a postcolonial reimagination of colonial culture. The nightclub singer, with an alluring public

Figure 2.6. Helen as the Chinese girl in *Howrah Bridge* (Samanta, 1958). Screenshot by author.

persona, seems to draw her lineage from the modern girl of the 1930s, conveying fluid religious and racial identities. For instance, Cuckoo Moray, who performed in *Awaara* and several films in the 1940s and the '50s, was an Anglo-Indian actress. Helen, born to an English father and a Burmese mother, became the most successful actress to play the role of the nightclub dancer/vamp right up to the 1970s. Helen was first noticed for her highly energized dance in "Mera naam chin chin choo" (My name is chin chin choo), in the film *Howrah Bridge* (Samanta, 1958), a cabaret number set in a nightclub in Calcutta, where she dances as a Chinese girl (figure 2.6). The choreography was based on different dancing styles borrowed from American swing (Chakravorty 2017, 76). The introductory musical section depicts four men playing a game of dice before they start dancing to the rhythm of the opening music. Helen enters the frame, clapping and dancing as she descends a staircase. When she reaches the center of the frame, the song is energetically channelized through the hook line sung by Helen/Geeta Dutt, followed quickly by a sonic attack of "Ba ba, ba ba," the gibberish words presented along with the sound of trumpets and hand claps. In the first *antara*, Geeta Dutt sings:

Babuji main cheen se aayi
Cheeni jaisa dil lai
Singapore ka joban mera
Shanghai ki angdai

Sir, I come from China
My heart sweet as sugar
My youth appealing like Singapore
My body sensuous like Shanghai

"Mera naam chin chin chu" created a hyperactive space marked by flowing identities and an array of costumes, props, gestures, and bodily practices.

The female body's interaction with other sonic bodies, clapping, whistling, and singing in chorus, became a recurring trope in nightclub songs.[30] For instance, *China Town* (Samanta, 1962) opens with the sound of a ship's horn on a night shot of Calcutta, evoking the idea of a port city. The city is shown to us on a moving camera as Asha Bhosle's voice singing "Thandi baharon se gulzar China Town" (The breeze is cool here, this is China Town) is introduced with rolling credits. After almost two minutes of the song, we enter a nightclub with Helen dancing in a Chinese-style costume with a parasol. The singer invites the spectators to China Town, warning both the on-screen and off-screen onlookers of the dangers that lurk beneath.[31] This movement into the nightclub simulates the listener-spectator's entry into the exhibition theater where the sound/voice could create a three-dimensional space, exceeding the two-dimensionality of the image. Apart from foot tapping and whistling, the sonic field includes the sound of castanets in several Flamenco-themed songs, turning the nightclub into a place for the productive articulation of desire and infinite possibilities.[32]

An overriding feature of these songs was the supporting chorus deployed to add layers of nonverbal sounds with extended vowels. For example, in "Kitni badi mehfil, yeh dil isko dun usko dun" (In this large gathering, to whom should I give my heart), Asha Bhosle opens the song with "*uiiiiiii*," which is repeated through the song with many variations and elongations.[33] The song was a copy of Harry Belafonte's "Banana Boat (Day-O)," released in 1956. But the use of "*uiiiiiii*," rendered by Asha Bhosle with several improvisations, combined with Helen's attire, gave the song a Middle Eastern touch.[34] The female voice in the nightclub songs became an important trope to show how diverse sonic textures from transnational locations could be easily borrowed and integrated into postcolonial cultural imaginaries. For instance, "Kya ho jo din rangeela ho" (What happens when the day turns colorful and frisky), from *Nau Do Gyarah* (Anand, 1957), is introduced with an extended shot in a nightclub with an art deco setting. A relay of bodies and sounds introduces us to several modern girls, each playing a Western instrument such as the guitar, the trumpet, the saxophone, and the accordion. We see Helen dancing on a spiral-shaped artificial bridge as she descends to the club floor. This leads to a close-up of hands with a cigarette holder gently striking a ceramic mug in sync with the music. The next vocal section opens with a close-up of cigarette smoke, taking us to Shashi Kala singing in Geeta Dutt's voice. Instead of the usual *mukhda/antara* structure, the entire song flows as a conversation between Shashi Kala and Helen, with Bhosle singing for Helen. Toward the end of the song, we see how the two dancers share the floor with other dancing bodies, clapping and performing a choreographed movement. The song presents modern girls in a relay of movement to invoke the aural and visual markers of a transnational cosmopolitan body.

Voice as an Unruly Force

In terms of both aural and visual registers, the space of the nightclub was reconfigured by the end of the 1960s through the staging of the cabaret song. Staged in hotels and nightclubs, cabaret numbers were crafted by creating a geography of illicit passion as the dancer moved across tables, forging a tactile relationship with the guests. The performance of the lead dancer simulated desire and danger in the spatial setting of the nightclub. As Mazumdar (2007, 88) notes, "violence, intrigue, death and sex lurk[ed] close to the vamp" as her bodily performance was staged to create "both revulsion and fascination." I would like to demonstrate a marked transformation in the sonic field through dramatic, frenzied musical arrangements and an unusual shift in scale and tonalities in the playback voice in the films of the 1970s. This involved an enactment of sharp moral binaries between the heroine and the vamp figure seen in songs like "Mera naam hai Shabbo" (My name is Shabbo) from *Kati Patang* (Samanta, 1971).[35] Moreover, the cabaret song was stripped of the overlapping tonalities of chorus voices, the rhythmic clapping, or the sound of the castanets that made the earlier nightclub an inclusive and lighthearted space for modern girls.[36] This distinct shift in sonic registers was indicative of the seething sexual energy displayed by a lone female figure dancing to music with dark undertones. Though Asha Bhosle had already established herself as a versatile singer with a facility for sensuous songs, it was in this decade that she acquired a monopoly over cabaret numbers. The introduction of multiple-track recordings in the Bombay film studios in the 1970s also played an important role in the creation of soundtracks with greater density (Booth 2008). Marked by the use of unlimited bass, experimentation with scale, variations in rhythm, and the use of whispering, breathing, tittering, and grunting sounds, Asha's malleable voice worked as an unruly force to produce the space of the nightclub. Unlike the nightclub songs of the 1950s and the early '60s, the cabaret was now introduced through an extended musical section accompanied by fragmented shots of the dancer's body. Choreographed movements like slithering, crawling, or lying on the floor or on a rotating deck became part of the dancer's repertoire of gestures. This contact of the body with the floor was combined with overwhelming shifts in the scale of the voice with an emphasis on the lower registers.

The themed acts depicted in the cabaret numbers of the 1970s that spectacularized racial violence were often borrowed from the nightclubs of Paris. "Aa janane ja," from *Intaqam* (Nayyar, 1969), a sensational number sung by Lata Mangeshkar, presents Helen with an ostrich feather fan, contact lenses, and exaggerated makeup as she starts enticing an encaged black-faced man. After an extended instrumental section with frenzied use of brass and string sections, Lata's voice is introduced with an elongated vowel sound of *Aaaaa*, in a low register, bringing out the sensuality of the voice. The elaborate set, lighting, costumes, and diegetic presence of a brass band formed an important backdrop for Helen's sensuous but highly intricate body movements, including slithering on the floor.[37] The song illustrates Usha Iyer's (2020, 18–19) argument about the scaling of the production number in terms of its music, dance choreography, set design, and camera movements, to match the movement vocabularies of an accomplished dancer. The playback singer's persona is stretched to "intensify the display of the female body," especially when the body is that of an "acclaimed dancer."

Kelley Conway (2001, 135) has elaborated on the cabaret song sequences of French films of the 1930s, incorporating live popular entertainment forms such as *chanteuse réaliste*, drawing upon the cabarets of Montmartre that emerged in France in the late nineteenth century. This realist genre became a shorthand for "female transgression" by depicting the lives of prostitutes navigating the Parisian underworld, and voicing "the intense emotions of sexual desire, melancholy, and despair" (137). In the cabaret songs of Bombay cinema, however, the song's structure; the elliptical, staccato style of singing; and the inclusion of nonverbal breathy sounds created a fragmented aural terrain. In "Mera naam hai Jameela" (My name is Jameela) from *Night in London* (Brij, 1967), Helen enters the nightclub in a latex raincoat with her face covered by a parasol. As she turns to the camera, we see her lip-synching to Lata's utterance of her name "Jameela, Jameela" (figure 2.7).

The traditional use of refrain/*mukhda* with meaningful lyrics is delayed by an extended instrumental section backed by Lata's voice singing the 'O' vowels. The fragmented style of vocal production, with an accent on breath as part of the song's rhythmic style, signals a breach between what is captured on-screen and what remains veiled and unarticulated. In several cabaret numbers, the choreographic style is woven around a dark narrative theme: we see backup male dancers violently pinning down the female performer on the floor as the lead dancer moves to set herself free of their clutches. In "Mera kya sanam, meri khushi hai tumhari" (Oh what of me? My happiness is linked to yours) in *Talash* (Ralhan, 1969), a set piece captures Rita/Helen, a lone female figure, dancing with a group of men who appear intimidating, violent, and exhilarating all at once. Asha's voice constantly moves between a deep, somber, and restrained quality and excessive and frenzied energy, thus playing a crucial role in producing the space of the nightclub, overlaid with danger and excitement. The alternating visual strategy of revealing and blocking our view in several songs is created through lighting, swish pans on bare fluorescent-colored surfaces, and blurred movements. In "Meri jawani pyaar ko tarse" (My youthful self is thirsty for love) in *Upasana* (Mohan, 1971), we are introduced to Helen slithering on the floor and moving toward her object of desire, a sculpted figure of a well-built, muscular, dark-skinned man. Following the *mukhda*, Helen

Figure 2.7. Helen performing "Mera naam hai Jameela" in *Night in London* (Brij, 1967). Screenshot by author.

wraps her body around this sculpted figure, proceeding to kiss him on the lips. The lights go off, followed by a swish pan, as we return to Helen's moving body framed behind the sculpture, denying us an unrestrained view. In the next shot, Helen enters the frame laughing seductively. This sexualized laughter became a hallmark of Asha Bhosle's vocal strategy in cabaret songs.

Bhosle's vocal performances, deployed with volatile movements in pitch, volume, and timbre, played a crucial role in crafting the soundscape of the nightclub. We can compare this to the female vocality of confessional songs, where the lyrics, melody, and use of sustained notes worked to bring out the interiority of the woman. In the cabaret song, the aural strategies of fragmentary voice, language, breath, and pitch enable the woman to express both pain and pleasure. In the song "Kaanp rahi main" (I tremble, I shudder) in *Joshila* (Chopra, 1973), however, Asha's vocalization of a scream foregrounds the dark undertones of the nightclub. This cabaret number is introduced in the film when the hero (Dev Anand) learns through a newspaper advertisement that his sister (Padma Khanna) has become a nightclub dancer. Once again, the scream in the sonic landscape alludes to much more than what can be revealed in the visual frame. This connects with Chion's argument that the screaming stands for "unrepresentability inside representation" (1999, 77). The song opens with Asha's scream on the soundtrack in sync with a close-up of Padma Khanna screaming and running toward the camera.[38] The scream repeated in each *antara* of the song alludes to rape, subtly addressed in the lyrics of the song and the choreographed movement of Padma Khanna and her male accomplice (figure 2.8).[39] An

Figure 2.8. Choreographed violence and the disjunctive voice in the cabaret sequence of *Joshila* (Chopra, 1973). Screenshot by author.

image of Padma Khanna lying on her back on a circular deck, slithering in rhythm, is repeated in the song sequence several times. Asha sings the *mukhda* in a mellowed tone at a lower range while she sings the *antara* at a higher octave, accompanied by a sudden frenzied shift to a faster tempo in the drum section. Crucial here is the way the music/rhythm and Asha's disjunctive voice gesture toward the experience of the dancing girl, exceeding the moral overtones of the narrative.

In *Anamika* (Jalani, 1973), themes of rape and violence are introduced in "Aaj ki raat koi aane ko hai" (Tonight I will have a visitor), where we see Helen performing an act as part of her cabaret in a nightclub. The setting is of a lone woman who, while waiting for her lover on a rainy night, is accosted by a lewd man. In the first interlude, she manages to shake him off with the help of a policeman, who looks at her with suspicion. The vocal inflections of "Shugu shugu shugu" and "na na a na," performed by Bhosle, simultaneously articulate both desire and aversion. In the second interlude, which lasts for almost two minutes, the wait continues, and the lewd man returns and pushes Helen into a telephone booth. What happens inside the booth is left to the imagination of both the on-screen and off-screen spectators. Though the cabaret sequence mirrors the sexual violence that the heroine is trying to escape, its presentation is mounted as a spectacle to entertain the guests at the nightclub. Since rape narratives could never be directly or fully explored, a dual register of masking and revelation emerged through an evolved and orchestrated performance. In this, Asha's unique vocal performativity showcased frenzied scale, rhythm variations, and unusual shifts from whispering and breathing sounds to a full-blown sonic attack. These sound variations played a significant role in alluding to the ellipsis between the main narrative and the minor voice of the vamp, and the oscillation between pain and pleasure.

Asha's sonic register in the nightclubs of the 1970s resonated in several other songs, like "Dum maro dum" (Take another drag) from the film *Hare Rama Hare Krishna* (Anand, 1971), where she lent her voice to Zeenat Aman's uninhibited dance movements. The song became an instant rage with the new generation, as it captured the youthful defiance associated with the late sixties The female voice's use of the lower registers in "Dum maro dum" was striking. The *mukhda* of the song was teased out in the lower range while at the end of the refrain "Hare

Krishna Hare Ram" was repeated by the chorus in the higher octave. In the interlude, Asha's higher-octave singing of "tar a ri ra a ra ri," or rhythmic syllables, is cut to exterior shots, providing us a sense of the incredible reach of her voice. In this sonic flow, we see the voice liberated "from the constraints of formal singing," bringing to the fore a dynamic sense of being (Biswarup Sen 2008, 95). The architectural space mapped by Asha's voice extends and defies the space mapped by the camera. While following the sonic trace of the voice, Zeenat's brother, played by Dev Anand, arrives at the hippies' shack. In the *antara*, "Duniya ne hum ko diya kya? Duniya se humne liya kya? Hum sub ki parvah kare kyon, sab ne hamara kiya kya?" (What has this world given us? What have we ever got from this world? Why should we care for others, what have they done for us?), Asha again sings at a high pitch, giving the lyrics a dramatic edge, and then glides down to return to the original scale by singing extended vowels—"aaaaaa." When we return to the line "Dum maro dum," we see a calmer Zeenat Aman smoking a chillum, sharing it with her hippie friends, conveying the visceral effect of her intoxication. Adding to the innovative registers of the song is its mise-en-scène, with the song located among a group of hippies in a night shack in Kathmandu. A constantly moving camera deploying pan, zoom, and tracking shots, and an out-of-focus shot coming into focus, creates a psychedelic effect, underlining the song's raw and edgy character.

In *Hare Rama Hare Krishna*, R. D. Burman introduced Usha Uthup to sing "I love you," a duet with Asha that has been described as an "extra cheese" version of "Dum maro dum" (Bhattacharjee and Vittal 2011, 113). What is interesting about the song is its unbounded structure and spirit, with Asha singing for Zeenat Aman in the upper octave and Usha in the lower for a white hippie woman, one in the crowd who sings and dances with Zeenat in the Kathmandu night shack.[40] The lip sync to Usha Uthup's lines is casual, reinforcing the industry norm of making a distinction between "minor" voices and playback stars. However, the inclusion of her baritone voice itself is an important landmark pointing us toward R. D. Burman's innovative approach to vocality in songs.[41] In his analysis of R. D.'s music of the 1970s, Pankaj Rag has referred to the underlying psychic impulses in his music. According to Rag (2006, 637), through the use of unlimited bass in voice, experiments with scale and rhythm, and the introduction of whispering, breathing, and grunting sounds, R. D. brought out the alienation and edginess of the urban youth as well as their rejection of outmoded expressions of sexuality and love.

What is often missed in these analyses is R. D. Burman's use of female vocals in the opening credit sequences of crime films like *The Train* (Nagaich, 1970, Usha Uthup); *Caravan* (Hussain, 1971, Asha Bhosle); *Raja Rani* (Bhowmik, 1973, Asha Bhosle); and *Shaan* (Sippy, 1980, Usha Uthup), declaring a new sensibility that combined urbanity with modernity. In these musical sections, Asha used an unusually bluesy low-pitched voice, synchronized with the fast-paced music to draw attention to crime in the city, thus setting the pace for things to follow. In *Raja Rani*, Raja (Rajesh Khanna) runs through the streets of Bombay chased by the police at night, as Asha and Bhupinder's voices map the cityscape with "Jab andhera hota hai" (When it gets dark) marking it as a place of danger, anxiety as well as adventure. The track opens with an eerie sound of the vibraslap, followed by heavy use of brass, lead voice, and a frenzied tempo that creates movement as well as rhythm to match Raja's escapades in the city, jumping across rooftops, scaling walls of buildings, and running along the streets. The moon at night, a recurring motif in the films of the 1950s, is no longer a witness to the dalliance of young lovers; the cinematic night in film songs is explored as a site of sexual transgression and ambivalent morality. The voice of the nightclub dancer hitherto confined to the interiors of the nightclub explodes out on the streets in this new constellation of bodies, voices, and urban spaces.

By subtly pushing similar vocal tonalities for both the cabaret dancer as well as the heroine, R. D. managed to push the boundaries further. The use of whispering by the female voices needs to be seen in the context of the promiscuous quality of sound as well as a sign of lived, desiring bodies. Lata's embodied performance in "Bahon mein chale aao" (Come into my arms) in the film *Anamika* (Jalani, 1973), visualized on Jaya Bhaduri, shows how she adapted to Burman's style to bring out a somatic performance with a whisper-like tone. Performing the song in the middle of the night in a bedroom, Jaya invites Sanjeev Kumar for a romantic dalliance. Lata's susurrant tone draws attention to both the space of the enactment and the off-screen space that lies outside. This is further accentuated by Sanjeev Kumar's use of "shu shu shushu" at the end of each refrain, asking Jaya to keep her voice low, gesturing to the listening bodies outside the bedroom oblivious to this clandestine encounter. The interweaving of verbal and nonverbal sounds lent spatiality to the voice, providing us with a sense of space located both inside and outside the privacy of the bedroom.

The Crooner in the Nightclub

The domination of the playback system in Indian popular music overlapped with the monopoly of the Gramophone Company of India and hegemonic control by a few playback singers. Further, the playback era also coincided with the domination of film music over other genres of popular music. This was no less undergirded by the overwhelming broadcast of film songs on the commercial channels of All India Radio. Countdown shows like the "Geetmala" became popular on Vividh Bharati. The sponsored programs on the commercial service introduced listeners to film songs of newly released films, prompting them to watch the film in the theaters or to buy its LP records. As I have argued elsewhere (Jhingan 2016), close networks between cinema, the radio, and the Gramophone Company of India underwent a critical transition in response to the arrival of new music-publishing companies and delivery technologies such as cassettes. This process began in the 1970s with the arrival of Polydor to slowly usher in an end to GCI's monopoly over the Indian music industry. It is perhaps no coincidence that in the '70s popular albums brought out by Polydor changed the auditory projection of the female voice in the Indian subcontinent, ushering in a distinct shift toward global trends in music. In 1974, Polydor introduced Preeti Sagar with her sultry whisper-like tone in "My heart is beating," a number from the film *Julie* (Sethumadhavan, 1975), that created ripples among the youth. This song carried forward what R. D. Burman had already innovated with Asha Bhosle's and Usha Uthup's voices. Incidentally, *Julie* was a remake of *Chattakari* (Sethumadhavan, 1974), a Malayalam film with a similar English number sung by Usha Uthup. Another notable song in *Julie* was "Bhool gaya sab kuch" (I forgot everything), with Lata singing "Julie, Julie Loves You" with a pronounced erotic register, showing how she could mold her voice to the scene being enacted by the actor on screen.

Polydor's other sensational release was *Qurbani* (Khan, 1980), which introduced listeners to Nazia Hassan and disco beats. Songs like "Laila

O' laila" (Laila, you are a laila) and "Aap jaisa koi" (Someone like you) reestablished the youth as the primary audience for Hindi film songs.[42] These songs introduced a fascination for the female crooner, pushing the industry to look for different kinds of voices and bodies to be presented in the nightclubs. The crooner was dressed up in a naturalized Western look: gone were the elaborate accoutrements, feathers, fishnet stockings, and skin-colored bodysuits associated with the cabaret dancer. The mutation of the cabaret dance was in response to the global popularity of disco music identified with the youth. Moreover, the role of the crooner was played by the heroine, who could now perform in the nightclub. Further, what set the crooner apart from the cabaret dancer was the visible presence of the microphone.

The erotic dancing performance of the heroine in the 1990s has been seen as an emergent form after the decline of the westernized vamp in the 1980s (Mazumdar 2007; Gopal 2011). I want to signpost the crooner as a cusp figure carrying two distinct visual and sonic registers, the westernized vamp of the nightclub, located in the past, and the dancing heroine of the 1990s, still to come in the future. The staging of the crooner's performance as a musicking body involved the creation of a shifting landscape involving the voice, the body, musical genres, and audile technologies. With a microphone as a key device, firmly placed in her hand, the crooner's bodily movements were far more restricted, unlike those of the mobile cabaret dancer, who could slither on the floor or make physical contact with the guests in the nightclub. The production history of *Qurbani* establishes how a growing interaction with global popular music had become significant. Feroze Khan, the director of *Qurbani*, traveled to the UK to approach Biddu to compose a disco number. As the story goes, Biddu agreed but with two conditions (Biddu, 2010). He did not want to work with any of the playback singers from "back home," and he insisted on London as the venue for the recording. Khan introduced Biddu to Nazia Hassan, a Pakistani teenager from Karachi in London. According to Biddu, "I took my guitar and asked her (Nazia) to sing anything and I would accompany her. She sang a verse and chorus of Dance Little Lady Dance. It was one of my songs. This girl was smart. Her voice did not have the piercing sharpness of most Asian singers. The pleasantness of her voice was around C3 . . . warm, expressive and nubile.

Figure 2.9. Nazia Hassan on an album cover of *Disco Deewane*, a nonfilm album of disco songs.

It wasn't a great voice. But it was different, and it was this that made the difference between using her and someone from the old school in India" (Biddu, 2010, 210).

Despite *not having* a "great voice" or the "piercing sharpness" of most Asian singers, Nazia was invited to sing simply because her voice was different. The aural registers of the song point us toward a distinct shift in sound mixing practices. Deploying twenty-four tracks for the song, Biddu backed Nazia's voice with an echo effect. Her nasal tone was blended into the layers of music, thus denying her voice the frontality afforded to the playback singers.

The popularity of "Aap jaia koi" turned Nazia Hassan into a sensation among the youth across the entire subcontinent (figure 2.9).[43] The song was a significant departure because it brought a Pakistani-born female singer to Hindi cinema. The influence of disco music and British club/dance music enabled the female crooner's embodied presence in Bombay cinema. In tracking Nazia Hassan's vocal presence, Ajay Gehlawat (2023) has argued that despite the popularity of "Aap jaisa koi," Hassan's voice could not find a sustained presence in Hindi cinema. He suggests that her decision to work for the pop music industry could have played a role in these developments, but also attributes this to the "attendant on-screen performer's inability to effectively match [with] this new female sound" (2023, 286). However, I want to highlight the context that pushed the industry to incorporate new sonic registers. Nazia Hassan's sonic presence, though limited, needs to be placed in the interconnected force field of new technologies, the rise of regional genres that expanded vocal registers, and an outward expansion of musical cultures. For instance, the music directors of *Qurbani* were the duo Kalyanji Anandji, who composed "Laila O' Laila," another disco-crooning number performed by Zeenat Aman in the film with a microphone in her hand (figure 2.10). Feroze Khan's decision to hire Biddu for a special disco number in the soundtrack shows his keen desire to create a new sound, even if that required a break from the industry norm. These strategies were meant to woo listeners who were getting a taste of different genres, voices, and musical styles. The hiring of Kanchan, a relatively new singer to sing

Figure 2.10. Zeenat Aman performing "Laila O' Laila" in *Qurbani* (Khan, 1980). Screenshot by author.

"Laila O' Laila," also points us toward a pressing need to include unusual voices. It is therefore no coincidence that in the 1980s, singers like Usha Uthup, Runa Laila, Salma Agha, Reshma, Nazia Hassan, Kanchan, and Preeti Sagar could enter the domain of Hindi film music to accompany their sonic presence in nonfilm genres.

Films like *Naseeb* (Desai, 1981), *Shaan* (Sippy, 1981), and *Namak Halal* (Mehra, 1982) made leading stars like Hema Malini and Parveen Babi play female crooners on-screen, singing at nightclubs with a musical band. Though dancing was an important part of the crooners' performance, the gestural economy was very distinct from the dancing style developed by the cabaret dancers. In *Naseeb*, though the lines between singing and dancing became blurred, the crooner's primary identity as a singer was highlighted in other ways: in *Naseeb*, Hema Malini is shown advertising for cough lozenges; in *Qurbani*, Shiela (Zeenat Aman) sings "Aap jaisa koi" without a microphone, but as soon as the song is over, she is complimented by a fan for her beautiful voice. In "Laila O' Laila," the other club number, Shiela sings with the microphone, playing with it, as well as dancing on the floor. In *Shaan*, Parveen Babi sings "Pyar karne wale" (Those who are in love) in the nightclub with a microphone in her hands. The dancing is minimal but is enhanced through swish pan and tracking shots. Visual drama is created through the choreographed presence of the two accompanying dancers, the camera focusing on their heaving and swaying bodies. What marks a clear shift through the figure of the crooner in the '80s is an investment in the surface phenomenon, moving away from the song's ability to express the singer's interiority. The quality of lyrics and the perfect pronunciation were forfeited for a "big sound" in which the music, the rhythm, the orchestration, and the voice competed with one another.[44]

The crooners were public women on-screen who sang to earn a living. Unlike the classically trained professional singer (*Abhimaan*), or the figure of the *tawaif*, the crooner conveyed in her songs a sense of urbanity and a westernized soundscape. Until the 1980s, the crooners on-screen were marginal figures, often played by Anglo-Indian women with a westernized appearance. The classic example is "Aage bhi jaane na tu" (You don't know what the future holds for you) from *Waqt* (Chopra, 1965), where the crooner, while remaining detached from the narrative events, seems to encapsulate the intensity of that moment. As I have demonstrated, in the 1980s, the female crooner became an important part of the narrative community, taking over the space of the nightclub from the westernized vamp. The heady mix of visual and musical artifacts mimicked the performative registers of female-led Western bands in the disco era. Instead of splitting the voice between the heroine and the vamp, the crooner's performance with a microphone effected a consolidation of the female voice in the space of the nightclub.

Musicking Bodies on the Street

The courtesans, nightclub dancers, and crooners fashioned by Bombay cinema were public entertainers who brought to life a dense ecology of leisure, desire, and libidinal energies through their labor. I now turn my attention to the "women of the street," whose songs carry intersecting registers of romantic playfulness, layered with an ability to prophesize, tease, comment, or even provoke the listening bodies around them. Dynamically negotiating the bazaars, streets, construction sites, or city parks, these street performers brought into relief subaltern and provincial bodies in the public domain as mobile sonic citizens. This reminds us of the role of the Mirasans, women of the hereditary community of genealogists and musicians in many regions of North India who traditionally performed the role of the intermediary figures for their patrons in life-cycle rituals (Jhingan 2001). The Mirasans, in popular parlance, were known for their uninhibited and witty performances that could embarrass the patrons at public functions. At weddings, led by the Mirasans, women sang *sithni*, or verses meant to lampoon the bridegroom's family (Jhingan 2001).

Film songs visualized on street performers also gesture toward the itinerant communities, such as quirky saleswomen, street entertainers, and alms seekers, who earned their livelihood by performing while on the move. In films directed by Guru Dutt in the 1950s, footpaths, streets, and public parks were used as locations for song sequences to stage encounters with a range of bodies. In *Aar Paar* (1954), Guru Dutt creates a vista of the street, when a woman construction worker sings "Kabhi aar kabhi paar laga teere nazar" (They hit or they miss, the piercing arrows of your eyes) gesturing toward the hero and the heroine, while kids in the neighborhood break into an impromptu dance (figure 2.11).

Figure 2.11. The construction worker's song in *Aar Paar* (Dutt, 1954). Screenshot by author.

The ludic song suddenly expands the frame, incorporating the community into its intimate space. One can recall Ashis Nandy's (2001, 25) discussion on the public life on the streets of the city that evokes the idea of a "home away from home." In *Mr. and Mrs. 55* (Dutt, 1955), a toy seller sings "Ab toh ji hone laga" (Now, it is happening), a playful song in a public park, addressing a young couple. The camera frames her body through low-angle shots, emphasizing her voluptuous torso and her embodied knowledge about being a sensuous body (figure 2.12). In the song, the performer teases the upper-class modern woman for not being able to express her attraction toward her male companion while elaborating on various enchanting stages of a passionate romance. In "Leke pehla pehla pyar" (Armed with his first love), in *CID* (Khosla, 1956), the hero and the heroine are accosted by two diegetic singers who carry legible signs of being low-brow street performers, through their attire and bodily gestures. The song opens with a shot of a harmonium, with the performer punching its keys while his female companion starts dancing: the addressee is the heroine, whom they start wooing on behalf of the hero. The selection of musical instruments, the attire, and the gestural performance become a marker of the caste and class identity of the performers.[45] All three songs are sung by Shamshad Begum, a playback

Figure 2.12. The toy seller sings in *Mr. and Mrs. 55* (Dutt, 1955). Screenshot by author.

singer who was overlooked by the industry after Lata's rise to aural stardom and sang for marginal figures in the film narratives.

Darshana Shreedhar Mini (2021, 39) notes that caste, gender, and class "hierarchies determine what kind of bodies are allowed to take up screen space (and time)." The performers in the songs as discussed above, play the role of mediators whose very act of enunciation through their expressive bodies and voices creates sensory geographies (Schreffler 2011). This resonates with the figure of the Mirasan, an intermediary figure whose primary task was to inject fun at events like weddings and enable the guests to shed their inhibitions. The songs convey an enthusiastic entanglement of the female performer in the streetscape, demonstrating her ability to sing, speculate, and comment on the lives of others in the public domain. However, this facility to sing and dance in a public setting is also a kind of disenfranchisement. The street performers are not singing about themselves, nor are their voices tied to the exteriorization of emotions as identified with melodramatic songs.

The playback system, argues Pavitra Sundar (2017, 70), was designed to mask the bodily labor involved in singing.[46] I would like to draw attention to songs where the playback singer's vocal performance is inventively used to accentuate the materiality of the female body at the site of work, in an attempt to provide a sonic universe to her labor. For example, in "Jaanu jaanu re" (O my darling) from the film *Insaan Jaag Utha* (Samanta, 1959), two women working as laborers on a construction site tease each other about a new romance in their lives. This female duet sung by Geeta Dutt and Asha Bhosle presents a vibrant interaction between the two characters, animated by teasing, laughing, and jesting tonalities. The accentuated nasal twang highlights a vernacular sonority. The harshness of the spatial setting and the labor it involves is blunted by the muted sounds of the construction site. Instead, the musical orchestration of the song mimics and amplifies the sound of anklets and bells, signaling the restlessness and constant mobility of the two women. What adds to the song is the placing of nonverbal sounds in the sonic chain running into sonorous words like *kangna*, *angana*, *jhumka*, and *payaliya*, before and beyond their meaning. Though there are diverse strategies at work here, what becomes pertinent is the distribution of bodily energies and facial expressions across two performers, to signal subaltern caste and class identity, even though as only a surface-level typology.

In Bimal Roy's *Bandini* (1963), we hear the voice of a woman prisoner who is working on a grinding wheel. In the realist style of this film, Roy's camera remains distant, slowly expanding the frame by locating other female inmates as listening bodies, immobilized by the affective registers of the song.[47] The folk song is crafted with poetic imagery of a woman trapped in her conjugal home, asking her parents to send her brother to secure her release from this confinement. The woman is a marginal character in the film, and the song works as a break from the narrative, allowing us to soak in the poignancy of the moment. However, songs filmed with working-class women, street vendors,[48] construction workers, and nautch girls at rural fairs overwhelmingly worked to showcase a boisterous performance in a public setting. The aural registers of

Figure 2.13. The acrobat in *Seeta Aur Geeta* (Sippy, 1972). Screenshot by author.

these songs were laden with an accented use of local dialects, folk instruments, and nonverbal vocalization. In *Seeta Aur Geeta* (Sippy, 1972), we are introduced to the free-spirited Geeta (Hema Malini) singing "Zindagi hai khel koi paas koi phel" (Life is a game, you win or lose) while performing acrobatic feats on a tightrope in front of a crowd (figure 2.13).

Asha's vocal style enhances Geeta's kinetic working-class body through an exaggerated vibrato, adding to the thrill of the tightrope walking. After the act, Geeta uses a shrill voice to fight and abuse her teammates over her share of the booty that has been collected from the crowd.[49] Other notable songs in this genre are "Chakoo churiyan tez kara lo" (Come get your knives sharpened), as Asha sings for Jaya Bhaduri as a knife sharpener in *Zanjeer* (Mehra, 1973), or "Paisa phenko tamasha dekho" (Throw a dime and watch the show), sung by Lata Mangeshkar for Mumtaz as a bioscope girl in *Dushman* (Guha, 1971). In the latter song, Mumtaz plays the *Raavan Hatha*, or a bowed string instrument, as an accompaniment to folk music by itinerant communities.

By focusing on bodies that enact the songs on-screen we can move away from dominant narratives about singers like Lata Mangeshkar and listen to them anew, uncovering the exclusions from her recorded repertoire.[50] In *Mera Gaon Mera Desh* (Khosla, 1971), Laxmi Chaya plays the

Figure 2.14. Munni Bai in *Mera Gaon Mera Desh* (Khosla, 1971). Screenshot by author.

role of Munni Bai, a village nautch girl caught between the police and the dacoits. In this situational song, performed at a mela (fair), Munni Bai cleverly offers clues to the police about the villain's identity, even as she pretends to be loyal to the bandits (figure 2.14). The bodily gestures and facial expressions and Lata's kinetic vocal performance bear testimony to Munni Bai's anxiety as a double agent negotiating the space between the police and the outlawed figure. The camera's point of view is harnessed to the clues provided by the singer as her voice mobilizes a spatial geography of the mela. Through a clever play of lyrics and shifting vocal tonalities, Munni Bai seeks aural and visual attention, keeping both the protagonist and the bandit on their toes.

Performative role-play in film songs became an important device to challenge gendered hierarchies and heteronormative formations through the use of parody and the grotesque. Besides the investment in attire, movements, and gestures, the body's liminal status in these songs is conveyed through the heroine's pretense of drunken wantonness in a public setting. Shohini Ghosh (2002, 211) points toward the masquerade as an enabler of "excess, badness, abandon and revelry" for the female protagonist. In *Intaqam* (Nayyar, 1969), Sadhana begins to sing during a soiree thrown by her father-in-law, while pretending to be inebriated.

The masquerade relies on Lata Mangeshkar's vocal inflections, like hiccupping, aligned with irreverent bodily practices, including bumping into men, throwing her slippers in the air, balancing a glass of whiskey on her head, and lying down and slithering on the floor, "lowly" acts of the body and the voice, not befitting the daughter-in-law of a so-called respectable, elite family.[51] The sheer exhibitionism is accentuated by the use of microgestures, intercut with the shocked expressions of the community. In *Roti Kapda Aur Makaan* (Kumar, 1974), we see Zeenat Aman dancing with abandon in a rain-soaked sari as she lip-synchs to Lata's voice in "Hai hai yeh majboori" (Oh this cruel compulsion), teasing the hero for being too shy and wasting the romantic, monsoon season by worrying about his search for a job. The use of colloquial words like "do takya di Naukri" (your two-penny job), Aman's bodily gestures such as jiggling her backside to attract attention of the hero, Lata's vocal modulation, and the hero's shocked expression evoke the masquerade of street performance.

In his work on music's representation in visual art, Richard Leppert (1993, XXVI) focuses on the "sight of the sound-producing body" and its enmeshment in the discourses of power, desire, and identity. I read the masquerade in film songs as a hypervisualization of the sound-producing body that draws attention to the anxieties about the blurring of caste, class, and gender identities. Further, the female singer's availability for all kinds of gendered bodies decenters its exclusive attachment to a normative female body. Asha Bhosle and Shamshad Begum became the chosen singers for gender-swapping songs such as the popular "Kajra mohabbat wala," (The kohl of love) where Biswajeet and Babita swap gender roles and sneak into a staged performance to dodge some goons.[52] In *Pyaar ka Saagar* (Goel, 1961), O. P. Ralhan makes a desperate bid to meet his beloved, kept under a watchful eye by her father, in the garb of a woman. But with a twist in the events, the girl's father takes a fancy to this "woman" and asks her to sing a song. Asha's deployment of a false, high-pitched voice in "Chahe koi bandook dikhaye" (Even if someone points a gun) draws upon the audience's knowledge and audio training about the visual and sonic elements that go into the performance of a masquerade in Bombay cinema. In this display of homosociality, Ralhan's facial expressions and grotesque body movements, miming the lyrics sung by Asha in a falsetto, rehearse what Chion (1999, 131) has described as a "a burlesque assemblage of body and voice." What ruptures the sonic voice is the moment when Ralhan temporarily loses his balance and trips: this momentary lapse not only reveals his false hairdo but also the corporeality of the voice. In this fleeting moment, the voice that sings for Ralhan is that of Mahendra Kapoor, a popular male playback singer. At the outset, this may seem to be a return to the normative voice-body relationship expected from the playback system, but it also demonstrates how bodies enact various cultural norms (Grosz 1994, 118).

By lending her voice to songs that play out false identities, Asha Bhosle created a new template of sonic performance, questioning the notion of an "authentic voice" as the locus of interiority. In *Rafoochakkar* (Bedi, 1975), Asha lent her voice to Rishi Kapoor, a leading male star of the 1970s. In "Chuk chuk chak chak chuk chuk chak chak" (The train chugs), Paintal and Rishi Kapoor disguise themselves as two young women and join a band of girls on a train on their way to perform in Kashmir. Replete with nonverbal sonic elements that mimic the sound of a train, this racy, comic song highlights the indexical relationship between the voice and the body. Paintal's wardrobe malfunction results in a momentary lapse of the voice, which has to be quickly restored to maintain the disguise. Further, Asha's vocals are distributed over two bodies. In the final *antara*, Asha sings for both Neetu Singh and Rishi Kapoor, adding a falsetto to Rishi Kapoor's lines. As we can see, Asha Bhosle's voice became a preferred choice for cross-dressed and contingent bodies.

Cassettes and Corporeality

The intersecting relations between cinema, the music industry, and public culture created the conditions for breaking the hegemony of the leading playback singers. The explosion of cassettes in the 1980s brought about cataclysmic changes in listening practices, expanding the aural textures and genres of female-driven songs. The *ghazal*'s robust presence in the nonfilm music market through cassettes created a demand for live concerts, thus enabling several artists from Pakistan to perform in India (Jhingan 2016). Voices of singers like Runa Laila, Salma Agha, Nazia Hassan, and Reshma, from Bangladesh and Pakistan, became part of the aural public sphere with their inimitable vocal textures. The *ghazal* boom pushed filmmakers and music directors to enter into complex negotiations with the film industry when selecting singers and recording this genre. In *Gaman* (Ali, 1978), Muzzaffar Ali relied on *ghazals* written by Shahryar and Makhdoom Mohiuddin to bring poignancy to the struggle of a migrant taxi driver in the city of Bombay and his wife, who eagerly awaits his return in a village near Lucknow. The film ends with "Apki yaad aati rahi, raat bhar" (Your memories kept me awake the whole night), a *ghazal* in Chhaya Ganguly's voice sung with a bare minimum use of musical instruments.[53] To play the titular role in *Umrao Jaan* (Ali, 1981), a film about a nineteenth-century *tawaif* in Lucknow, Muzaffar Ali approached Rekha to play the role of Umrao, while Asha Bhosle was hired to sing all of the songs for the character, which were written and composed as *ghazals*.[54] Khayyam, the music director, who was concerned about creating the right tonal inflections, asked Asha to "sing at one note lower than her normal *sur* to get a full-throated effect that went so well" with the character of *Umrao Jaan* (Rajendran 1986, 49). As he notes, "I wanted Asha to sing not as Asha but as Umrao Jaan, who comes from a certain historical context. She was a singer, a dancer and a poetess. I wanted the voice to embrace all these qualities."[55]

Asha, however, was skeptical about this change. During the recording of "Dil cheez kya hai," it was decided that if the singer was unhappy with the results, the *ghazal* could be re-recorded in her normal *sur*. As the story goes, once the recording was played back, Asha was convinced, and all of the songs of *Umrao Jaan* were sung on this lowered note (Khayyam 1992, 24). If the singing voice conveyed the lived, embodied experience of the *tawaif*, it was also deeply connected to the transformations in the popular music market. A deeper voice could now become part of the musical imagination, as demanded by the characters in the narrative. Concomitantly, the proliferation of music through cassettes created the space for a syncretic meld between folk and regional popular music, a genre distinct from film music (Manuel 1993).

By the second half of the 1970s, parallel cinema also helped in expanding sonic textures, bringing in region-specific song genres, local dialects, and auditory habits. In *Manthan* (1976), the director, Shyam Benegal introduced "Mharo gaon Katha Parey" (My village Katha Parey) in Preeti Sagar's voice, a song that gained immense popularity on the radio. Several filmmakers in the Bombay industry used innovative techniques to open their films with semiclassical songs like the *thumri*, with deeper, heavier voices like that of Shobha Gurtu in "Saiyyan rooth gaye" in the film *Main Tulsi Tere Angan Ki* (Khosla, 1978), Hira Devi Mishra in "Aaja sanwariya" in the film *Gaman* (1978),[56] and Sharda Sinha, a Bhojpuri singer, in "Kahe tohe sajna," in the film *Maine Pyar Kiya* (Barjatya, 1989). The folk singer/dancer's forceful aural (and visual) presence in song sequences became a popular trend in the 1990s.

The diversification of the musical market led to the increasing mobility of song genres with regional inflections, with greater room for titillating and erotic content that appealed to "lower- and lower-middle-class men" (Manuel 1993, 159).[57] While noting the robust presence of women's folk songs, or other female genres, Manuel argues that cassettes mainly provided leisure to men, as women did not have any control over their production, nor did they have access to cassettes (160). This argument misses out on the sonic presence of bawdy folk music in the public sphere in bazaars, on the streets, or in domestic spaces: given the porosity of sound, recorded music would be available to diverse kinds of listeners, including women. Further, as Manuel himself notes, cassette technology led to a greater demand for live performances of regional music, allowing artists to directly connect with their fans. I locate the emergence of the figure of the ethnic folk singer in Bombay cinema from the late 1980s, in the context of these transformations. The dispersal of cassettes riding on new genres, musical instruments, rhythms, and vocal textures bolstered the female sonic body. The incorporation of the rural/folk voice of the woman involved a series of self-conscious enactments of acoustic transference from the husky-voiced rural, ethnic woman to that of the heroine. Natalie Sarrazin (2009, 213) has remarked that the folk/tribal timbre, with its distinctly rough quality, was used in songs to evoke the expressions of lower castes and class groups.[58] Many of these songs were duets presented in two vocal registers—one to go with the body of the folk/rural dancer and the other to match heroines like Madhuri Dixit and Sridevi. The female duets piggybacked on a folk/rural setting, allowing the middle-class heroine to enter that space through citation or impersonation. For instance, "Morni baga ma" (When the pea hen calls out in the forest) in the film *Lamhe* (Chopra, 1990) introduced Ila Arun as an ethnic Rajasthani woman singing with an open-throated style. Her energetic aural and visual style is followed by Sridevi taking over the song with Lata's playback voice. The female voice was thus split, with two distinct tonalities performed by Ila Arun and Sridevi on-screen.

Shot on the sand dunes of Rajasthan, the song captures a cartographic imagination of Rajasthan's deserts. Viren (Anil Kapoor), who belongs to a landed Rajput clan, comes back to Rajasthan from the UK to formally take charge of his family's legacy. Soon, he becomes fascinated by Pallavi (Sridevi), his next-door neighbor. Sitting in his *haveli* one afternoon, Viren overhears the strains of a woman's (Lata Mangeshkar's) singing voice. He follows the trail of the voice to catch a glimpse of Pallavi dancing in the rain with her friends.[59] Driven by his attraction to Pallavi, he extends his stay in Rajasthan and persuades Pallavi to show him around.[60] The film introduces us to the vast landscape of the desert through a series of acoustic transfers, beginning with Ila Arun's voice as we see her leading a group of itinerant performers on the dunes. Ila Arun's short musical prelude describes the beauty of *Registan*.[61] We see a distant shot of Viren and Pallavi riding on camels with the sunset framing the landscape in the background. The music shifts briefly to the typical sounds of "Bollywood," with a guitar and flute riff, leading us to an alap by a male singer. Ila Arun takes over the song as the camera reveals her singing with abandon, her hands outstretched toward the sky, her body swaying languorously. In the next shot, we see Pallavi and Viren sitting in the dunes at a distance, with the folk singers framed in the background in soft focus. The song is made accessible to Viren and the spectator through translation provided by Pallavi, followed by

Figure 2.15. Ila Arun performs "Morni baga ma" in *Lamhe* (Chopra, 1991). Screenshot by author.

her performance, relying on Lata's playback voice.[62] Even though Pallavi/ Sridevi appropriates the provincial woman's song in "Morni," Ila Arun's powerful presence through a heightened vocal and bodily performance challenges the song's bounded status (figure 2.15). If Sridevi's section in the song resembles an intelligible structure, Ila Arun's vocal performance and body movements point to a defiant, open-ended, oral form.

Ila Arun consolidated her position in the industry both as a singer and as an actor after the popular reception of "Morni."[63] However, the significance of "Morni" lies in its ability to inaugurate a transformation in the song's structure, giving space to the voice of the Banjaran to undermine the *mukhda/antara* demarcation.[64] Further, I want to draw attention to the way these mediations were engendered through women's voices. "Morni" set an important trend for duet songs to be presented in two very distinct female vocal timbres. As a reciprocal form, as I have discussed, the conversational style of singing in duets evokes liveness where two bodies interact with each other as musicking bodies. An exceedingly popular "Choli ke peeche kya hai" (What's under your blouse) from the film *Khalnayak* (Ghai, 1993), for instance, was structured like a conversation between two women, Champa (Neena Gupta) and Ganga (Madhuri Dixit) on-screen, with Ila Arun and Alka Yagnik, respectively, singing for them. The song was mounted as an aural and visual spectacle, with extended choreographed rhythmic sections, hybrid musical arrangement, and a *sawal-jawab* (question and answer) styled conversation between two women with distinct vocal registers.[65] Each *antara* of the song concluded with Ila Arun's "Haaiii," in a distinctive style associated with rustic women.[66]

Charting the transformations in female voices with the arrival of satellite television in the 1990s, Pavitra Sundar (2017, 72) has discussed the rise of Ila Arun, noting her distinctive "full-throated style, uninhibited vocal performance and suggestive dance moves." Sundar describes the "othering" of Arun's voice in duet songs such as "Choli ke peeche," and notes that though a bawdy and bodily singer like Ila Arun was "allowed into the world of playback singing," she could never be the voice of the heroine (73). On the other hand, the dancing body of the heroine remained attached to a voice similar to Lata Mangeshkar's (74). Elaborating on "Choli ke peeche," she writes, "Except in a few fleeting moments, playback singer Alka Yagnik's vocal performance for Ganga hews closely to the 'pure' and 'smooth' Mangeshkar ideal. The vocal burden of difference and desire thus falls on Ila Arun. While Arun's voice does not require translation in this song as it does in 'Morni bagama,' it still needs to be properly contained" (75).

Further, Sundar argues that though the body of the heroine (Madhuri Dixit) is presented in a highly sexualized manner, her "chaste voice and lyrics manage to push against the bawdy, bodily voice of her friend and the sexualized visual and dance choreography" (75). However, this analysis overlooks the song's assemblage form and the auditory terrain it foments where singing, performing, and listening fold into one another. Though Madhuri Dixit is lip-synching to Alka Yagnik's voice in the "Choli" song, her dynamic presence as a dancing, musicking body involves responding to Ila Arun's charged vocal performance and Neena Gupta's corporeal bodily gestures. Further, the constant deployment of onomatopoeic words like "kukukuku" and "Haiiii" enables an intermeshing of tonalities, creating a layered soundscape. I recall Eidsheim's (2019, 11) important assertion that the voice "does not arise solely from the vocalizer; it is created just as much within the process of listening." Following Brandon LaBelle's (2010) conceptualization of an acoustic territory, and sound's ability to create a relational space, I contend that songs like "Choli" gave rise to an interlaced experience where the bodily performance of the middle-class heroine was enmeshed with the vocal and gestural performances of the subaltern body of the ethnic singer. In inaugurating the risqué body of the dancing heroine of the 1990s, the aural force of regional music, along with the emergence of new auditory habits, played a crucial role.

The popularity of Dixit's dancing songs in the 1990s brought about what Anna Morcom (2016) describes as Bollywood's dance revolution. The postliberalization era, according to Morcom, allowed middle-class girls to perform sensual dance in the public domain, bringing in a more Western sensibility with fashion, fitness clothing, and new ideas of the body.[67] Through my discussion of the sonic and visual landscapes of film songs, I have traced the way cinema responded to the transformations in the auditory landscape, riding on the expansion of popular music industries through the 1970s and the long '80s. The influence of rock, jazz, and disco music through a new entrant like Polydor can be seen in the cabaret songs of the 1970s, as well as the development of the crooner in the 1980s. This auditory framework has also allowed me to examine the transformations in the female voice through the popularity of genres like the *ghazal* and regionally inflected folk music, that changed the way the female musicking body was seen and heard in the postcassette period. In the next chapter, I turn toward print media archives to examine the music critic as a specialist kind of listener, an intermediary figure, who played an important role in shaping the gendered soundscape of the Bombay film song.

Part II

FROM SINGERS TO LISTENERS

3

The Critic as Biographer

The previous chapters have addressed the technological and material practices that shaped the journey of the female voice of the Bombay film song. Songs work as independent artifacts, beyond the narrative and industrial logic of films. Thus, the voice of the playback singer remains in the aural domain via memory as well as through various modes of circulation. In this chapter, I move away from the textual analysis of song sequences to analyze the writings of music critics that emerged in popular magazines like *Filmfare* and *Madhuri*. However, the emergence of these "music specialist" writers in magazines needs to be placed within an overall context of the public discourse on film music and its intermedial footprints. The release of song booklets, the circulation of gramophone records, the marketing of chap books, and the popularity of radio shows showcasing innovative curations of film songs created a secondary layer of film music leisure economy in which the music critics, the industry, and the listeners participated.

Given the overall domination of Hindi film music on radio and in India's music publishing industry, the music critic's role in our cultural landscape cannot be underestimated. I engage with special columns dedicated to film music and with biographical accounts by music critics and journalists to signpost the creation of moral and aesthetic categories around the female playback voice. I argue that, through this discursive formation, music critics pushed for a private, acoustic space for the consumption of the female playback voice. As a self-conscious, urban figure with a degree of cultural competence, the music critic mediated between the industry and listeners to produce a regime of taste. At the same time, the critic often came across as a starstruck fan and listener, deeply moved by the affective voice and aural stardom of the female singer. In this regard, I discuss melodrama as an important force field in print media, intimately tied to the discourses on female payback stars, and their presence in the "shadowy" space of the sound studio. I argue that by focusing on the sentimentality of the voice, or the "excessive" erotic appeal, the critics could easily build stories about female singers' personal lives based on speculation and gossip.

In his typology of listeners, Theodore Adorno (1988, 4) refers to the expert listener as a "fully conscious" figure who gives a meaningful context to listening by turning it into a narrative. In the Indic aesthetic tradition, the connoisseur is framed as a *rasika*, a figure who can savor the "nine rasas, [or] affective essences" that are manifested in music, poetry and other arts (Schofield 2015, 409).[1] A *rasika* must "learn to taste the *rasas* not merely intellectually, as might be possible with poetry but also experientially, as is central to musical understanding" (408). In a provocative discussion, Kalpana Ram (2011) has shown how the Sanskrit aesthetic discourse was deployed to invite a wider class of spectators to occupy the position of the *rasika* in Indian modernity. As I will demonstrate, the *rasika* in the print discourse was deeply invested in sharing with the reader the affective pleasures of listening to film songs. The object of the *rasikas* auditory attention was the composition of the song (the tune) and the timbral quality of the playback singer's voice. However, this engagement was intimately tied to technologies of sound recording and the dispersal of film songs in the public domain. The reader being addressed by the critic was imagined as a consumer of gramophone records.[2] With the arrival of new technologies of music consumption, such as audiocassettes, the critic intervened even more vociferously to create moral hierarchies and aesthetic classifications. Thus, the intermedial context of film music, and its diverse and unstable materiality, provided a crucial layer for discussions on print media.

Music Critics, Listening Practices, and the Formation of Taste

Jonathan Sterne (2006, 23) has reflected on the genealogy of various audile technologies that connected listening to science, reason, and rationality. Sterne suggests that listening was intensified and separated from the other senses in the nineteenth century due to the arrival of audile instruments like the telegraph and the stethoscope. For the sound media industry to flourish, acoustic space had to be transformed and reconceptualized as a private bourgeois space (2006, 24). Sterne's ideas are useful for analyzing the figure of the Hindi film music critic. The critic's writings on the female voice were deeply implicated in sound reproduction technologies. Like the medical practitioner who trained himself to listen to the sound of the body with the stethoscope, the critic learned to distinguish between the "interior" sounds of the phonograph and "exterior" sounds on the gramophone record. The term "taste" is deeply embedded in questions of class, social distinction, and educational status. Bourdieu (1984, 18) has underscored classificatory practices like attending concerts or playing "noble" instruments as indicators of "class" and "taste in music." Armed with his musical knowledge and backed by his access to a personal collection of gramophone records, the critic emerged as a self-conscious rational figure, shaping notions around film songs, their tunes, their vocal style, and so on, by advocating the importance of discernment in listening.[3] However, as I will demonstrate, while writing biographical articles or review pieces on female playback singers, the critic never shied away from giving his own opinions based on innuendo, speculation, and a personalized affective response.

Scholars have noted that as public intellectuals, music critics can play a dominant role during periods of cultural transition. Lakshmi Subramanian (2008, 63) has shown that the rise of music criticism in modern South India was a response to "the emergence of new consumers and patrons" of music. Critics and commentators intervened in the public domain to shape standards of performance and pedagogy, consolidating a "new aesthetic of classicism" (63). However, while vocal music in India was always valued, the language of emerging criticism around vocal practices remained "vague and general" (69). While navigating special articles on playback singers in film magazines on Bombay cinema, we can notice a similar lack of consistency in discussing the merits of a performance. It was in the mid-1960s that regular reviews of gramophone records and concerts and sketches of composers and playback singers began to appear in magazines like *Filmfare*. Raju Bharatan managed to draw attention to his reports through his sheer knowledge of film music and quirky style of writing that often relied on speculation.[4] In special columns like "On Record" and "Keeping Track," Bharatan covered events related to film music, reviewed music albums, and commented on declining standards of film music. Moreover, by writing consistently on the Mangeshkar monopoly with bold headlines like "Who's Afraid of the Mangeshkars?" and "Has Asha Forgotten O.P.?"[5] he managed to create controversies inviting robust responses from the readers. For instance, when the music of *Pakeezah* (Amrohi, 1972) became extremely popular in the 1970s, Bharatan claimed this was a clear indication that

> a generation which otherwise has time for *Dum Maro Dum*, discerns a serene sweetness in the out-of-this-world music created for "Pakeezah" by this out-of-this-world Ghulam Mohammed. . . . which proves that there is nothing wrong with public taste that good taste cannot put right. For who shall deny that "Pakeezah" for all its "dated" look, is a film done with taste by Kamal Amrohi, and that its music, composed in admirable taste, has about it a lyrical charm. Taste to be sure, is not something to be foisted; it is something to be cultivated. (1972b, 33)

Through his assertive style, replete with adjectives, Bharatan tried to privilege film songs that drew on classical music, citing his knowledge of ragas. For instance, he wrote hagiographic accounts of Vasant Desai for using classical music as an important resource for his compositions (1976, 46). While writing columns on Lata Mangeshkar, he speculated that Lata's real love was for classical music. As he wrote:

> Her eyes become misty. Obviously, she was thinking of the *tanpura* her father had bequeathed her. In doing so nearly 30 years ago, Master Dina Nath had naturally hoped that Lata would go on to be something more than a film singer. Though

> she didn't say so in so many words, I could see that this is a vacuum that Lata has begun to feel. For all her name and fame, the realization is dawning on her that, with the quality of film music being so debased she has not been able to carry forward her father's classical tradition. (1971c, 46)

Bharatan's eloquent description of what Lata was beginning to feel is an indulgence in speculative territory. Through his columns, Bharatan often reminded his readers about Lata's cherished and hidden desire to devote all of her time to classical music. In his biography on Lata (1995), which drew upon his columns and articles, he opined that it was time she retired from film music and devoted herself to singing classical and devotional songs. However, I contend that there was no consistently deployed aesthetic standard for the articulation and cultivation of "good taste" in Bharatan's journalistic writings. For instance, though biased toward songs based on classical music, he often wrote favorable articles on O. P. Nayyar, a music director known for composing fluffy, romantic numbers. His numerous pieces on the Mangeshkar sisters ranged from hagiographic to hypercritical. While he often praised younger playback singers for sounding like Lata, there were frequent criticisms as well of their attempt at cloning Lata.[6] How do we then conceptualize the ideas around taste and social aesthetics projected by the critic in the light of these inconsistencies?

Ben Highmore (2010, 135) has insightfully drawn our attention to the importance of affect in the field of cultural experience. For Highmore, aesthetics in its initial impetus was concerned with material experiences and sensate perceptions.[7] Questioning the preoccupation of aesthetics with high art, Highmore asks, "How does a form of inquiry that once aimed at the entire creaturely world end up as a specialized discourse about fine art? How did an ambitious curiosity about the affects, the body and the senses end up fixated on only one tiny area of sensual life—beauty and the sublime?" (121–22). Though primarily concerned with the question of taste in food and its links with the sensate, creaturely body, Highmore's interventions provide me with a framework to not only locate inconsistencies in the writings of critics but also engage with the overtly affective response to the female voice.

Melodramatic Readings and Female Stars

In her work on female stardom in Indian cinema, Neepa Majumdar (2001, 171) alerts us to the dual pleasures of stardom in song sequences, enabled by playback technology. Lata's voice monopoly, according to Majumdar, demonstrates how aural stardom gained its currency not through glamour but through "voice recognizability" and the circulation of "extra textual knowledge about the singers" (171). In discussing the specific modalities of the audiovisual contract of Bombay cinema, Pavitra Sundar (2023, 37) has highlighted the role of paratexts and public discourses in shaping the way "audiences put together sound and image in a meaningful relationship." In the following pages, I will examine biographical pieces on Asha Bhosle, Lata Mangeshkar, and Geeta Dutt, accompanied by photographs that appeared regularly in magazines like *Madhuri* and *Filmfare*, to demonstrate how the music critic mediated this relationship. *Madhuri* devoted an entire issue to playback singers in 1971, giving text and photographs equal space, while *Filmfare* carried cover page stories on Lata Mangeshkar in March 1971 and June 1987. Both issues relied on the biographical form, giving importance to Lata's early days of struggle in the industry and showcasing her ability to survive in challenging circumstances to become a star. The critics writing on aural stars had no official access to information about their private lives and drew on oral gossip to write biographical pieces. One of the key strategies deployed by the music critics was to draw attention to the sentimentality of the songs in order to write about the singer's private self. The critic used his own listening experience—foregrounding the "affect" in the playback voice—to recuperate earlier regimes of listening associated with musical genres like the *thumri*, traditionally performed by the courtesan. Through the use of speculation and innuendo, the private selves of the singers were conflated with the narrative address of film songs. For instance, a piece that Raju Bharatan wrote on the release of a compilation of Geeta Dutt's songs brought out by HMV covered an entire span of Geeta Dutt's career, laced with episodes that described her troubled relationship with her husband, Guru Dutt. Bharatan (1985a, 89) opened his review with the following lines: "Any LP of Geeta Dutt must come like that cloud burst accompanying a cool monsoon breeze. For Geeta was 'thandi hawa and kali ghata' rolled into one. The moment she came you got the refreshing feeling of 'aa hi gayi jhoom ke.' There was a rare swing in her voice . . . she never sang. She just glided through a tune." Bharatan ended his piece by writing about Geeta Dutt's poignant songs, directly linking them to her biography. He wrote, "Geeta soon had neither her singing nor her man with her. So, she drank herself to a point of no return. Like Chhoti Bahu Meena Kumari. From 'Mera Sundar Sapna Beet Gaya' to 'Waqt Ne Kiya' she had come full circle. Only to discover that in films it's a man's world in which a woman's voice counts for only so much and no more" (89).

Although this article appeared as an album review, the opening page displayed a photograph of Geeta Dutt with her husband. The title, "She Stopped Singing to Save Her Marriage," clearly provided a biographical stance to the review, with Bharatan focusing on the story of a victim, selectively recalling songs like "Mera sundar sapna beet gaya" (My beautiful dream is a thing of the past) and "Waqt ne kiya kya haseen sitam" (Time unleashed an alluring, yet cruel fate), both pensive songs sung by Geeta Dutt. In sharp contrast to Bharatan's piece, an article in *Madhuri* on Geeta Dutt, though describing a similar narrative of decline, gave enough space to the singer to articulate her dilemma. In Geeta Dutt's (1971) own words:

> My husband did not want me to sing for films. Singing was not just a career for me, it was my passion. It was difficult for me to stay away from singing . . . I tried my best to continue in the industry. . . . My husband would go to work and return home by 6 or 7 pm. I would reach the studio by the afternoon. There were days when the recording would finish in a couple of hours, and I could return home before my husband was back home. But sometimes the song recording would take much longer. As the clock inched towards 6 pm I would get so anxious to lose all control over my voice; the notes would go haywire and the sense of rhythm would escape me. I realized that I was not doing justice to my music, that is when I decided to quit singing.

Before the arrival of the multitrack system, singers had to record the song along with a live orchestra, and a minor mistake could lead to a retake of the entire song. Geeta Dutt's account foregrounds the anxiety of the singer caught between the demands of industry and family, both pushing her toward a disciplined body governed by the regimes of time. Insightfully, Geeta Dutt connects this to the production of voice, techniques of aligning with other musicians, and her sense of musical aesthetics. For the singer, the recording room thus became a space for creative possibilities as well as profound anxieties.

While Geeta Dutt was usually depicted as a victim, the critics had an ambivalent relationship with the Mangeshkar sisters. Both Lata and Asha remained the focus of discussion in popular magazines from the 1950s to the '90s. In the "Star Focus" series in *Filmfare*, an article by Lata (1964) carried photographs of her puja room and a large picture of Swami Vivekananda at her home. This iconic framing was crucial in creating an image of the singer as a simple, sincere woman, devoted to her music. A special issue of *Madhuri* on playback singers gave special treatment to Lata by carrying a full-page color photograph of her standing next to the sculpted figure of Meera Bai, a mediaeval saint poetess, holding a *tambura* in her hand. On the other hand, Asha Bhosle's image in the same series was largely constructed around her successful partnership with music composer O. P. Nayyar, who played an important role in giving her the heroine's songs. Later, two kinds of narratives dominated the print media: one related to the Asha/O. P. Nayyar breakup and the other about her relationship and creative partnership with R. D. Burman.[8]

In analyzing the coverage of the Nanavati case in the tabloid press in the 1950s, Sabeena Gadihoke (2011, 105) has highlighted how sensationalism, press photography, and speculative speech were mobilized to foment a melodramatic sensorium in the press.[9] The photographs and their placement with captions were key to relaying the visceral experience of the scandal (106). In biographical stories on Lata and Asha, magazines relied on clever placement of photographs, combined with selective recall of lyrics from romantic songs, in an attempt to uncover their private lives. For instance, when Asha Bhosle won her first *Filmfare* award for "Chain se humko kabhi, aapne jeene na diya" (Never did you let me enjoy a moment of peace) from the film *Pran Jaye Par Vachan Na Jaaye* (Raza, 1974), Bharatan (1975, 39) wrote a column focusing on Asha's personal life, giving details of her relationship with O. P. Nayyar. As he wrote:

> [and] now O.P brings her to us with a pang in "chain se hum ko kabhi." With a pang because the song was recorded when both Asha and OP knew their break was final and complete. Yet the regret remained that it had to end this way—that is why the lilt is so full of feeling as Asha sighs: Aapne jo hai diya voh to kisine na diya [What you gave me, no one else could]; and when she concludes: kaash na aati apni judaai maut hi aa jaati [alas, death didn't come knocking before our final parting].

Bharatan's description highlights his own listening experience to mark out the expressive quality of a particular song, suggesting that it indexes the singer's private emotional state toward Nayyar. Christine Gledhill has alerted us to the overlaps between melodrama and the construction of stars. For Gledhill (1991, 210), melodramatic characterizations are performed "through a process of personification whereby actors—fictional characters conceived as actors in their diegetic world—*embody* ethical forces." What is common to melodramatic characters and stars is the use of gestures, facial expressions, and body language that provide a link between "moral stances and personal desires" (210). Neepa Majumdar (2010, 141) has noted the "typecasting of stars as a form of genre identification," similar to melodrama's reliance on broad, legible, and emblematic characterizations. On the other hand, in discussing playback as part of a gendered cultural system, Amanda Weidman (2021, 10) observes that "Singing is constructed as the voicing of words and melodies that others have written and composed—and that therefore doesn't involve the singer's self in the same way as speaking does." Discussing the gender asymmetries in playback, Weidman (10) acknowledges that the singing voice and the speaking voice can at times come together for male singers, while it remains far "more risky for women." However, in the writings of biographers and music critics, as I will demonstrate, this gendered construction was reversed: the lyrics of the song, their melodic tone, and the affective registers of the voice were constantly being invoked to speculate on the inner landscape of the female playback singer. In a review of *Mellow Gold*, an album of Asha's selected songs, Bharatan framed Asha's entire career through the registers of speculation (figure 3.1). Even though the *Mellow Gold* LP carried songs sung by Asha

Figure 3.1. Album cover of "Mellow Gold." Author's personal collection.

Bhosle for several composers, Bharatan (1985a, 88) highlighted O. P. Nayyar's unique contribution to Asha's career. As he wrote:

> "Yeh hai Asha" came only after O. P Nayyar had given Asha Bhosle a singing personality she could call her own. Before that Asha at best was the poor man's Geeta, just as Suman Kalyanpur was the poor man's Lata. There was no consolidated record as to how Asha sounded during those days of struggle when she was cutting her musical teeth. We have such a record now in Gramco "Mellow Gold" ECLP 5939. Its sound quality is excellent.

By citing "Yeh hai Asha," the title of a popular television show in which Asha performed with R. D. Burman on Doordarshan in 1975, Bharatan tries to remind the reader that it was O. P. Nayyar who paved the way for Asha's success in her present run of popularity with R. D. Burman. Toward the latter part of the review, Bharatan writes, "[Like] in Jayen

Jahan Meri Nazar from *Kalpana* you get to feel the touch that O.P. Nayyar reserved for Asha." A photograph of Asha dialing a telephone (figure 3.2), lying next to O. P. Nayyar's framed photograph, accompanied the text. This visual enactment, encoded with liveness, suggests an intimate connection between Asha and Nayyar through the telephone. Curiously, this photograph had been used by *Filmfare* in an article on Asha Bhosle in 1964.[10] Bharatan's stance and the reuse of this photograph more than a decade after its first appearance allude to an overriding investment in the singer's personal life, mediated through the melodramatic register of the confessional songs she performed.

In articles on Asha Bhosle with accompanying photographs, the speculation about her private life were bolstered by selectively citing the genres and lyrics of her songs. Though critics and biographers often described Asha Bhosle as a versatile singer, the notion of versatility was deployed to underline her facility in singing seductive songs (Jhingan 2022, 214).[11] The song lists on popular radio countdown shows, however, point us toward the popularity of Asha's songs in diverse genres that were performed by children, prepubescent boys and girls, alms seekers, and queer bodies on-screen. However, this repertoire of songs performed by Asha was given scant attention by the print media, thus eliding her versatility (Jhingan 2022, 211). Magazines like *Filmfare* frequently carried pictures of her lighthearted interactions with O. P. Nayyar and other co-singers in music studios.[12] The array of gestures and facial expressions

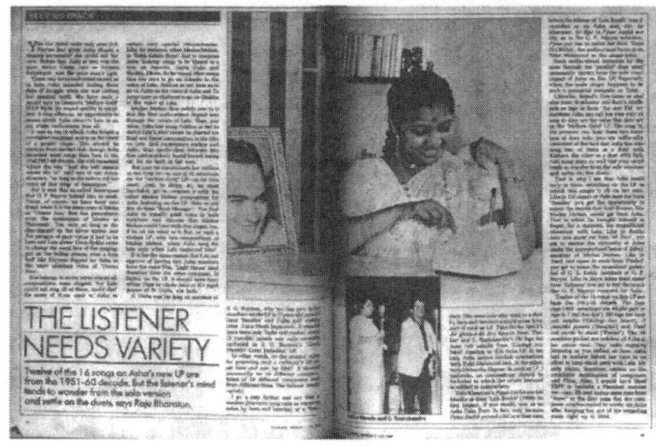

THE LISTENER NEEDS VARIETY

Twelve of the 16 songs on Asha's new LP are from the 1951-60 decade. But the listener's mind tends to wonder from the solo version and settle on the duets, says Raju Bharatan.

Figure 3.2. Bharatan's review of "Mellow Gold" in *Filmfare*. Author's personal collection.

in these photographs conveyed a sense of abandonment and alluded to her relationship with Nayyar (figure 3.3). Her overriding performance of "bad girl" songs like *mujras* and cabaret dance numbers was often conflated with her off-screen persona, relayed primarily through photographs in film magazines.

In constructing Lata, on the other hand, the dominant narrative was that of a devotee of music and her purity of style, an image that could not have been created without her own involvement. Her photograph with the tanpura became an iconic image. Other recurring images showed her with her head covered, and pictures of her puja room in her Pedder Road house. Often called the woman in white, Lata had self-consciously created an image of simplicity with her white saris. This process of exteriorization illustrates how stars are cast in broad moral and emblematic terms where the use of the body relayed through photographs short-circuits linguistic constraints (Gledhill, 1991, 213).

In representing Lata, critics often used arbitrary adjectives to describe the voices of other female singers, while attempting to establish her superiority over them. For instance, in an attempt to defend Lata on the monopoly issue, Arvind Dhurandhar, a regular Lata enthusiast, wrote, "Lata's *sugar and spice* voice scored easily over the *rustic and harsh* voice of Shamshad Begum, the *earthy and seductive* voice of Geeta Dutt and the nasal and *courtesan voice* of Amirbai" (1983, 26; emphasis

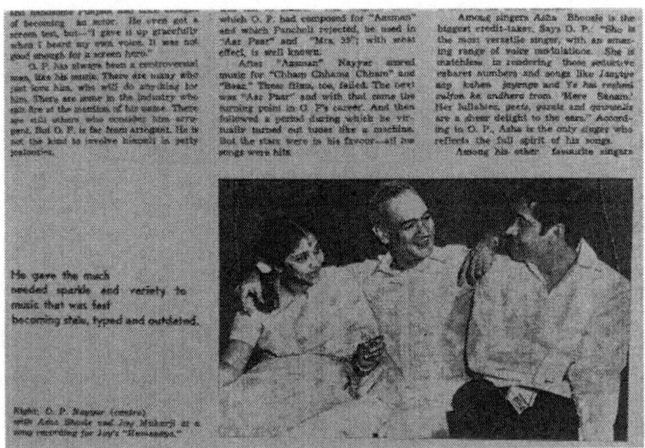

[illegible] of becoming an actor. He even got a screen test, but—"I gave it up gracefully when I heard my own voice. It was not good enough for a screen hero."

O. P. has always been a controversial man, like his music. There are many who just love him, who will do anything for him. There are some in the industry who spit fire at the mention of his name. There are still others who consider him arrogant. But O. P. is far from arrogant. He is not the kind to involve himself in petty jealousies.

which O. P. had composed for "Aasman" and which Pancholi rejected, he used in "Aar Paar" and "Mrs. 55"; with what effect, is well known.

After "Aasman" Nayyar scored music for "Chham Chhama Chham" and "Baaz." These films, too, failed. The next was "Aar Paar" and with that came the turning point in O. P.'s career. And then followed a period during which he virtually turned out tunes like a machine. But the stars were in his favour—all his songs were hits.

Among singers Asha Bhosle is the biggest credit-taker. Says O. P.: "She is the most versatile singer, with an amazing range of voice modulation. She is matchless in rendering those seductive cabaret numbers and songs like *Jaiye aap kahan jayenge* and *Ye hai reshmi zulfon ka andhera* from 'Mere Sanam.' Her lullabies, geets, gazals and qawwalis are a sheer delight to the ears." According to O. P., Asha is the only singer who reflects the full spirit of his songs.

Among his other favourite singers

He gave the much needed sparkle and variety to music that was fast becoming stale, typed and outdated.

Right: O. P. Nayyar (centre) with Asha Bhosle and Joy Mukerji at a song recording for Joy's "[illegible]."

Figure 3.3. A photograph of Asha Bhosle with O. P. Nayyar in *Filmfare*. Author's personal collection.

mine). A recurring trope was to write about the expression of *dard*, or pain and suffering, in Lata's voice. Dhurandhar's piece evoked several letters by readers, some defending his account, while others criticized him for "weeping into his own pathos," (S. Mohan 1983, 6). In another article, Dhurandhar tried to make speculative connections between Lata's "heart-rending" personal life and the early days of struggle in the industry. He writes:

> I rate "Bichade Hue Pardesi" (*Barsaat*) and "Tod Diya Dil Mera" (*Andaz*) among my favourites of Lata. Note the utter helplessness in Lata's voice in both these songs. One's heart reaches out to Lata in her anguish and grief and one wants to envelope her and protect her from the vagaries of this cruel world. No Noor Jehan, no Shamshad Begum, no Amirbai Karnataki, no Khurshid, no Suraiyya, no Geeta Roy had ever sung with such heartfelt conviction. (Dhurandhar 1988, 15)

By citing some of Lata's "sad songs," Dhurandhar attempts to draw attention to Lata's "helplessness" by subtly referring to her struggle as the oldest daughter who took care of her family after she lost her father. Lata's image as a single woman was based on either a recurring motif of grief and trauma or speculation about some hidden unfulfilled desires. We can recall Ira Bhaskar's (2018, 168) insightful assertion that songs in Indian melodramas amplify the interiority of character and make intelligible the emotion that the world outside would rather ignore or repress. However, in this instance, we see how the melodramatic form seeps into print cultures through the interconnected, affective force field of the voice, star discourses, and the cinematic form. By citing Lata's "sad" songs, critics attempted to give the readers a comprehensive image of the aural star.[13] This involved a subjective engagement with the voice undergirded by the conventions of melodrama. For example, in the same article, Dhurandhar wrote, "Lata never got an opportunity to experience motherhood herself. However every line of her in 'O mere lal Aja' drips with rare brand of 'mamta.' It is hidden mother in Lata that has surfaced in the song" (1988, 16).[14]

Dhurandhar's contrived and selective recall of Lata's songs about maternal love points us toward a highly gendered discourse. Reading strategies that attempted to collapse the subjective voice of the playback singer with the emotional and narrative import of film songs were applied only to female singers. Further, the narratives on Lata were built by a complete disavowal of her erotic songs: cabarets, mela songs, boisterous numbers like "Hai hai majboori," "Hai sharmayun," or "Bahon mein chale Aao," discussed in the last chapter. To be clear, I am not suggesting that playback singers could never dip into their inner selves while recording a song. My argument is that print media's speculative and intrusive interest in playback singers' "interiority" was skewed toward women singers, reifying an essential notion of femininity.

During the 1970s, the discussion around Lata and Asha in film magazines started referring to their hegemonic control over the industry.[15] Leading the attack, Bharatan used his columns to accuse the two sisters of blocking the careers of upcoming playback singers like Vani Jairam and Sulakshna Pandit.[16] In a sharp response carried by *Filmfare*, Surinder Singh (1974) referred to Bharatan as a "half-baked music expert misusing his skills to spite two of the finest singers of all times."[17] Singh (1974, 31) added:

> Lata Mangeshkar scores over her contemporaries in her capacity to imbue songs with a meaning deeper than the words. Add to this her superb musicianship and you get some idea of her greatness. She does not merely reproduce, she creates music. She can be dreamily wistful as in "Raina beeti jaye," teasing as in Saqia qarib aa, girlishly buoyant as in "Yeh dil unki nigahon ke saye." She can be the picture of simplicity in Allah tero naam or a musical virtuoso as in piya bin piya bin. Her emotional range is phenomenal. Next only to Lata in popularity is Asha Bhosle. Asha's voice contains peals of laughter, pangs of adolescent love and the devil may care abandon of a non-conformist bohemian . . . she can yoddle [*sic*], titter, sob, staccato, yell, cry and laugh with absolute abandon.

In describing the vocal style of the two sisters, Singh claims that the formidable range between the two made the presence of any other singer in the industry almost redundant. Lata's emotionalism and creativity are contrasted with Asha's spontaneity and a sense of abandonment. Asha's ability to yodel, titter or, laugh is invoked to draw attention to her voice's sonic and material production, connecting it with her bodily gestures and practices. The debate continued to take an unpleasant turn when Bharatan responded with "Who's Afraid of the Mangeshkars?" (1974b), accusing the Mangeshkar sisters of using Surinder Singh for "playback," adding that it was his job to question the monopoly of the two sisters, so that newer singers could get a fair chance. Somewhat reversing his stance, Bharatan cited the popularity of "Bole re papihara" on *farmaish*, or request, programs of Vividh Bharti, to contest Surinder Singh's claim that Vani was no match for the Mangeshkar sisters.[18] By citing specific incidents and anecdotes to build his case, Bharatan displayed his skillful ability to get insider information from his networks in the industry. In journalistic accounts on aural stars and their dramatic posturing, the female singer's voice thus emerges through the interface between musical, lyrical, and extramusical, gendered discourses. In the next section, I focus on the affective intensities of the female voice as distilled through the writings of the critics.

Ambiguous Address, Shadowy Spaces

In "The Mass Production of the Senses: Classical Cinema as Vernacular Modernism," Miriam Hansen (2000, 342) discusses Kracauer's theorization of early cinema as an alternative public sphere, an imaginative horizon that engaged with "the contradictions of modernity at the level of the senses, the level at which the impact of modern technology on human experience was most palpable and irreversible." Hansen suggests that cinema's relationship with modernity is reflexively articulated by the medium's aesthetic and sensorial regime. Taking a cue from Hansen, I suggest that film songs work as artifacts that draw on the contradictions of modernity, illuminating in the process the subjective voice of the female protagonist. But this illumination also creates a drama of shadows, speculation, and ambiguity.

The female solo songs, as discussed earlier, were uniquely placed to express women's subjective experiences and desire in public settings. In song sequences, spectators were addressed as key figures in this interplay between transparency and opacity, through a privileged access, that was denied to the narrative community. This enigmatic quality of the romantic song draws on older forms of music like the *thumri*. Both Vidya Rao and Lalita Du Peron have examined *thumri*'s shifting address as a form where the performer moves fluidly between the text and a real audience outside the text (Du Peron 2002).[19] The play with address and the ambiguity around the addressee heightened the reception of the performance. In film songs, the ambivalence around the addressee is embedded in a range of words used to address the beloved, like *sawanriya*, *raja*, *piya*, *balma*, *pardesiya*, or *sajna*.[20] In several film songs the naming of the lover is deferred or couched with indistinctness. For instance, songs like "O O O mujhe kisisi se pyaar ho gaya" (I have fallen in love with someone) from the film *Barsaat* (Kapoor, 1949) are associated with the female narrative voice in which the woman confesses to the camera/spectator her first feelings of love and desire. Songs like "Kaun aaya ki nigahon mein chamak jag uthi" (Whose arrival has brought a bright sparkle in my eyes?) from the film *Waqt* (Chopra, 1965) are pleasurable because they lead you into a nebulous territory. Moreover, the ambiguity is staged and expressed through the camera and shot distribution to emphasize the acoustic relay between the singer and the listener. In "Kaun aaya," while the spectators are aware that Sadhana is expressing her excitement about Sunil Dutt's impending visit, the sequence shows Raj Kumar entering her home as he starts to respond to her singing. The desire expressed in the song acquires a sensory edge as the spectator is directed to hear the voice from Raj Kumar's point of view and its misdirection.

This recurring idea of ambiguity in the narrative voice of the female singer needs to be placed within a wider context of the female singer's techno-material voice. There are two important points that I would like to raise here. The first has to do with frontality in Indian cinema, which is connected to the notion of the iconic in Indian art. Geeta Kapur (1987, 80) has suggested that the frontality of word, image, design, and the performative act yields forms of direct address. Ashish Rajadhyaksha has analyzed Phalke's work in early cinema as a negotiation of new technologies and space through the deployment of a frontal frame. According to Rajadhyaksha (1987), this neotraditionalist mode, adopted by filmmakers like Phalke, helped restabilize the viewing subject. Ravi Vasudevan (2000) identifies the frontal mode in Indian cinema as a mode operating through the spectator's knowledge of existing narrative paradigms and performance traditions such as film songs.

I am borrowing this concept of frontality in film music to highlight how the sonic amplification of the singer's voice emptied out the soundtrack of incidental sounds, thus giving primacy to the voice. James Lastra (1992, 76) has suggested two models of sound representation: the fidelity model and the telephone model. In the fidelity approach, "all aspects of sound event are inherently significant," including direct and reflected sound. The telephonic approach assumes that "sound is internally hierarchized" (76). The voice in Hindi film songs has always been privileged to enable optimal registration, indicating a bias toward the telephone model.[21] Though orchestration and scoring were important, their primary role was seen in a limited way, to provide tonal color and a subtext to the song.[22] The musical instruments were rarely deployed to compete with the voice when the singers sang the *mukhda* and the *antara* of the song. Singers were expected to pronounce the Hindi or Urdu words "correctly" and give importance to the lyrics. All of these strategies were used to establish the frontality of the singing voice in the aural domain. The mise-en-scène of song sequences contributed to this projection of frontality by highlighting the facial expressions of the on-screen stars who mimed the voice, and of the key figures being addressed.

Let us now turn to the material conditions under which songs were produced. Since the songs were recorded live, along with the musicians, the singer had to spend a lot of time with the composer to rehearse the song prior to its recording. During recordings, the singer and the musicians shared the same space and the same microphone. Later, a separate microphone was introduced for the singers. Slowly, with transformations in technology, the recording booth became an exclusive space for the singer, while the musicians remained in the hall and the sound engineer in the console room. Thus, the recording room became a private and intimate space where the singer could shape the song.

In his work on the history of sound, Jonathan Sterne alerts us to the bodily dispositions and affective states involved in the studio. Recording studios are considered technical, social, and spatial, thus harnessing bodies and sounds in space, in "a particular ordering of practices and attitudes" (Sterne 2006, 236). Following Sterne, I argue that the recording studio was a space where the singer was expected to mobilize her voice to foreground the expressions of love, desire, and sensuality demanded by the song. At the same time, the process of recording songs in a "live take" along with the orchestra required a disciplining of the singer's body.[23] With the arrival of sensitive microphones, the singer had to learn to control her breathing and ensure that the throw of her voice reached the microphone in the right manner. The conflict between the demands for a disciplined body and the intensity of desire, love, and intimacy expressed by the singing voice in a frontal manner turned the recording studio into an enigmatic space open to speculation and gossip.

Mark Katz's distinction between live and recorded music also becomes productive here. Katz (2004, 5) shows that while performing live, musical sound is "fleeting, evanescent." The process of recording turns these fugitive sounds into tangible media that can be sold and circulated (5). The contingent feelings of desire, longing, and anguish as expressed by the song get inscribed in recordings, to create varying possibilities of decipherment. These fleeting emotions become further complicated by the production protocols of the recording studio as a shadowy space. The production of songs until recently remained hidden from public view, while the playback voice has often been referred to as a "ghost" voice. Majumdar (2010, 154) has shown that speculation about a "real life" romance between the actors/stars, performing as lovers in the film, resulted in their off-screen and on-screen lives coming together at certain moments in films. In contrast, the idea of a relationship between the singer and the music director could find resonance through the aural and affective traces of the song where the voice was lionized over other sonic elements through the mode of frontality. The industrial process of sound recording, combined with the aesthetics of ambiguity in the lyrics and the sonic character of the song, turned the studios into sensual, shadowy spaces. The end product of this process was the song, an aural text that could be heard, but not seen. It is this obscure quality of the romantic song that opened it up for muted speculation, especially regarding the relationship between the music director and the singer. Further, the ambivalent narrative address in the female voice gave ample scope for conjecture and gossip. For instance, in a review of an album of Lata's favorite songs, Arvind Dhurandhar chose to rely on the lyrics of the songs to speculate on Lata's relationship with C. Ramachandra. According to Dhurandhar, "Lata has chosen a very symbolic Ramachandra number as her favourite, 'Tum Kya Jano' from *Shin Shinaki Boobla Boo* (Santoshi, 1952). If you mark the lyrics of the song closely, you will realise why. Ramachandra is no more today, but the torch that he carried for Lata in his heart is still alive in his songs. Whether Lata reciprocated Ramachandra's feelings for her, I don't know, but I do know that Lata managed to impart a rare sentimental touch to his songs" (1988, 16).

By underlining the sentimentality of "Tum kya jano tumhari yaad mein hum kitna roye" (How would you know how much I cried in your memory), Dhurandhar tries to connect the singer's inner landscape with the lyrics of the song, imbuing it with ambivalence. He builds his suggestive narrative through partial revelation, privileging his emotional response to a song that Lata *sang for* C. Ramachandra (emphasis mine).[24]

While Dhurandhar restricted himself to subtle references, Ishaq Muzavar created drama around the alleged relationships between Lata and C. Ramachandra in a three-part series in *Madhuri*.[25] "Daastan adhure pyaar ki" (Story of an unfulfilled love) focused on Lata Mangeshkar as being Ramachandra's muse. The entry point for Muzavar was C. Ramachandra's Marathi autobiography, in which he described his love for a woman named "Sita," his favorite playback singer. According to Ramachandra, once Sita came into his life he could not imagine his music without her voice. The mythological names Ram and Sita were evoked to instill some ambiguity, yet according to Muzavar, Ramachandra left enough clues for the reader to deduce whom he was referring to. Muzavar identified "Sita" for the readers by using several photographs of Lata Mangeshkar to "unmask" this mystery woman. According to Muzavar (1988), even after Lata stopped working for Ramachandra, he composed all of his songs imagining her as the singer. In one interesting image, Lata's photograph was layered with notations of a song. A small-sized photograph of C. Ramachandra completed the graphic to suggest that Lata's musical voice was flowing toward Ramachandra. Another clever filmic strategy employed in the series was the display of a full-page photograph of Lata Mangeshkar speaking on the telephone (figure 3.4). The text on the image is attributed to C. Ramachandra from his autobiography, sharing that Lata's voice still echoes in his ears. The visualization of the page with the text was meant to create an impression that Lata was trying to establish contact with the composer through the

दास्तान अधूरे प्यार की

सी.रामचंद्र

तुम्हारे एक सुर की खातिर...

Figure 3.4. A visual from Ishaq Muzavar's article in *Madhuri*. Source: National Film Archive of India.

telephone. In both of the photographs, visual strategies were used to highlight the sonorous and sensory registers of the voice.

Nostalgia for Live *Mehfils*

Let us recall a sequence from *Mirch Masala* (Mehta, 1987), where the mise-en-scène establishes the arrogant subahdar, or tax collector, showing off his new gramophone player to a gathering of men. When the first record breaks accidently, the mercurial subahdar beats his attendant mercilessly. He then goes inside the tent to get another disc and returns. The acts like pulling out the disc from the jacket, hand cranking the player, and placing the needle on the disc are stretched in the sequence, drawing attention to the machinic assemblage. The men, lined up in order of caste and class hierarchy of the village, are all ears at a strange hissing sound: the subahdar gestures toward them to remain silent until we hear the sharp voice of the singer. Through an array of gestures and their timing, the subahdar performs the role of a *rasika*, or connoisseur, who understands the nuances of this recorded performance while also claiming ownership over the woman's voice. The breaking of the record disc demands attention to its materiality, its *thingness*, that can break or become worn out over time.

The above sequence also underlines the ephemerality of musical sound. As Richard Leppert (1993, 22) has observed, music is a mythical substance, it "disappears as absolutely as a shadow, once light fades." Listening practices as described by the critics evoked pleasurable yearnings for the recorded female singer that would disappear as soon as the needle had completed its rotational cycles on the groove of the record. Through his columns and sketches, Bharatan alluded to the narratives of loss by focusing on female-centric songs. Interestingly, he often added layers of meaning by describing the context in which he had heard the gramophone recording. For instance, in writing about an alleged relationship between Lata Mangeshkar and C. Ramachandra, he particularly focused on one song:

> That pang, the tang was to be felt in the music Lata and C Ramachandra made together. From the moment he came into her life, she sang for him like she did for no one before and the two conquered our hearts to become engraved in our minds as the numero-uno "meludo." There were tears in his eyes as with great difficulty, I got him for an all night soiree at which we played around midnight, his torch-melody for Lata from "Yasmin": Aankhon mein sama jaao is dil mein raha karna [Let me behold you with my eyes, come, dwell in my heart]. It was obvious to all present that the number must have been composed by C. Ramachandra for Lata in a moony moment of tender togetherness. (Bharatan 1995, 116)

This "romantic" encounter at midnight with Lata's voice gestures toward a nostalgia for live *mehfils*, all-night sessions where courtesans performed for their patrons, or the male connoisseurs, who often asked the artist for a repeat performance. Here, the live performance of the courtesan is replaced by an acousmatic voice of the singer evoking personal memories and a sense of loss. The voice within the text and the sonic voice of the singer seem to overlap as he writes: "she sang for him like she did for no one." In another column, Bharatan describes a listening session with O. P. Nayyar that evokes the idea of a *mehfil*:

> I get so many letters—letters from as far away as East Africa and the West Indies—asking whatever happened to O.P Nayyar. I met O.P to find things out for myself. And the big change I found in him is that he has left his past behind. . . . A far cry from the time he played "Raton ko Chori Chori" six times over and wouldn't stop even when I told him I'd had enough. Today you can discuss musical matters with him frankly. . . . Not that Nayyar is blameless—if anything, he is only paying the logical price for having identified himself with the voice of Asha so completely. (Bharatan 1977, 50)

Bharatan's reference to Nayyar's obsessive listening to "Raton ko chori chori" (Slyly at night) sung by Asha Bhosle points significantly to a yearning for private consumption of the voice and an attempt to hold on to that fleeting moment.[26] The lyrics of this song express a woman's desire and yearning for physical intimacy:

Raton ko chori chori bole mora kangana
Ab ke jo barkha aayi aayenge sajna

Slyly at night my bracelets whisper to me
This time when it rains my beloved will return

In her work on print culture in North India, Francesca Orsini (2009, 80) discusses the popularity of songbooks of *Barahmasas* that described the sexuality and the sensuality of the *virahini*. The *Barahmasas*, literally meaning twelve months, were written by male poets, centered on the figure of the woman, who is flatteringly dependent on men for her fulfilment. Gramophone recordings and film music further popularized the genre. "Raton ko chori chori" expresses the woman's interiority addressed to the listener: her bracelets, the clouds, the rain, and the moon bearing witness to her longing become an integral part of the sensuous experience. Bharatan describes the song as a locus for pleasure, evoking memories of the past: the presence of the "spurned" lover (O. P.

Nayyar) in this act of repeated listening reinforces the affective registers of the voice. The themes of desire and yearning combined with the ambiguity of address, show how the Hindi film song relied overtly on the female voice to generate memories and murmurs, evoking the specter of the courtesan. The enchantment with the female recorded voice became a recurring motif in Bharatan's writings, where the boundaries between the critic and a fan became increasingly blurred. The act of listening described by Bharatan reinforces Simon Frith's (1989, 139) ideas about popular music, which spurs the listener toward personal and affective engagement. The *mehfil* described here evokes the image of an entitled male listener, demanding unmediated access to the voice, in a mode of listening that is both intense and ephemeral.

One of the biggest controversies Bharatan got involved in during his journalistic career was related to the *Guinness Book of World Records* with its announcement that Lata Mangeshkar had recorded the highest number of songs in India. In an article in *Illustrated Weekly of India* in 1970, Bharatan credited Lata with sixteen thousand songs and set off a number game.[27] Following Rafi's challenge to the Guinness claim, a fierce debate raged on this issue in *Filmfare*.[28] Later, Bharatan admitted to the error in his judgment, failing to live by the standards he had set for himself as a musical aesthete. In his biography of Lata Mangeshkar, he writes:

> How did I go wrong? It is a testament to Lata Mangeshkar's surpassing vocal skill that, each time you and I heard something like *Kuch Dil Ne Kaha* (Anupama) from her silver throat, it sounded, to both you and me, a wholly fresh listening experience. Not only I, therefore, but each one of us listening mentally calculated each such record of Lata as equal to 10, the multiplier effect working unconsciously in our minds in times when there was no ready reckoner in which to check out. This very simply, is how the figure got inflated to 16,000 in my mind. If you are honest, you will admit that it got so inflated in your mind too. The one thing that you and I can say in defence of such a guestimate, having lived through those lilting listening times is that the figure, if got inflated, at least got mentally stimulatingly inflated. (1995, 284–85)

Bharatan underlines his intense engagement with Lata's voice as a fetishized object: as in Freud's understanding—a sign of an insistence on something being present when it is not.[29] The critic turns into a fan, allowing the "multiplier effect" of the voice to invoke collective listening as a scaffold for collective memories. However, it is important to add that throughout his writing, Bharatan's accounts evoke aural perceptions, mediated through sound technologies intersecting with social imaginaries.

Music, Mediation, and Technology

According to Antoine Hennion (2003, 90), taste becomes a mutually transformative force in the mediation between the music lover and musical sound, as cultivated through a range of practices and techniques.[30] An important intervention by the critic was a self-conscious mediation between the listener and the music industry. The critic stood at a vantage point drawing on experiential and cognitive elements in his writings. I signpost the emergence of a highly gendered discourse, articulated by creating a hierarchy of media technologies as music delivery devices.

Through his columns in film magazines, Bharatan addressed an elite listener who accessed film music through gramophone records, or the contingent experience of radio broadcasts. For instance, in one of his columns, he attacked the industry for ignoring composers like Hridayanath Mangeshkar, blaming All India Radio's Vividh Bharti service for promoting "catchpenny commercialism," riding on the wave of "transistorization" of film music (Bharatan 1971b, 46). Identifying the Vividh Bharati service with the arrival of transistors was a familiar trope that betrayed anxieties about new delivery technologies. In reviewing vinyl albums, Bharatan's approach was to make sure that the "needs of the listeners" were taken seriously by music publishing companies like HMV. Bharatan insisted that compilation albums brought out by HMV should showcase the rarest of film songs, not accessible on the radio, as this would help listeners to assess the voices of the singers. As he wrote about *Mellow Gold*:

> She belongs to an era when almost all compositions were elegant. Yet Lata could not sing all of them, could she? So some

> of them went to Asha in certain special circumstances. Like for instance, when Madan Mohan, in "Dekh Kabira Roya" had to compose three "linking" songs to be filmed in a row on Ameeta, Anita Guha and Shubha Khote. So he tuned "Meri veena tum bin roye" to go on Ameeta in the voice of Lata, *Ashkon se teri humne* to go on Anita in the voice of Asha and *Tu pyaar kare ya thukraye* to go on Shubha in the voice of Lata. Madan Mohan thus subtly saw to it that the first audio-visual impact was through the vocals of Lata. Then, just when Asha had sung "Ashkon se teri" to match Lata's "Meri veena," he planted his final and finest composition in the film on Lata.[31] End impressions endure and Asha, thus sandwiched between two fine Lata numbers found herself losing out for no fault of her own. But now we can evaluate her Ashkon se teri hum ne—as one of 16 selections on the "Mellow Gold" LP on its own merit. (Bharatan 1985a)

This review came out in *Filmfare* in March 1985, at a time when gramophone records were slowly being eroded to make way for the cassette boom (figure 3.5). Bharatan's analysis gives weight to his approach toward compilation albums that would allow listeners to assess Asha's voice without getting distracted by other voices, which wasn't possible while watching the film. The compilation album record was coveted, as it could offer an unmediated experience between the singer and the listener. In 1984, HMV brought out *I Remember Madan Mohan*, an LP with fourteen songs, selected by Lata Mangeshkar as her tribute to the late composer. In his review, prominently splashed in *Filmfare*, Bharatan sharply criticized the selections made by Lata, referring to them as "commonplace," while attributing this to an overexposure on radio. According to him, "the object [of this album] should have been to bring to the listeners a selection calculated to put back on record some of the most prized gems from Madan Mohan's treasure trove. True, this would have meant going to no end of trouble in hunting out numbers with the never-never touch. But the end product would have been a record truly rare, not something commonplace, as we have here" (1984, 85).

In working out his argument that HMV's compilations should avoid being "commonplace," Bharatan articulated his bias toward privileging

'I REMEMBER MADAN MOHAN'

LIKE TUNING TO VIVIDH BHARATI

Take away Lata and what is left of Madan? Ghazal Ka Shehzada is what Lata now calls him as she picks 14 numbers to make up her 'I Remember Madan Mohan' album. Are these 14 numbers Lata's best ever for Madan Mohan?Raju Bharatan asks.

Figure 3.5. Bharatan's review of Lata Mangeshkar's tribute album in *Filmfare*. Author's personal collection.

regimes of listening that were addressed toward the respectable elite. Presenting an alternative list of fourteen film songs composed by Madan Mohan, he wrote, "Madan's achievement lay in the fact that through Lata, he took the ghazal to the masses *without coarsening it*" (1984, 85; emphasis mine). One must recall that the partnership between Lata and

Madan Mohan in the 1950s and the '60s played a crucial role in distancing the *ghazal* of Bombay cinema from its association with the courtesan. By raising the pitch of her voice, Lata offered an antidote to the open-throated style of singing in the *kotha*. The use of high-pitched violins and the sitar in place of the sarangi, traditionally used as accompanying instruments in *ghazal* singing, further contributed toward the recalibration of the genre sans its "coarseness." Moreover, highlighting the conjunction between spatial practices in the consumption of music and its aesthetic and moral hierarchies, Bharatan (1971b) referred to Madan Mohan as a "drawing room composer" and not a "bedroom composer." Later, in Lata's biography (1995, 224) he wrote, "The ghazal could get so transcendently transplanted on Lata's lips only as long as Madan Mohan was storing it on that spool tape recorder. He was an aristocratic product of his age. And his age was the age of taste."

Bharatan privileged the gramophone record and spool tape over cassettes, sharpening the divisions between formats on social, cultural, and spatial lines. The excessive proliferation of musical commodities due to the arrival of cassette technology meant that listening to music at one's own will was no longer a privilege of the upper middle class. Jonathan Sterne (2006) has alluded to the significance of sound turning into a commodity through the ideas around private, individual acoustic space as created by sound reproduction technologies. For the critics, the ideal place for consuming the voice of women on gramophone records was the living room, a space associated with elite homes, with a clear separation between inner and outer spaces. The gramophone player was a symbol of social and cultural capital, and though gramophone companies advertised their products for both male and female listeners, and their extended families, for the music critic the ideal listeners continued to be imagined as elite men with a discerning taste.

The anxieties displayed by the critics were commensurate with Lata Mangeshkar's carefully built persona in the industry. As Neepa Majumdar (2010, 192) has suggested, Lata's star persona was defined by the absence of beauty and glamour. Though her film songs covered diverse genres like romantic numbers, *mujras*, seduction songs, cabarets, picnic/leisure songs, *qawwalis*, bawdy numbers, patriotic and devotional numbers, the songs selectively recalled by the music critics were largely *bhajans*, mother's songs, and "sad songs." With the popularity of cassettes and the disco genre, music critics used the language of decline to primarily target female singers. For instance, in an article on Lata, Dhurandhar (1983, 27) advised her not to "lower her standards by singing cheap disco songs." Similarly, commenting on the new trend of film music in Lata's biography, Bharatan (1995, 191) lamented, "Was this all Lata Mangeshkar wanted from her singing life?" As he wrote, "That was the era of composing giants. This is the era of composing ants. That was the era when song was queen, this is the era in which what we have in the name of music, is 'tuneless pornography'" (314).

In this moral discourse, the "bazaar" was often evoked as a space responsible for the decline in music. In this context, the question asked repeatedly by the critics was how a soulful singer like Lata could be so easily available in cassettes in bazaars, paan shops and slums. More significantly, the word "bazaar" itself raised the specter of the courtesan, evoking the cultural memory of the *gaane wali*, or singing girl, in the *kotha*. As Bharatan (1995, 319) wrote, "It sounds so tasteless to listen to Lata in the cinema of today. She sounds elevating enough in the non-film singing she is doing, you may say. Let her stick to that. Let her sustain at least there the standards she so scrupulously maintained in films, until music became merchandise in our films and those clips on satellite television made our song and dance sequences look like something done for the bazaar."

Bharatan's references to the spatial and social practices of music production and consumption revealed a deep apprehension of the mass proliferation of recorded music. The emergence of new listening publics with access to "cheaper" devices led to deep anxieties, as the female playback singer now seemed to move away from the private, exclusive domain of the music critic.

The Critic and the Hagiographic Turn

On the heels of Bharatan's biography, Harish Bhimani brought out *In Search of Lata Mangeshkar* in 1995. The biography can be considered as a sharp reply to Bharatan by the "Lata camp," as Bhimani (1995, 11) described it as a "concert travelogue, point of view, a revelation of her true self," in which his agenda was to foreground the "real Lata," as opposed to the one shaped by misunderstandings or malicious rumors.

The author and fan captures Lata in various stages of her concert tours, sharing details of the planning, rehearsals, and nervous expectations for and audience reactions to the concerts covered in the travelogue. These accounts are interspersed with other narratives on her life that move between deep appreciation and close observation. This strategy, he claims, helped him access the singer's life, a feat that would not have been possible for any other biographer. The significance of the book lay in opening up for readers the expanding spatial geographies of Bombay film songs, in overseas locations, where Bhimani could invoke his claim on Lata, via liminal spaces, such as airports, hotel rooms, or the moments in the green room, just before her live shows. The conversations with Lata were molded into a surrogate autobiography, where she could respond to a slew of criticisms that she had been facing, primarily regarding her "monopolistic control" over the industry and her refusal to quit "tasteless" film music. In this process, Bhimani's work was aligned with Lata's attempt to assert control over her own image and the dispersal of her voice. One of the recurring motifs in Bhimani's book was giving significance to Lata's attempt to distance herself selectively from some of her songs. The author played his part by amplifying Lata's aversion to and disavowal of some of her songs, adding his own moralistic attitude. As Bhimani wrote:

> The frolicsome number *Buddha Mil Gaya* from *Sangam* got recorded only because she was not aware of what she was supposed to sing until she reached the recording studio. She found both the lyric and the situation of the song distasteful. . . . Again if she has liked a song but found the picturisation bawdy, she will not sing it. If she does sing the song "hai hai yeh majboori" from the film *Roti Kapda Aur Makaan*, it is always half-heartedly. And the song "Bindiya Chamkegi" from *Do Raaste* puts her off because spectators from some corner invariably begin to dance in response to the rhythm. She is even known to act as a one-woman censor and edits portions of her songs which she thinks are unbecoming of her age and stature. I wonder if those of you have heard her sing "*Mere hathon mein nau nau choodiyan hain*" from *Chandni* on stage, have noticed that she astutely avoids the stanza which

> has a naughty reference to the heroine's choli and the tailor! I have always maintained that instead of overt description of sex on screen, it's more tasteful to employ music and dance to draw out this delicate emotion. (289)

The passage elaborates various strategies employed by Lata to contain the erotic registers of her voice, while betraying Bhimani's compelling anxieties about the depiction of sex on-screen. In another passage of the book, Bhimani provides a list of song genres that Lata does not sing, including, *qawwalis*, "cheap and saucy mujras," "cabaret numbers," and "songs with double entendre" (160). However, after mentioning each genre, Bhimani cites a few songs as exceptions, while leaving out several others.

The timing of the biographies by Bharatan and Bhimani overlapped with HMV's successful attempt at reaching out to its listeners by bringing Lata back into the aural domain. As I will discuss in the next chapter, the gramophone company tried to recalibrate its image by bringing out special compilations in collaboration with Lata. Through my discussions on the print media discourse, I have shown how the recorded voice of the female playback singer available on gramophone records fascinated the music critic. Guided by affective registers of romantic song and the circulation of private information about the lives of singers, the critics often speculated on the singers' private lives, or subjectivities by privileging his own listening experiences. The critic alternated between a discerning listener/ public intellectual and a star-struck fan, who was deeply moved by the disembodied voice of the female singer, to cull out in the public domain a substantive discussion around the female voice. Moreover, the critic played a crucial role in mediating between the film and music industries and listeners to articulate a highly gendered, hierarchical, and value-driven aesthetic. In the next chapter, I will discuss the intersections between the music industry and the emergence of a new community of version singers in the wake of the cassette revolution. For the critic, the space to explore the interiority of the singer, laced with the yearning for her voice, was no longer available. In the new taste economies, the music publishing industry was poised to enter the domain of cassette distribution by piggybacking on new voices, or through a recalibrated packaging of old voices, in a desperate bid to reach out to the listeners.

4

Cassettes, Fans, and Singers

For almost six decades HMV dominated the world of Hindi film music.[1] In the first three decades after India's independence, the gramophone records published by HMV enabled the circulation of the female voice. Significant transformations in the media economy marked the 1980s, largely due to the arrival of cassette technology. The decade is referred to as a period of decline in Hindi film music, a claim based on a complete disregard for the diverse cluster of experiences offered to the expanding community of listeners. As we will see, the arrival of new technologies for the consumption of music gave listeners the chance to participate in a range of activities in the dispersion of popular film songs. This process involved mobilization of aural memories, musical training through intense listening by fan devotees, and marketing of nostalgia. In this chapter, I discuss the recirculation of Lata Mangeshkar's voice during this period of the cassette revolution. I look at the proliferation of her songs not in *her* voice but that of "copy artists." The industrial boom in version recordings drew upon embodied memory and sensual knowledge of the star singers' voices, questioning the boundaries between fans/listeners and playback stars. I will demonstrate how version recordings force us to acknowledge an earlier practice of "dubbing" or scratch singing that formed the underbelly of the music industry. This brings to the surface an ambivalent relationship that the younger aspiring singers had with Lata Mangeshkar, simultaneously marked with anxiety and deep devotion. The clever marketing of version recordings piggybacked on the names and photographs of star singers, resulting in quick sales, and also destabilized the easy connections between the aura of the voice and its auditory presence as a techno-material recording. Finally, the chapter examines the strategies adopted by the Gramophone Company of India (HMV) in staking its claim over the rightful ownership of the most treasured archive—the authentic voice of Lata Mangeshkar. I unravel the textual, visual, and aural strategies adopted by HMV for recirculating Lata Mangeshkar's "original" voice through the dual registers of nostalgia and subjective memory. In this complicated journey, music companies were not just staking a claim over the "authentic" but also reordering the past.

From the arrival of sound cinema in 1931, the marketing and dispersal of film song recordings in India were monopolized by the British-owned Gramophone Company of India (GCI) under the label HMV. This monopoly remained unchallenged until Polydor entered the Indian market in the late 1960s. The biggest pressing factory of GCI was located in Calcutta and, until the early 1940s, Calcutta remained the most important hub for the music industry. Later, with Bombay becoming the stronghold of the Hindi film industry, GCI began shifting its operations to Bombay. In the 1950s, as Bombay cinema became the most important resource for providing musical content to the recording industry, the city of Bombay became the preferred location for music companies, recording studios, and other ancillary units. Images of leading stars/actors on the jackets and covers of film music products point to the pervasiveness of film culture, with film songs firmly aligned with their cinematic contexts (Manuel 1993).[2] The arrival of cassette technology revolutionized the Indian music industry in commercial viability.

The arrival of cassette technology created a new hunger for music. The market was quickly flooded with cheaply produced music in diverse genres like *bhajans*, *ghazals*, and folk and regional music and film songs. One of the emerging players in the cassette-driven music industry was Gulshan Kumar, who entered the business by marketing pirated versions of popular film songs through parallel networks. According to Lawrence Liang (2005, 10), Super Cassettes Industry Limited (SCIL), the company owned by Kumar, was involved in "obtaining film scores even before the release of the film to ensure that their recordings were the first to hit the market." These commodities with the label of T-series were sold in bazaars, at petrol pumps, in *kirana* stores and in paan shops, at prices much lower than those sold by upmarket retailers.

In his detailed work on the traffic of images, sounds, and objects, Ravi Sundaram underscores the destabilizing nature of piracy, riding on the dynamic networks of pirate production and distribution. Piracy, according to Sundaram (2010, 112), "escapes the boundaries of space, of particular networks, of form, a before and after, a *limit*." In the 1980s, piracy made its appearance in diverse and ancillary forms. SCI began recirculating popular film songs in the market as "cover versions," with the help of local singers and musicians in Delhi.[3] The boom in cover version recordings has been attributed to the "inability of HMV to meet the demand for [the] release of its vast catalogue of past film songs" (Manuel 1993, 146–47). Following the success of cover version products, SCIL started publishing advertisements in local newspapers inviting aspiring singers for auditions.[4] Soon, the voices of singers like Vandana Vajpayee, Wasim Raza, and Alka (from Delhi), through popular songs of films like *Karma* (Ghai, 1986) and *Ram Teri Ganga Maili* (Kapoor, 1985) became a recursive force in the aural domain.[5] According to Anuradha Paudwal (2010), "When I went to Delhi for the first time after joining T Series, everywhere, every petrol pump, every nukkad it was only Vandana Vajpayee. I said to myself, not Lataji but, how am I going to have any chance with Vandana Vajpayee around? How will I penetrate this voice? They were all versions. People in the North knew only Vandana Vajpayee."

In defending their decision to bring out version recordings of old film songs in the voice of copy artists, music companies like SCIL used a fair use clause in section 52–1 (j) of the Indian Copyright Act. "My company has always promoted new talent," Gulshan Kumar claimed in an interview (1990). The rapid foray of cassettes into the music market enabled many new singers to enter the industry. Singers like Uttara Kelkar, Vandana Vajpayee, Anupama Deshpande, and Bela Sulakhe were among many who made a foothold in the music industry through version recordings. These musical commodities were recorded on stereo, with far superior quality of sound fidelity. Bela Sulakhe became associated with Gulshan Kumar's company in the mid-eighties. Bela had been singing for stage shows for a group called *Melody Makers*, performing regularly in the small towns and cities of Maharashtra and Gujarat. This was followed by an offer to record duet songs with Manhar Udhas for SCI. Later, Gulshan Kumar invited her to their studio in Delhi. As Sulakhe (2011) recalls:

> He [Gulshan Kumar] said, "We have some tracks ready, what would you like to sing?" I sang "bahon mein chale aao" from *Anamika* and one more song. Then we recorded a lot of songs live with live music, as the tracks were being prepared at that time. Later, I started recording for T-series in Bombay at Sudeep and then at Golden Chariot. I did a lot of recordings for them. I sang *bhajans*, cabarets, sad songs, *ghazals*, *qawwali*, all the diverse genres, and, since I had started recording so much I cut down on my shows. Because when you do shows your voice gets strained. When you travel, and have late nights, it affects the voice so I started concentrating on studio recordings.

Despite their prolific aural presence, artists like Bela Sulakhe and Vandana Vajpayee were referred to as "poor copies" of established aural stars, waiting endlessly for a "big break." In this recursive mode, singers were expected to be good listeners in order to be able to reproduce a voice that could come as close to the "original" singer as possible. This fluid relationship between listening and singing, hearing and recording, became a hallmark of the booming music industry in the wake of an ever-expanding listenership.

The Inaudible Voice of the Dubbing Artist

The circulation of film songs through an imitative mode was not a new phenomenon. Several discursive practices in use since the 1950s encouraged listeners to sing songs imitating the style of their favorite playback singers: song booklets with lyrics of songs were available through cheaply produced chapbooks; notations of film songs appeared in magazines like *Madhuri* and publications of Sangeet Karyalaya, Hathras; and events like live music shows and *antakshari* sessions were organized by amateur music radio clubs and fan-based groups.[6] Outfits like *Melody Makers* successfully organized live shows of film songs in India and abroad, working with lesser-known singers and artists. Reproducing the playback singer's style through imitation was recognized as a legitimate activity for young girls, as a sign of both their talent and middle-class femininity.

It would be fallacious to believe that version recordings inaugurated the production of a mimetic voice in its material form. Discussions around the practice of imitation have dominated the Bombay film music industry since the 1940s. For instance, there was a discussion in film magazines about Noor Jahan's influence on Lata Mangeshkar in the early years of her career.[7] Later, as discussed in chapter 1, the soft, intimate style of singing developed by Lata Mangeshkar, referred to as her distinctive voice, became a template for heroine's songs. Most of the new generation of singers who entered the industry in the 1960s and the '70s modulated their singing style to be as close to Lata's as possible by listening to her songs on the radio.[8] Sulakshana Pandit (1980, 27), trained in classical music, admitted in an interview that it was only after listening to Lata Mangeshkar on the radio that she realized that her vocals were "inclined to sing soft, melodious numbers." Similarly, Sadhana Sargam worked for several years under the tutelage of Kalyanji Anandji to get accepted as a playback singer. This required her to tone down the effect of her training in Hindustani classical music and introduce new stylistic elements in her vocal performance. As she notes:

> See, when we sing classical music we sing at a lower scale, because we have to sing for a long time. So the scale is usually kali panch or safed saat. But for film songs I had to sing and practice at a higher scale, at least, by one or two notes. I had to work on my diction and see to it that I do not get the Marathi accent in my voice. I learnt Urdu to improve my pronunciation. In classical singing vibrato is not accepted/ usko dosh mana jaata hai [it is considered to be incorrect]. But for playback singing I had to develop vibrato (*kampan*) because that brings out the expressions. I used to listen to Lata ji, and my range was ok. It was neither too wide nor too limited but I had to work a bit. I think every singer has to work around a bit according to her limitations to become a playback singer. (Sargam 2011)

Sadhana Sargam worked as a dubbing artist for several years before she could make a mark as a playback singer. This implies that for several years her film song recordings could not reach the public domain. The practice of dubbing gained currency when singing stars like Lata Mangeshkar and Asha Bhosle started traveling extensively for overseas shows.[9] To examine the dubbing system, I recall Martin Daughtry's (2017, 48) ideas on the acoustic palimpsest, as a "micromethodology for thick description" that allows us to uncover "moments of inscription and erasure that lie beneath acoustic phenomenon and auditory practices." With the tracking system in place, the voice of the dubbing artist was recorded on a separate track. The song was created by mixing this scratch voice with the music tracks and used as a referent for on-screen stars to perform the song during its "picturization." Finally, just before the release of the film, along with its music, the voice of the dubbing artist was replaced by that of the star singers. Marked by erasures, the dubbing system was meant to perpetuate the hegemony of leading playback singers like Lata Mangeshkar, but, in its wake, it consolidated imitative singing as a normative practice.[10] Dubbing artists learned, rehearsed, and recorded film songs in studios along with the musicians. The technique adopted by female copy singers was to produce a voice that simulated those tonal inflections best suited to articulate women's desires, betrayals, and confessions, as a template of the female voice in popular film songs.

Version recordings by copy singers pulled the dubbing system inside out—giving a public face to a practice that formed the underbelly of the music industry. As I have shown, by lending her voice, the dubbing artist facilitated the production of the song in its musical and visual form. The voice of the scratch singer was temporarily inscribed on the tracks, but this sonic material was rendered inaudible in the final version. Like the figure of the extra and the body double, the labor provided by the scratch singer remained invisible, or unheard.

Affective Constellation: From the Listening Fan to the Singing Devotee

Chronologically and materially, the dubbing singer's voice prefigured the voice of the playback star, creating fissures between the notions of originality and authenticity. The sonic voice of the dubbing artist not only got recorded on the vocal tracks but also left its trace on the performance of the on-screen star.[11] Since the dubbing artists and the star singers shared the same musical tracks, the only way a singer could get a chance to become a dubbing artist was with her ability to sing at the same scale as the Mangeshkar sisters and produce similar tonalities. Moreover, songs were composed according to the vocal range of the main artist.[12] It is therefore not surprising that singers who started working as dubbing artists claimed to be deeply influenced by Lata Mangeshkar's singing. Alka Yagnik has referred to herself as an ardent fan of Lata's singing. "I wanted to sing like her. I used to listen to her songs carefully and hum them. That's when my mother spotted my aptitude for singing," recounts Alka (2000, 93). It was this quality, to be able to "*sing like her*" that qualified a new entrant in the industry to become a dubbing artist. More importantly, the practice of dubbing allowed a singer to cross over and become a playback singer in her own right. Facilitated by the multitrack system, the material voice of the dubbing artist could be heard, analyzed, appreciated, and accepted and finally upstage the imagined voice of the singing star. As Anuradha Paudwal (2010) recalls:

> I always used to say no to offers for dubbing. For *Satyam Shivam Sundaram*, I was asked to sing but I refused since I did not want Raj Kapoor to hear my voice as a dubbing artist. But when they [Laxmikant Pyarelal] were recording for *Hero*, I learnt that they are recording for Lata Ji and she was not in town and I just felt that day that let me do it. I called Lakshmiji and said, "I would like to sing this song." But they said, "No this is for a dubbing artist. It will not be retained." I said, "Doesn't matter, I would like to sing it." They gave me the song. It was "Tu Mera Janu hai." The tracks were good and I worked hard on it and my first take was okayed, although, they were also not spending too much time because for them this was just a scratch voice. But in the evening when they heard the song they said that this is sounding fine so let us retain it. That is how it was retained, it was meant for Lataji. Immediately, after 15 days, they recorded "Ding dong" and that too was retained, though it was a dubbing song. Then

> I sang "Pyar Karne Wale Kabhi Darte Nahin," but that was dubbed by Lataji the next day.

The huge popularity of songs like "Ding-dong" and "Tu mera janu hai" (You are dear to me) pushed Anuradha Paudwal into the limelight, ending her ten-year struggle in the industry (figure 4.1). The popularity of these songs was a clear indication that the listeners had accepted her voice. With the demand for musical content on the rise, the industry required a new brand of trained singers who could quickly and efficiently produce a voice by adjusting to the set patterns of the film song.[13] Working as dubbing artists became a part of this training, allowing new entrants to showcase their mimetic voice. In return, what excited the new singers was the opportunity to sing with a live orchestra following the discipline demanded from a studio recording. In industry parlance, this is referred to as a "period of struggle" that every successful singer has to go through. Kavita Krishnamurthy (1987), who worked as a dubbing artist for several years, reminisces, "Occasionally I'd feel emotional about certain songs. But this was good for me as a singer. Since I had never struggled for anything, I thought it was good to know some pain. I think struggle is essential for an artist."

Moving away from the concepts framed by critical sociology to a pragmatic approach toward taste in music, Antoine Hennion (2004, 131–32) has perceptively pointed toward the rise of the amateur, the spectator, the fan as a new competent figure employing "highly elaborate formats and procedures" to display productive as well as creative capacities. In the case of Lata Mangeshkar's recursive voice, we can see the emergence of a range of listening and fan practices that, spurred by the cassette boom, led to the proliferation of song recordings through heterogeneous material practices. But the journey undertaken by the amateur, aspiring singer was never easy: singers like Kavita Krishnamurthy were confronted by memories associated with songs they had sung as scratch artists. These songs were now material objects available in the public domain through another voice. For instance, in an interview, Kavita shares her initial reaction when Vidhu Vinod Chopra, the director of *1942, A Love Story* (1994), informed her that "Kuch na kaho," a song that she had sung for the film, would now be recorded by Lata Mangeshkar. As she recollects:

When the makers of *Utsav* were entering the film for the National Awards, Anuradha's name had been mentioned for the song "*Mere man baje mridang*," when she learnt this her instant reaction was: "I have only sung four lines that too in background, so where's the question of an award?" Producer Shashi Kapoor's reply was: "why not? What's important is how effectively you've rendered the four lines."

"Can you believe it, I have won the Filmfare Award for the same four lines," said a surprised Anuradha.

Anuradha describes the song composed by Vasant Dev as an exceptional one "composed with the period of the film in mind." And "for the first time", she observes, "sounds recorded on three separate tracks were fused to achieve the most enchanting piece of music I have ever heard. There have been lots of *mela* songs but this one is so different."

Anuradha, who was at one stage accused of "aping" Lata, is gradually evolving a style of her own and is among the sought-after singers of today. About that initial phase she says: "Since I didn't have any formal training in singing I had to follow somebody, who could be a better model than Lata*ji*..? I am now trying my best to establish an identity of my own."

I am trying my best to establish an identity of my own..

ANURADHA PAUDVAL: BEST PLAYBACK SINGER (FEMALE): UTSAV

FILMFARE, FEBRUARY 16—28, 1987

Figure 4.1. Anuradha Paudwal in *Filmfare*. Source: National Film Archive of India.

> I was stunned. First of all I hadn't recovered from Dada's [R. D Burman's] death and then this. It was as if the clock had been turned back to make me a dubbing artist all over again. Still, I consoled myself that it was the divine Lata Mangeshkar who was singing for me. I got over my disappointment. As far as I am concerned I will be eternally grateful to Lataji. I started my career singing her songs which she would dub over later. *Unko sab maaf hai*. I owe everything to her. (Krishnamurthy 1996, 81–82)

Kavita's account alerts us to the complexity of the relationship the aspiring singers of the industry shared with Lata. This ambivalent bond was marked by both devotion and anxiety, gesturing toward the intricate ways in which fandom played itself out in relationship to the star on the one hand and the music industry on the other.

As a dubbing artist, a singer had to imagine the voice of the aural star, as the referent was not available. In version recordings, on the other hand, copy artists relied upon listening to the original song. As Steven Feld (2003, 226) has proclaimed, through an experience of embodied listening, one hears oneself in the act of voicing and one resonates the physicality of voicing in acts of hearing. The use of imitation in both cases was as much about the self as about the other. In these affective constellations, aural memories and sensations were mobilized to keep alive the connection between the dubbing/copy artist and her role model. Further, the techniques required for version recordings challenged the notion of voice as a locus of subjectivity. Bela Sulakhe molded her voice by closely following Lata Mangeshkar. As she remarked:

> I have the same scale as Lataji. I grew up listening to her and I can say that I am her biggest devotee. It is not possible to sing like her. She is so great an artist but I have tried to listen to her and to follow her technique in the way she sings *murkis*. I think I am a good listener. Jaise arjun ko sirf machli ki aankh dikhti hai vaise mujhe sirf unka gana sunai deta hai [The way Arjun could see nothing but the eye of the fish, I pay attention to her songs]. My whole body listens to her. (Sulakhe 2011)

Bela's insights point toward a deep investment by a fan/devotee in listening, imitating, rehearsing, and recording as a relay in an active engagement in the sonic field.[14] In replicating Lata's voice, Bela followed the sonic trace of Lata's recorded voice. This could be achieved by excavating her aural perceptions and memories, as reflected in her remark, "my whole body listens to her."

In their influential philosophical treatise *A Thousand Plateaus*, Gilles Deleuze and Felix Guattari (1987, 504) used the term "assemblage," to foreground the movement of experiences through connections and affective alliances. Assemblage is "simultaneously and inseparably a machinic assemblage and an assemblage of enunciation." This formulation has been discussed by many scholars working on music and technology (Hemment, 2004; Rai, 2009). In India, cassette technology brought together an inventory of machines, cultural networks, and human bodies to alter our listening experience, reorienting us toward familiar songs through different voices. In this discursive form, the voice of the copy artist connected with the machinic, spilling out into new territories and forms. The imitative style in version recordings can be better understood as bodies immersed in the process of "becoming." Following Deleuze, Melissa Gregg and Gregory J. Seigworth (2010, 1) locate affect in intensities that move from body to body (human, nonhuman, part-body, and otherwise), in resonances that circulate and "stick to bodies and worlds," creating new passageways and variations between different intensities. Bela's sensual engagement with Lata Mangeshkar's voice foregrounds the myriad connections and loops within which music, voices, and bodies are entangled. The performance and material practices involved in version recordings emerged through affective constellations as the bodies of fans/listeners and a new generation of singers were immersed in recuperating aural memories associated with the original song. It was this affective alliance that remained at the core of the copy singer's investment in the production of an imitative voice. Sharing the same repertoire, having the same scale, singing the same songs—this articulation of the self, bodily practices, and aesthetic achievements were all cast in a mimetic mode.

Mimesis, Memory, and Market

The regurgitation of older film songs in the form of version recordings was anchored through the "voice" of the original singer in the market. Audio companies adopted two key strategies to attract buyers: the first was to keep the prices of these musical commodities very low; and the second was to highlight the names and photographs of the original artists on the covers of these musical commodities, which resulted in quick sales. The success of this venture created new demands for cover version artists.[15] While the jacket covers of these cassettes and CDs carried photographs of the original singers/stars, the names of version singers were mentioned only in small print. For instance, the CD cover of *Lata ke sadabahar geet* (Lata's evergreen songs: Volume 7) gives prominence to Lata's name and photograph on the front cover while, Bela Sulakhe's name appears on the back cover (figure 4.2) As Zaheer Ahmed of SCI remarked, "now-a-days even the company label does not matter. The buyer doesn't care who the artists are as long as he gets the original names right" (S. Mukherji 1994).

The transmission of artistic skill through mimesis involves activating the aura of the star singer. We also need to consider how the copy can assume the name and power of the original to enter the mass market

Figure 4.2. Front and back cover of an audio CD of Lata Mangeshkar's songs produced and marketed by T-series as version recordings. Bela Sulakhe, the copy artist's name, appears only on the back cover. Author's personal collection.

through a specific mode of fandom that is based on devotion and intense listening.[16] The escalation of sales of version recordings led to a scathing attack by critics, who labeled them as low forms that threatened to destabilize the moral and aesthetic categories as fashioned by singers like Lata Mangeshkar. In reviews written by Subhash K. Jha, listeners were not spared either. As he wrote, "having built an inbuilt aversion to version recordings, I have so far desisted from viewing them. I mean if people like to hear Lata's songs in the voice of Uttara Kelkar, surely it is their funeral" (Jha 1988). Another journalist called the copy artists, "pitiful clones" who were "desperately trying to match his/her vocal cords with the original divine singer" (A. Purushottam, 1998). The chasm between the original singers and copy artists seemed particularly "unbridgeable" when the artist being copied was Lata Mangeshkar. While comparing voices, critics drew upon their force field of memory. As Jha (1988) wrote, "The duets with Bela Sulakhe are less painful to consume. But even as I heard her and Manhar doing Jeevan Saathi (*Amrit*), Aap se humko bichde hue (*Vishwas*), Loote koi man ka nagar (*Abhimaan*), and Pyar karnewale (*Hero*), I was subconsciously comparing the substitute voice with the original one. And believe me, the original won!"

Despite the moral high ground displayed by the critics, the music directors of the film industry continued to fall back on familiar vocal tonalities. Younger singers could enter the industry after getting suitable training to become playback singers. For romantic numbers, confessional songs, and sad songs Lata Mangeshkar's style was followed; for nightclub or sensuous numbers the template was Asha Bhosle's vocal style. The industry's expectations were met by listening, remembering, rehearsing, and recording based on the original singer's voice.

Friedrich Kittler (1999) has proclaimed that Gutenberg's writing monopoly ended with the arrival of the gramophone, film, and the typewriter, by effecting a clear division between the real and the symbolic. These apparatuses could record "the very time flow of acoustic and optical data," free from any concerns about its symbolization (1999, 3). For Kittler, it was the real that escaped into the phonograph. Drawing upon Guyau's argument that the human brain is an "infinitely perfected phonograph—a conscious phonograph," Kittler argues that the phonograph is superior to all other media. As he writes, "It [the phonograph] alone can combine the two actions indispensable to any universal machine, discrete or not: writing and reading, storing and scanning, recording and replaying. In principle even though Edison for practical reasons later separated recording units from replaying ones, it is one and the same stylus that engraves and later traces the phonographic grove" (1999, 33).

Taking a cue from Kittler, I would like to signpost the deployment of acoustic memory as an important tactic in imitative practice. By following the trace of the sonic voice of the aural star, the copy artist enters into a creative relationship with that voice and makes it her own. Making connections between memory and voice, Rudolph Lothar writes, "Nothing excites the memory more strongly than the human voice, maybe because nothing is forgotten as quickly as a voice. Our memory of it however, does not die—its timbre and character sink into our subconscious where they await their arrival."[17] This idea of memory, linked with consciousness, has been challenged by scholars. In a detailed discussion on memory and mimesis, Laura Marks (2000) revisits Bergson's understanding of memory, to underscore his idea of habitual memory. Bergson makes a distinction between habitual or impulsive memory, which is "immediately and unselectively actualized in the body" and "selective memory that actualizes what is useful" (cited by Marks 2000, 142). Drawing on Taussig's theory of bodily mimesis, Marks places greater value on embodied memory and sensuous forms of knowledge. Marks's intervention is useful for understanding the play of memory in the aural field and helps to unravel the relationship between musical memory and sense experience. For the younger singers, the conjunction between the activation of aural memory and the molding of the voice was crucial for getting a foothold in the Bombay music industry. This memory was refracted from listening to the dominant and mechanical voice of the "other"—the singing star of the industry. To sing like Lata Mangeshkar meant an active recalling of the memory of her voice. Mahalakshmi Iyer, who began her singing career by singing advertising jingles, recalls her experience of singing for films in the late 1990s: "I came in at a time when these voices were still around and music directors would invariably say, 'aap yeh gana Lata ji ko vaad kar ke gaiyye [please remember Lataji when you sing this song]'" (Iyer 2010).

In a similar vein Alka Yagnik shares her early experiences of being in the industry:

> If you have admired a singer all your life, subconsciously you do tend to imitate the person. But what ultimately sets you apart is your voice quality. I've held the examples of Lata ji and Asha ji before me. My aim has been to try and sing the way they do, to come as close to them as possible. . . . In fact in the beginning music directors would say, "voh Lataji vali baat aani chahiye, voh Asha ji vali baat aani chahiye [give us the same magic as Lata ji, give us the same magic as Asha ji]." I tried to achieve "voh baat" but voh baat to unhee mein hai [that magic is only in them]. (Yagnik 1990, 36)

This desire to "come as close to them as possible" brings us to the core idea of mimesis, which, according to Walter Benjamin, is driven by a powerful compulsion to become and behave like something else. Benjamin alerted us to the resurgence of the mimetic faculty during the period of modernity—in the presence of "everyday life rhythms of montage and shock alongside the revelation of the optical unconscious that is made possible by mimetic machinery such as the camera and the movies" (cited in Taussig 1993, 20). The technologies of sound reproduction, enabling the proliferation of film music through cheaply available cassettes, led to the expansion of affective alliances, mimetic faculties, and sensuous knowledge. Imitating the tonality and the voice modulation of an aural star to enter the networks of recorded sound was as much about acknowledging the aura of the playback singer's voice (*voh baat*) as the desire to sing "as close to her as possible."

Musical commodities such as cover versions, available in abundance, are targeted at buyers in crowded bazaars, a space that becomes a force field for numerous aural, visual, and bodily sensations. Listening bodies respond to a familiar song by following its sonic trace. This experience of listening is as much about memory as about the flow of sounds. I suggest that the copy singer's voice activates impersonal, nomadic memory that gets inserted into the flux of everyday life of bazaars, paan shops, transport vehicles, and a larger auditory environment. Version recordings can thus be seen as cultural forms that created new modes of listening through distraction, expanding the recursive field of Hindi film songs.

Re-Performing the Authentic: HMV and the Production of Nostalgia

After enjoying a monopoly over the film music market for almost fifty years, HMV faced its biggest challenge with the arrival of cassette technology. The Gramophone Company of India (HMV) was unable to capitalize on this opportune moment because it "dismissed cassettes as just a technology" (Kohli-Khandekar 2010, 181). The circulation of version recordings placed the company on the back foot. Restrictions placed on HMV to get a license to manufacture audiocassettes further hampered its business interests. To establish its distinctiveness, HMV started adding "original soundtrack recording" as a prominent label on its cassettes and advertisements, warning buyers to beware of imitations (figure 4.3). More specifically, to meet the challenge of version recordings the company stepped up its production of special film song compilations. It was becoming evident that a new kind of listenership had to be imagined to regain its position in the market. Piggybacking on star singers like Lata Mangeshkar, Asha Bhosle, Mohammed Rafi, and Kishore Kumar, HMV repackaged musical content from its archive and released it as new, innovative, and authentic content. *Moods and Memories*, *Enchanting Hour*, *Magic Moments*, and *Best Of* with various artists were released during this phase. The increased proliferation of version recordings in the post-1985 phase resulted in HMV/RPG introducing special series like *All Time Greats* and *Golden Collection* from the "golden era" of Indian cinema.[18] The *Golden Collection* series was publicized as the work of "legendary and rare artists" that was "digitally cleaned on premium quality hardware."[19] Vanita Kohli-Khandekar (2010, 184) attributes these changes to Pradeep Chanda, who took charge of the company after it was taken over by the RPG group in 1985. According to Kohli-Khandekar, "the collector's series of Indian greats was retailed to institutions like Citibank, which used them for promotions" (184). By the 1990s, 45 percent of HMV's sales, according to a journalist, were through the compilation route (Syed 1994).

One of the hurdles faced by the company was the poor quality of its archival material. A major fire had destroyed the masters, and though it owned the rights to the majority of the Hindi film songs, it did not have access to its original recordings. Realizing the demand for compilations of songs from the 1950s to the '70s, the company decided to source

Figure 4.3. An HMV advertisement wooing customers to buy its cassettes with the label "Original Soundtrack Recording." Source: National Film Archive of India.

film songs of older films from the owners of gramophone records. But the hiss, or the noisy scratches on these records, interfered with their musical effect. On the other hand, SCI tried to leverage the arrival of new technologies by publishing version recordings of new artists with better sound fidelity. According to Ajit Kohli (2007), the artist and repertoire manager of SCI, "How can you repair something? What we were doing was redoing the whole song with freshness of voice, with fresh orchestration and [the] latest equipment."

How did HMV respond to the T-series claim about its access to new technology and "freshness of sound"? HMV's biggest asset was its access to "original" recordings of film songs, and this notion had to be pushed to lay its claim over the past. For Benjamin (1969, 220), "the presence of the original is central to any concept of the authentic." Benjamin writes, "The whole sphere of authenticity is outside technical—and, of course, not only technical—reproducibility" (220). Rey Chow (1989, 70) has suggested that for Benjamin authenticity was a cultural construct, produced at a chronological moment when what is "authentic" is already superseded. Simon Frith suggests authenticity to be the most misleading term in cultural theory. According to Frith (1989, 137), what we should be examining is "not how true a piece of music is to something else, but how it sets up the idea of 'truth' in the first place." The idea of the original, so intimately tied to the concept of authenticity, needs to be seen as part of a discursive practice involving artists, music companies, retailers, consumers, critics, and law-making and enforcing bodies.

The notion of authenticity for Bombay film songs has been constructed around the voice of the playback singer. Among all of the other sonic elements, the voice is privileged and referred to as the "soul of the song."[20] Neepa Majumdar (2010) has cogently argued that the pleasure associated with listening to the playback singer's voice in Bombay cinema involves knowledge about the technology of playback as well as its disavowal. In contrast, in the Hollywood system, playback technology was seen as artifice, meant to deceive the audience. Following this logic, an article in *Time* magazine referred to Lata Mangeshkar as a singer who had been "putting on soundtracks the songs that Indian actresses fake when they appear on screen."[21]

In a detailed discussion of Benjamin's ideas on authenticity, Jonathan Sterne suggests that the nature of originality and authenticity is transformed in the context of reproducibility. According to Sterne (2006, 220), "Reproduction does not really separate copies from originals but instead results in the creation of a distinctive form of originality: the possibility of reproduction transforms the practice of production." The privileging of the playback voice and its synchronicity with the notion of authenticity is linked to the events around Lata's rise as a playback singer in 1949. As suggested in chapter 1, while playback technology was in vogue since the early 1930s, it got public recognition only in the late 1940s. The discourses around playback technology obsessively converge around the rise of Lata Mangeshkar as an aural star, emerging from the shadows of invisibility. By dispelling the myth that it was not Kamini, the character played by Madhubala in the film *Mahal* (Amrohi, 1949), but Lata who sang "Aayega aanewala," radio announcements allowed Lata's voice to become an eternal sign of authenticity. This unmasking of identity helped build an aura around Lata Mangeshkar's voice and paved the way for her aural stardom.

HMV used this idea of authenticity to its advantage when faced with a crisis in the 1980s. Drawing on its archive of stockpiled music, HMV flooded the music market with compilations of film songs of the 1950s and '60s, evoking a nostalgia for the past. A substantial number of these albums contained songs exclusively sung by Lata Mangeshkar. In fact, during this period HMV was often unofficially referred to as LMV (Lata Mangeshkar's Voice) because of these albums. What Lata Mangeshkar symbolized for HMV was not just the golden period of Hindi film songs over which they had enjoyed a monopoly for more than fifty years but also the fact that they were owners of her authentic recorded voice. Not only was she known for her great voice and musicality but she had also had the experience of working with "great masters" like Ghulam Haider, Khem Chand Prakash, Anil Biswas, and Sajjad Hussain. She had grown up listening to K. L. Saigal, Kannan Devi, and Pankaj Mallik and had sung duets with singers like Mohammed Rafi, Geeta Dutt, and Mukesh during the golden period of the playback music era. If HMV wanted to sell repackaged music based on nostalgia, Lata Mangeshkar could not be bypassed.

To establish that their music was authentic, a set of networks, social relations, and symbols had to be created. The strategy was to woo middle-class listeners ready to pay more for the "authentic" voice. In 1987, HMV (now under the RPG group) hosted a public event in Bombay honoring Lata Mangeshkar for completing forty years in the industry.[22] This was followed by an advertising campaign projecting Lata Mangeshkar as the "Voice of a Nation." With Lata's photograph in the foreground, the visual was crafted by layering an image of India's map on a gramophone record. A horned gramophone player and the text "Voice of a Nation" in the middle of the record was also part of the visual schema (figure 4.4). The copy of the advertisement carried in *Filmfare* and other magazines read as follows:

> The year, 1947, *dil mera toda mujhe kahin ka na choda*, the film *Majboor*. Unobtrusively one afternoon, the Lata legend was born. In making that quiet transition from NoorJahan to Lata Mangeshkar, Hindi film music turned a corner. Things would never be the same again. Lata's music cast a spell that would outlast several generations of actresses. From Nimmi in *Barsaat* to Mandakini in *Ram Teri Ganga Maili*, actresses have used Lata's voice. (*Filmfare* 1987c)

Figure 4.4. "Voice of the Nation" advertisement by HMV in *Filmfare*. Source: National Film Archive of India.

The print advertisement carefully evoked the past of 1947, when Lata sang "Dil mera toda" for Ghulam Haider in *Majboor* (Ajmeri, 1948). Several biographical accounts, including Lata's own, have acknowledged Haider as an important figure who was quick to discern the unique quality in Lata's voice, despite its "thinness." It is also well known that Haider asked Lata to sing "Dil mera toda" on the same evening that S. Mukherjee rejected her voice.[23] More importantly, the association of Lata's music with 1947 as a marker of new beginnings was aligned with the phrase "voice of the nation" and lent credibility to HMV. The period evoked in the advertisement is bookended with *Ram Teri Ganga Maili* (Kapoor, 1985). The significance of this citation cannot be missed since Lata's popular "Sun sahiba sun" from the film was exponentially circulating in the voice of copy artists as version recordings.[24]

According to Baudrillard (1983, 12–13), "When the real is no longer what it used to be, nostalgia assumes its full meaning. There is a proliferation of myths of origin, and signs of reality; of second-hand truth, objectivity and authenticity." In her work on gender and modernity, Rita Felski (1995) writes insightfully on the debates around nostalgia, drawing on the ideas of Georg Stauth and Bryan Turner as developed in classical European sociology. Nostalgia, according to Stauth and Turner, has four broad themes: the idea of history as a process of decline from a lost golden age; an absence of wholeness and moral certainty, the loss of simplicity, spontaneity, and authenticity; and the belief that individual autonomy and genuine relations have collapsed (Felski 1995, 54–55). For Felski, the "woman is undoubtedly one of the central figures" in the nostalgic paradigm in sociology (55). Critiquing nostalgia from a gender perspective, Felski traces the yearning for the feminine as emblematic of a nonalienated, nonfragmentary identity as an important motif in the history of cultural representations of the nature of modernity.

At the core of nostalgia are the stimulation of memory and the creation of myths. When in the 1980s music was brought back into the market through song compilations, the context of the on-screen star was no longer available. HMV had to restrategize itself to push a certain kind of subjectivity that could evoke memories of the past and nostalgia for the acousmatic voice of the singer. The market was confusing, volatile, and flooded with diverse genres of music, including film music, pop *ghazals*, devotional music, folk music, and regional music. Lata Mangeshkar became an overarching stable figure, pushing the notion of authenticity through the use of her voice. To push forward the notion of authenticity of voice in its musical commodities, HMV relied on the insertion of biographical and autobiographical material that chronicled Lata Mangeshkar's early struggle and devotion to her art. Personal memories of Lata Mangeshkar in first-person narration and black-and-white photographs covering her life from childhood to her rise to stardom were pushed forward in the public domain.

William Mazzarella (2003) suggests that branding can inject an emotionally textured relationship into the impersonality of commodity exchange. One of the strategies in this direction was to bring out compilations of Lata Mangeshkar's songs as unique, premium products by pushing her subjectivity. Several albums/cassettes were brought out in the market in which her personal selections were strung together with a thematic idea. Most of these compilations were introduced with exclusive jacket covers and accompanied by her first-person introductory commentary. What was underscored through these compilations were her memories and personal association with these songs. For instance, in 1987, HMV brought out *My Favourites*, Lata Mangeshkar, in an album and a set of four cassettes that did well in the market.[25] The launch was strategically timed to coincide with the celebrations commemorating Lata's forty years in the industry. But what made this album stand apart was using Lata Mangeshkar's signature on the album cover, accompanied by her photograph and the title *My Favourites*. The album contained fifty songs with a first-person commentary by Lata. It may not be coincidence that *Filmfare* carried the "Voice of the Nation" advertisement just three months after it carried a twelve-page cover story on Lata Mangeshkar in June 1987 (figure 4.5). The story, titled "The Lata Legend," was accompanied by several photographs of the singer chronicling her life (Punita Bhatt, 1987).[26] Bhatt (1987, 31) suggested, "we, who have become a nation of second raters and compromisers, we would do better to imitate her [Lata Mangeshkar] in unabashed pursuit of excellence and achievement." The timing of the advertising campaign was also close to the release of *My Favourites* by Lata, and *Filmfare* carried Dhurandhar's review of the album in February 1988. Later that year, the magazine carried a review of *My Favourites* Volume II, referring to the selection as spellbinding.[27] The review addressed the criticism that had been leveled against the first volume of the album and noted, "[But] the singer makes it clear for the benefit of professional quibblers that her choice is based on association: in a certain song it was the tune that attracted her, in another it was the lyric. In a third, it was the memory triggered off by the melody" (Dhurandhar, 1988, 72). The reviewer is referring here to Lata's opening words on the album *My Favourites*, Volume II, playing

Figure 4.5. Lata Mangeshkar on the cover of *Filmfare*. Source: National Film Archive of India.

the dual role of a singer and a storyteller. Lata's narrative account of her own experiences of recording the "original song" lends authenticity to the past. The insertion of personal memories and associations along with the songs in *My Favourites* creates a unique synthesis of meaning and wholeness.

Circulation of special musical commodities needs to be considered through the optics of knowledge and close relationship with the politics of value. Igor Kopytoff (1986, 73) refers to commoditization as "a process of becoming rather than as an all-or-none state of being." Further, excessive commoditization tends to homogenize value, "while the essence of culture is discrimination" (73). Susan Stewart (1984) explores the relationship between narratives and objects, giving us an insight into how we order ourselves into a relationship with these objects. Stewart proposes the production of two distinct kinds of narratives around the souvenir and the collection.[28] The souvenir carries within itself a trace of an authentic experience when it is associated with a "supplementary narrative discourse that both attaches it to its origins and creates a myth with regard to those origins" (Stewart 1984, 136). The collection, on the other hand, creates a world that is representative, but also erases the context of its origin (152). In order to meet the challenge posed by version recordings with an accent on imitations, HMV created special albums of Lata's songs not by erasing but by holding on to the trace of *her* voice as a locus of authenticity. The first-person narration worked like a glue to hold together musical and nonmusical elements of a narrative that articulated the authenticity of an idealized past. More importantly, the past in this construction began pointedly at 1947.

In the post-1985 period, each important event in Lata's life was celebrated by HMV, evoking nostalgia for the past. HMV released an advertisement marking Lata's birthday and the launch of the music album of *Lekin* (Gulzar, 1991).[29] In 1989, HMV released *Diamonds Forever*, another four-pack felicitation album, with songs from older films.[30] The album with sixty songs was released on the occasion of Lata's sixtieth birthday. The text on the album: "60 Years—60 Songs" was accompanied by a photograph of Lata ensconced in a diamond frame.[31]

Memory and the Selection of Time

HMV introduced *Shraddhanjali: My Tribute to the Immortals* in 1992.[32] In this exclusive collector's album, Lata Mangeshkar presented songs by "immortal artists" in her own voice as a "humble tribute" to these singers. The jacket covers of the album (LP, compact disc, and cassette) carried Lata's photograph accompanied by her signature.[33] A framed image with headshots of all of the six male artists who have been commemorated on the album completes the visual layout of the jacket cover. In the first volume, Lata paid tribute to K. L. Saigal, Pankaj Malik, Mohammed Rafi, Mukesh, Hemant Kumar, and Kishore Kumar. In her introductory commentary, she referred to the collection as a tribute not only to the singers and musicians of yesteryear but also to the musical history and the heritage of our great country. "I have not tried to surpass any of them, I have only tried to pay homage to them," adds Lata. The album opens with a haunting refrain in Lata's voice from *Lekin* (Gulzar, 1990). This short alap is significant since it symbolizes the fluid dispersal of Lata's disembodied voice into an abstract notion of space, as if we are being transported from the real into an imaginary world. Each artist's original singing voice is introduced briefly on the soundtrack. This is followed first by Lata's commentary about the artist, and then by her singing a selected song from the artists's repertoire. An example of this is the way the song "Babul mora naihar chhuto hi jaye" from the film *Street Singer* (Majumdar, 1938) in K. L. Saigal's voice plays in the background as Lata speaks about him. According to one reviewer, this, "takes one back to the Saigal era" (Kumatkar 1992).

The recirculation of songs from the past era through the framework of nostalgia and remembrance resonates with Kopytoff's (1986) notion of the compulsive drive for singularization amid homogenization. By pushing into the market special collections of Lata's songs from the past, HMV presented itself as a quasi-public institution, claiming its rightful ownership of the most treasured aural archive—the voice of Lata Mangeshkar. The "Voice of the Nation" advertisement, and Lata as a national symbol, became crucial for this public posturing. HMV was also symbolically presenting itself as playing a cultural role through its hold over an authentic aural archive—film music of the 1950s and the '60s.

One must recall here the contentious relationship between the state and the film industry in the 1950s when B. V. Keskar, India's first minister of information and broadcasting, curtailed the airing of film songs on All India Radio in his zeal to promote classical music. This relationship changed significantly after Keskar retracted his stand and All India Radio started Vividh Bharti, its first commercial service, in 1957, to broadcast film songs and other popular content. The state was now leaning on the film industry to commemorate important events in its cultural life, as can be gauged from the first public performance of the well-known nationalist song "Ae mere watan ke logon" (People of my country). The song was performed by Lata on India's Republic Day on January 26, 1963, at a public function in the presence of India's first prime minister, Jawahar Lal Nehru. It is well known that Nehru was moved to tears when Lata sang this song, written by Kavi Pradeep as a tribute to the Indian soldiers who had died in the Sino-Indian War of 1962. Subsequently, HMV's decision to release an album of the song turned it into an eternal sign of the nation's homage to the martyred soldiers in subsequent episodes of war with Pakistan. Nehru's reaction, as reported by the press and amplified by the film industry, contributed in no small measure to the aura as well as the iterability of the song. As Raju Bharatan (1995, 75) says, "the moment Nehru reacted, HMV acted," to release a special private record of the song.

Sonic events played an important role in HMV's collaborative alliance with the Bombay music industry to produce affective, politically laden cultural products for the nation-state. Patriotic songs like "Ae mere watan" are regularly reintroduced into the market by HMV during special events in the nation's cultural and political life. To mark India's fifty years of independence, for instance, HMV brought out *Mere Watan Ke Logo*, a special CD (CDNF 154027), as a compilation of Lata's film and nonfilm patriotic songs.[34]

What exactly is being remembered or effaced by these special premium musical albums or objects that seek to honor the dead and foreground the act of remembrance? More importantly, how are we being addressed as listeners through these products? For the French philosopher Bernard Stiegler (2010, 67), human memory requires a degree of externalization and has been "technical from the start." We rely on notes and traces, diaries and letters, sounds and objects, to jog our memory. Stiegler warns us against our reliance on artificial memory aids that can make us passive and vulnerable to manipulation, since "the technologies of memory are controlled by industries intent on exploiting our desire for the gain" (66). For Stiegler, memory is a "selection of time in the present, and its passing, its becoming past, is its diminution" (80). HMV's prolific investment in the song collections of remembrance and tribute was meant to push the discerning listener into the aural embrace of Lata Mangeshkar's voice.

As a tribute to "immortal singers" of the past, the *Shraddhanjali* album tried to evoke the memories of songs like "Ae mere watan," mourning the loss of a bygone era. What is important to note is that the past was an abstract naturalized category. In the second volume of *Shraddhanjali*, brought out in February 1994, Lata paid homage to women artists of the past, namely: Kanan Devi, Parul Ghosh, Zohrabai Ambalewali, Amirbai Karnataki, and Geeta Dutt. The criterion for selecting the artists was their legendary status even after their death. That is why singers like Noor Jahan and Suraiya were not part of this tribute.[35] A pronounced use of reverberation added to the nostalgic effect in the aural register of the album. Following the same template as the first volume, the voices of the older artists are recalled through a nostalgic reconstruction of the past. In her introductory commentary to this volume, Lata referred to her presentation as "not only . . . a tribute to the bygone artists but to that era itself in which this legendary music had been created." The first singer chosen for the tribute was Kanan Devi. Like Lata, we are expected to respond to the sensuous quality of Kanan Devi's soft and distant voice as it fades into the soundtrack. "Mujhe yaad aa rahi hai . . ." (I remember . . .) "this artist whom we all knew as Kanan Devi," carries on Lata. This encounter with memory is presented as a temporal journey we take with Lata as our guide. Kanan Devi's faint voice, when compared to Lata's bolder aural presence, simulates our struggle with memory and its fleeting and uneven nature. We are given a visceral sense that Kanan Devi's voice is being pulled out of Lata's reservoir of memories. In this mode of remembrance, the past gets reconstituted through the performance of the self. This engagement with the past, with its memory, reenacts the erasure of these voices and their effacement as suggested by Steigler. As soon as we connect with Kanan Devi's voice, it is gone. *Shraddhanjali* can be seen as an archive that relives the journey of the female voice in film songs and its ephemeral quality. The song in this archive emerges as a palimpsest carrying voices of the past, their textures, and their timbres. Ironically, HMV participated symbolically in the erasure of its own archive by bringing out this album.

Undoubtedly, *Shraddhanjali* was intended to be a tribute to the female singers of the erstwhile era, but there is also an underplaying of their professionalism. Parul Ghosh is introduced as Anil Biswas's sister and Pannal Lal Ghosh's wife. "Despite being a singer in films she was a

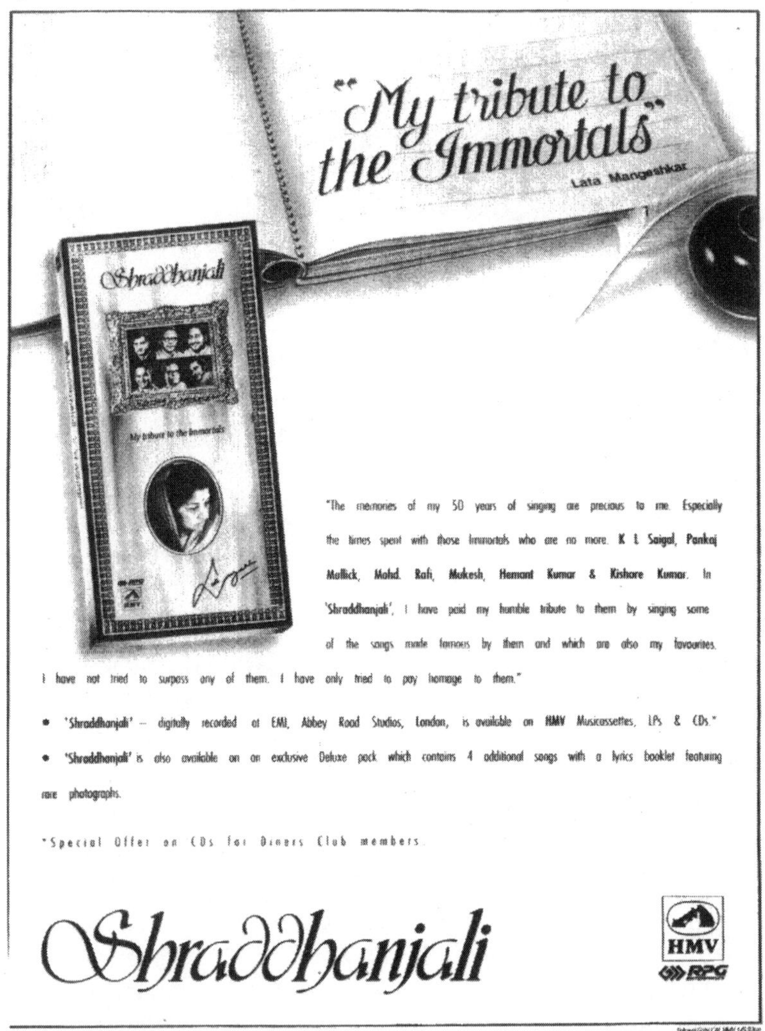

Figure 4.6. An advertisement for a special pack of *Shraddhanjali* for Diners Club members. Author's personal collection.

wife and homemaker," says Lata. In the case of Zohrabai, Lata chooses to highlight her mellifluous voice, while Geeta Dutt emerges as a vivacious woman but prone to anxiety due to her deep sense of responsibility. Kanan Devi is introduced as an actress/singer whose "voice had the magic of Bengal." Only Amirbai Karnataki is represented as a great singer whose popular songs had "created a stir." Crucially, Lata's commentary tends to naturalize the voices of the older artists. Missing in this narrative is any allusion to a textured relationship between music and performance; or more importantly, an affective alliance between voice and the technological and material practices that make this voice audible.

The reception of the album was mixed, as a few critics and singers referred to it as a version recording, though presented with distinctive taste.[36] For Harish Bhimani (1995, 242), this was an offering to the "new generation who had missed the magic of their [the legendary singers'] music, in Lata's voice." A more exclusive version of the collection with four extra songs was offered to Diners Club members, with a booklet containing lyrics and exclusive photographs. An HMV advertisement wooing the Diners Club members further underscored Lata's authorial vision over the product: an open notebook with "*My Tribute to the Immortals*," written by hand, along with Lata Mangeshkar's signature was framed with a quill and an inkpot (figure 4.6).

The competition between the T-series and HMV intensified in the 1990s in contemporary film music. Both companies were offering advance royalties to film producers against music rights. HMV had made a big turnaround with commercially (and musically) successful films like *Chandni* (Chopra, 1989) and *Maine Pyar Kiya* (Barjatya, 1989). Gulshan Kumar's Super Cassette Industries went one step forward by entering into film production, creating a stir in the film industry with the success of films like *Aashiqui* (Bhatt, 1990) and *Dil Hai Ki Manta Nahin* (Bhatt, 1991), both riding on the unparalleled popularity of their songs. By now, T-series had established itself as a company that got box office returns by feverishly promoting the music of its films. Producers were now lining up to give the music rights of their films to T-series. An intense rivalry broke out between Anuradha Paudwal and other female singers when T-series started aggressively promoting the former.[37] By the end of 1992, Paudwal had a ubiquitous presence on cassette covers, T-series advertisements, and television promotions of her film and nonfilm albums. Tips, Venus, Red Cat, Plus, Weston, Magnasound, Sony, and several other companies had already entered the film music business by the early '90s, each favoring one singer over the others.[38]

Despite a boom in contemporary film music, publishing companies continued to make the most of old film songs through special compilations. "The music industry is in a very reverential mood," wrote a journalist in the *Times of India* (S. Mukherjee 1994). In what can be seen as a mimetic interaction with HMV, T-series collaborated with Anuradha Paudwal to bring out a series of musical products, a tribute to legendary composers like Madan Mohan and Roshan. The positioning of these products was done with care to woo the "connoisseurs." As Paudwal reminisces, "When I did the tribute for Madan ji I never had the intention that I [had] to prove something. I wanted to sing those songs because I came at a time when those songs were not composed anymore and as a singer one has an aspiration to be able to sing particular songs. . . . If there is an orchestra playing Madan Mohan's songs I want to sing those and see how my voice sounds in them."[39]

Paudwal's description points toward her desire to insert herself retrospectively in the nostalgia economy and its affordances, inaugurating new ways to circulate film songs. T-series seized this moment to reach out to a "discerning" audience and change its image of a low-brow, mass-oriented audio company. The muted, aesthetically designed jacket covers were accompanied by booklets carrying the lyrics of the songs. The company released videos of the *Tribute to Madan Mohan* (SVCD1140) depicting Anuradha Paudwal singing in an off-white sari, standing on a somber but ornately designed stage set. An orchestra with string, brass, and rhythm sections completes the mise-en-scène. T-series roped in Ramesh Aiyyar, an ace arranger known to have researched for months to bring together a "full orchestra to give it that feel."[40] The impulse to record, create, and project a certain aesthetic value motivated the recordings. The overriding driving force was to enter a niche market with nostalgia, not through the claims of originality but through those of expertise. Access to new technologies, refurbished studios, a full-scale orchestra, and a skilled and motivated singer whose vocal tonalities matched that of Lata's allowed T-series to enter the arena of "enclaved" musical commodities. "I had never rehearsed the way I did for the tribute albums. . . . I knew we were doing something that stalwarts had done," said Paudwal (2010). These articulations reinforce the notion that discourses that shape taste and aesthetics in music are contingent upon not the inherent value of music but the materiality around it. They also demonstrate how important it was for a company like T-series, a late entrant in the business, to recreate the past and to insert itself in it. Several music companies started following the route of tribute albums: in 2000, Sony organized *Shraddhanjali*, a well-publicized concert by Lata, as a musical tribute to the last century. The company brought out *Lata: An Era in an Evening*, a concert-based album as a collector's item. A small booklet in sepia tone with "rare" black-and-white photographs of Lata Mangeshkar and the lyrics of the songs accompanied the album. The double spread in the center had Lata's signature scrawled on it. "This voice, this personality and this era has been captured by Sony music to create a Collector's Item. Listen. Enjoy. And Cherish an Era," is how the album was introduced to the listeners. In the latter half of the 1990s, HMV introduced *Classics Revival*, a series of compilations meant to give "enhanced listening pleasure for all those who value originality."[41] The emphasis was on the company's access to a combination of new technologies, modern studios, and original voices. The text on the jacket covers of CDs was carefully written, to emphasize both what the product was, and *what it was not*. It read as:

> **Original Voices, Original Music, Original Compositions**
>
> *Carefully re-recorded, in a modern studio, using the original instruments, and then overlaid with the original voice track. . . . So, these are not modern remixes or imitative recorded versions. Everything is original, as good as new.*

In a review of the series Jha (1998) wrote:

> HMV has discovered a fool proof method of beating the remix and cover version craze. The original sound track has been spruced up with brand new orchestral passages. "Woh Bhooli Dastaan" featuring the pensive melodies by Lata Mangeshkar makes us wonder why HMV didn't think of this idea before. . . . Purists may quibble about snatches of newly introduced incidental music that connect track to track. But not for a second do we forget that we're listening to the *original songs in the original unbeatable voices*. (Emphasis mine)

Through the *Classics Revival* HMV was responding to the criticism by its rivals that its recordings were dated and its archives in a "poor quality." Sound recording, notes Jonathan Sterne (2006, 310), is a way of dealing with time, involving the "retention of a certain sequence, isolation and repeatability of moments." In the sonic revival by HMV, studio re-recordings were deployed to circulate old songs in new forms by filtering out the noise that betrayed the trace of time—the decay of the recording. Once again, memory, mimesis, and technology were brought together to construct a semblance of originality. HMV's strategy was to push its "legitimate ownership" over the most authentic voice of the past and the institutionalization of its aural memory. Moreover, by the latter half of the 1990s, with the liberalization of media, HMV was also trying to resurrect the aural, faced as it was with the onslaught of the spectacular presence of the film song on satellite television. In the next chapter, I shall turn to the journey of the female voice in film songs on Indian television.

5

Television to Digital Data

Taking forward the thematic of media assemblage, this chapter considers the widening of sonic terrain of Bollywood songs through satellite and cable television, mobile telephony, and the internet. Sound recording technologies such as DAW (digital audio work station) effected seismic transformations that shaped the aural presence of the female voice in the new digital landscape. While bringing on board the convergence of cinematic, television, and computational media, I trace the circulation of women's voices as sonic material and the variable affects generated by this circulation on the expanded visual terrain of Bollywood. Neither radio nor the printed songbooks can give us the pleasure of listening to a song re-edited to a fresh set of images or connect us to the corporeal body of the singer. I focus on a new generation of singers who have actively intervened in the recreation of film songs on new media circuits. Singing contest shows on television and their afterlife on YouTube goad us to rethink not only the established voice/body relationship but also listening practices.

The transformations in the performances and practices of the female voice are part of a complicated narrative of Bollywood's arrival on the global stage, marked by a shifting media landscape that resulted in the fluid circulation of Hindi film songs.[1] Aswin Punathambekar's (2013, 12) geographical framework has been productive in highlighting Bollywood's spatial expansion through a transformation in media ecologies, with the emergence of the "consumerist television industry."[2] I build upon his discussions on the vast, networked realm of fans and their media-driven practices to signpost the recirculation of film songs through contest-based television shows (7). The expansion of sonic geographies through television played a key role in bringing singers into direct contact with their listeners. The voice of the playback singer, until then amplified by the gramophone, the radio, cassettes, and cinema, acquired a visible body that itself became an object of desire. With the recalibration of songs in music countdown shows, singing contest shows, film award functions, and other live performances of Bollywood events, television became a crucial apparatus for a first encounter with the performative bodies of singers. This was a new direction that was distinct from the playback system entrenched in the industry. Rather than see these as separate platforms, I read these as part of the sensory media infrastructures that made possible the emergence of new affective geographies, that destabilized the boundaries between singers and listeners.

The arrival of digital workstations, computational media, and "software culture" ushered in new production practices in the music studios of Bombay combining human and nonhuman energies (Manovich 2013, 33). The voice became a mediating surface for software performance, not just for the purpose of cleansing or fixing sound (pitch correction) but crucially for amplifying certain moods and sensations. I end the chapter with a discussion of the proliferation of background songs to demonstrate how they function as a dispersed and ever-mutating form not tied to any particular character or body in the film. Drawing on Anahid Kassabian's concept of ubiquitous listening, I argue that the retreat of the film song into the background is, at the core, a transformation in its aural ecology through sync sound recording. Non-lip-synch songs destabilize the relationship between the singer and the listener in film narratives, but in the process, stretch the relationship between image and sound, providing greater room for enunciating the screen body in its spatial context. However, the attenuation of the playback voice by forfeiting lip sync in Bollywood songs has had greater repercussions for the female voice.

Changing Dynamics of Television

The early 1990s saw an escalation in the production, dispersal and consumption of popular music, riding the wave of expanding media networks. Audiences could enjoy a diverse range of music, "regional, indipop and classical musics, and a fusion of these genres" that had a bearing on Hindi film music on television (Sundar 2023, 43). Parallelly, this moment transformed the sonic landscape of the Bollywood music industry and its para-textual footprint. Television allowed viewers to connect with the persona of erstwhile copy singers. As Anuradha Paudwal (1994) remarked, "Once TV took over from radio, the singer was more than just a voice." Gulshan Kumar, the founder of Super Cassette Industries, was quick to realize the potential of the visual media for providing a face to the voice, a technique that he used extensively for print media as well.[3] Another significant trend started by T-series, his music label, was to carry the photographs of the music composers and singers like Paudwal on film posters. According to Paudwal, "For me television was a big boon. It was crucial for me because unless the female voice was recognized by a knowledgeable person or a connoisseur, everyone was identified as Lata Mangeshkar. It's like asking for Colgate when you need a tooth paste even though you may actually be buying Aqua Fresh. So, until the expansion of visual media, people did not know the difference" (2010).

Anuradha Paudwal used the indexicality offered by television to enable her listeners to connect with both her voice and her visual identity. The viewers' experience of connecting to a song was now mediated through the body of the singer. Promotional clips of song sequences were used to market musical commodities as well as films, highlighting the face of the singer, with facial gestures, moving lips, and eye movements matching the sonic trace of the voice.

Richa Sharma, a well-known singer with a heavy voice, has spoken about her struggle to create a place in the industry, both aurally and visually. Desperate to get a foothold in the industry, Sharma started her career with cover versions of Ila Arun's songs. This meant imitating Arun's raw and heavy bass voice.[4] Though cover versions allowed singers to enter networks of sound production, they also pushed them into a vicious cycle of imitation and repetition. In her own words:

> [Arun's] style was folk, raw folk. . . . But I had to change my style completely. . . . I had to avoid short delicate ornamentation. So, I had to control my natural style of singing. There

Figure 5.1. A T-series audio CD of Ila Arun's songs sung by Richa Sharma as a copy artist.

> were songs where there was enough space to improvise. If I sing like that then the song becomes more beautiful. Payal Utardoongi [*sings*] . . . see how I use the delicate notes here to make the song more beautiful and give it some freshness. But I had to make my voice big and avoid these nuances. Also, I had to crack my voice a bit. (Sharma 2010; translated in parts by the author)

Richa Sharma's reflective analysis displays a self-awareness about her own singing style that had to be kept in check when she was imitating the voice of an already established aural star. Deleuze (2005, 25) has argued that "even the simplest of imitation involves a difference between the inside and outside." Following Deleuze's (2005, 26–27) ideas on difference and repetition, I suggest that Richa Sharma's version recordings of Ila Arun's songs, were based on repetition that included difference, thus animating a secret subject. To gain a foothold in the industry, Richa Sharma had to self-consciously mask her *own* vocal style to produce a voice like Ila Arun's. Parallelly, while the industry was looking for "big" and "powerful" voices to match the performances of sexualized heroines, the singers themselves were trying their best to find ways to present their own unique style. Music videos with their repetitive presence on television helped many of these singers to get their voice accepted, in sync with their bodies. To get accepted in the industry, a singer had to negotiate diverse practices of sound dispersion, quickly moving from one platform to another, creating new territories and networks. Television allowed singers to become visible, unsettling the practice of dubbing and imitation. As Sharma (2010) adds:

> I needed to establish my identity. So, I did a (private) album which became a big hit called *Ni Main yaar Nu SajdaKardi*. That was *me* and there was also a video, and that was the first time that a female song of that kind had come out. It was a Sufi song; today Sufi is very popular but at that time it was new and this song was appreciated. Then my voice got accepted by the music companies and the people. They could connect with *my* voice. Then I got a chance to sing in *Taal*.

The rise of Indi-pop and the hypervisibility of music videos offered instant visibility to the singer, along with voice recognizability. Moreover, the singer could look glamorous and move her body with abandon, breaking older codes of performance. Music publishing companies experimented with voices, providing viewers with an opportunity to hear new tonalities: singers like Shubha Mudgal, Shweta Shetty, Suchitra Krishnamurthy, Ila Arun, Richa Sharma, Jaspinder Narula, Alisha Chinai, Anamika, Falguni Pathak, and Sunita Rao expanded the vocal range of female singers. On the other hand, remixed versions of older numbers brought quick visibility to new female stars on television. Lata Mangeshkar's "Beri ke peeche" from the film *Samadhi* (Mehra, 1972) and "Kaliyon ka chaman" from the film *Jyoti* (Chakravarty, 1981) acquired an erotic charge on MTV shows and revitalized the remix industry. In fact, television shows created a space for enfolding the sonic trace of the female playback voice, even before the proliferation of digital technologies.

The decade of the 1980s was marked by the arrival of color television, followed by an exponential increase in the advertising of consumer products as a form of "public cultural production" (Mazzarella 2003, 4). In building a strong aural hook for their products, advertising companies experimented with new voices for products like coffee, cosmetics, polyester fabrics, and beer. A clear distinction was made in harnessing the acoustical properties of the female voice for jingles between domestic products like Nirma (detergent powder) or Rath (cooking oil) and upmarket products like Liril (bathing soap) and Sunsilk (hair shampoo). Many of the Indi-pop singers who were simultaneously singing jingles for commercials flaunted their fandom for global singing stars. Private channels with Hindi-language content were quick to realize the potential of film-based music on television. Zee TV cashed in on this popular segment with *Close-Up Antakshari*, a show that allowed film song enthusiasts to recognize tunes, recall lyrics, and sing in their amateurish style.[5] The follow up to this was *Sa Re Ga Ma*, to accommodate talented singers who could not fit into *Antakshari*'s game show format. *Sa Re Ga Ma* placed considerable emphasis on the quality of singing, as demanded from a playback singer. The contestants were judged by veterans of Hindustani classical music, music directors of the industry during the 1950s and '60s, and established playback singers. The mood in the studio was somber, with contestants touching the feet of the judges as a mark of respect. Although some contestants chose to sing contemporary songs, the show was heavily tilted toward songs of the 1950s and '60s, evoking a nostalgia for the past.

In 1995, Doordarshan's Metro commercial channel introduced *Meri Awaz Suno* (Listen to my voice), produced by Metavision, a company owned by Yash Chopra and spearheaded by Sanjeev Kohli. The lineup in this singing show separated female singers from male contestants. This was in line with the Bombay music industry's practice of creating different codes for judging male and female voices. The show was projected as a platform to search for an ideal playback voice that would match a Hindi film hero and heroine.[6] The studio backdrop in *Meri Awaz Suno* was designed with large posters of legendary playback singers like Lata Mangeshkar, Mohammed Rafi, Manna Dey, and Asha Bhosle. Contestants were invited to apply for the show with their demo tapes. Metavision reportedly received thirty to fifty cassette tapes every day from aspiring contestants (Karamblekar, 1997, 82).

In an important segment of the contest, singers were asked to sing with a video clip of a song, by matching the performance of the on-screen actor, as well as the vocal registers of the original playback singer. The show's idea was to select some talented singers who could do playback.[7] In the finale episode, Manpreet Akhtar, a singer from Punjab with a heavy bass voice, was asked to sing "Chale jhoom jhoom raat yeh suhaani" from the film *Love Marriage* (Mukherjee, 1959), a song originally sung by Lata Mangeshkar and performed by Mala Sinha in the film. As Akhtar struggled to match her voice with the video clip and the orchestra, in a pitch with which she was hardly comfortable, it became clear that the show legitimized an older playback voice aesthetic.[8] The segment exposed the gap between Akhtar's vocal tonalities and Mala Sinha's facial expressions, and as expected, Akhtar lost the contest in the finale. Moreover, the segment was designed to mask the singer's body, as she was made to face the projected screen, rather than the audience. This caused a dissonance with new cultural practices and performance codes that had already gained currency on channels like MTV. *Meri Awaz Suno* lasted for only two years (two seasons), but its rival, *Sa Re Ga Ma* on Zee, ran successfully until 2005, when it was reintroduced in a new format as *Sa Re Ga Ma Pa Challenge*. This remodeling was clearly exacerbated by the arrival of *Indian Idol*, introduced in 2004 on its rival channel, Sony Entertainment Television (SET).

Mauli as Shakira on Global Television

Indian Idol was introduced by Sony Entertainment Television (SET) in 2004 as part of a much larger media phenomenon following the opening of the Indian economy to foreign investment in the early 1990s.[9] The proliferation of global television in national markets, enabled by deregulation, privatization, and the advent of new technologies of distribution, created a new context for the expansion of the format market.[10] Talent contest shows on television pushed forward the singer's unique identity through image makeovers and vocal training (figure 5.2). The singer's corporeal performance on talent shows provided a corrective to the masking of playback stars and dubbing artists associated with older industrial practices, even as new discourses emerged around the production of the voice. Many of the judges or guest stars who were invited to comment on the singers had experienced their own marginalization in the music industry.

These transformations leaned on the mediating presence of wireless microphones, allowing singers to move their bodies and perform while making a connection with the listeners. Ankita Mishra, an eighteen-year-old contestant from *Indian Idol 3*, epitomized the convergence of singing and performing on live television, drawing a huge response from viewers on blogs and websites. Hailing from the provincial North India town of Kanpur, Ankita was appreciated by the judges for her performance, as she used the stage with great confidence, sometimes moving close to the judges.[11] Sporting a tomboyish image, wearing jackets, hats, belts, and other accessories, Ankita explained to me how she carved a niche for herself:

> I told the producers from day one, "I want to move on the stage." They kept telling me to wait . . . They knew I would not stop, so they would ask me, "What are you planning this time? How are you going to move on the stage?" Then there was this picture of mine on a motorbike in Kanpur, they started using that. I always had lots of jackets and told the costume designers, "I will not wear sleeveless [garments]." It was not my style. For my performance of the "Chamma chamma" song [*China Gate*, 1998], they gave me a butterfly dress. I refused to wear that and asked for a gypsy dress. For Helen's "Piya tu" [originally performed in a cage by Helen], I demanded a cage and performed with it. (A. Mishra 2008)[12]

Travel, mobility, fashion, and Hindi film songs' recursive presence on satellite television made a heady combination in the 1990s. Ranjani Mazumdar (2007, 96) has described song sequences as mini fashion shows that allow female spectators to explore the "world of consumption." The repeated circulation of these songs on television enabled them

Figure 5.2. Prajakta Shukre, a contestant on *Indian Idol 1*, performed "Mera naam chin chin choo" with a hand fan.

to "function like electronic catalogs" created through a "combination of travel, fashion photography, and the rhythmic movement of dancing" (96). Singing contest shows provided a platform for young girls to perform with a mobile dancing body, available for consumption on prime-time television. "Light has gone out from Indian Idol," wrote fan Poonam Sharma in 2007 following Ankita's elimination from the show: "Remember her . . . *Piyatu ab to aa ja* performances that had a *big cage* on the stage. Did I notice that she had few of her notes up and down? I was too captivated to notice while I watched her. The audio of her performance heard stand-alone retains that special enthusiasm and confidence. It is contagious."[13]

In 2005, Zee TV launched *Sa Re Ga Ma Pa Challenge*, inviting audiences to vote for their favorite singing contestants. The show's global reach becomes apparent when you examine the launch of the second season of *Sa Re Ga Ma Pa Challenge*, in 2007. It was introduced as the "first world war of music," and auditions for the show were conducted in Dubai, Johannesburg, London, Pakistan, and the United States, reiterating Zee TV's popularity among the Non-Resident Indians in different parts of the world. The logo of the show depicted a globe with headphones. The unique synergy between transnational television and the Hindi film song on the show enabled several interesting possibilities, demonstrating the expansion of cultural flows between diasporas and their home country (Sundaram 2013, 9). Contestant singers from Pakistan, Dubai, the United States, and South Africa entered the show and generated considerable popular support. Mauli Dave, a seventeen-year-old of Indian origin from Houston, became a rage on *Sa Re Ga Ma Pa Challenge* after winning the crown of Miss Teen Texas. Mauli was rechristened as India's Shakira by her mentor on the *Sa Re Ga Ma Pa Challenge* on Zee TV. Though eliminated in the thirty-seventh episode, Mauli Dave received a huge response on YouTube and other online forums, with several fans writing detailed blogs on her singing and style of performance, while others criticized her glamorous doll image and lack of singing talent. Here are two examples taken from the show's website:

> Hi Mauli I am a big fan of yours. And I love your voice, personality. And u r also a very good dancer. u r mind blowing.

> When you sing there is fire on the stage. I think u will win Saregamapa 2007.
>
> Mauli, you cannot sing. Listen to your own past performances, and you will realize this. All you are good at doing is "oo"- and "aah"-ing, and dancing. I'm surprised that you have made it this far in the competition, because quite frankly you really do not deserve to be there.[14]

In the show's second episode, Mauli created a sensation by singing "Mayya mayya" (Dear dear), a popular song by A. R. Rahman from the film *Guru* (Ratnam, 2007). The biographical details of "Mayya mayya" are important to an understanding of Mauli's performance. The lead vocals in the original version, with liberal doses of Arabic words, were performed by Maryam Tollar, a Canada-based Arabic singer, with vocal support provided by Chinmayi, a Tamil singer. In the film, "Mayya mayya" was performed by actress Mallika Sherawat in an Istanbul bar. Sherawat is known for her sultry performances in nightclubs and "item" songs of Bollywood. A few weeks after its release, the song track was cleverly edited with visuals from Shakira's music video for "Whenever, Whatever" and placed on YouTube. The coming together of a pool of talent as diverse as A. R. Rahman, Maryam Tollar, Chinmayi, Mallika Sherawat, Shakira, and now Mauli points us toward Bollywood music's transnational reach in the networks of production and consumption. The intermeshing of language, genres, and vocal registers created an enigma around the song, further pushing its circulation among global audiences. Mauli received an unprecedented response from online communities, with her fans claiming that her "Mayya mayya" performance was the most viewed clip among singing shows on YouTube, outnumbering Sherawat's original performance.

With the mobilization of new circuits, singing shows transformed the voice of the Hindi film song. Common to Mauli Dave, Mallika Sherawat, and Shakira was a style of performance that relied on the mobility of the dancing body and the articulation of desire on a transnational platform. Further, the reconfiguration of Bollywood songs to fit the demands of new media technologies pushed music directors and lyricists toward miniaturizing the aesthetics of the song. This strategy allowed the song's easy dispersal via television promos, radio shows, medley sequences in film award functions, and DJ mash-ups at weddings and college functions. Songs like "Tanha tanha" and "Yai re yai re" from the film *Rangeela* (Varma, 1995), "Humma humma" from the film *Bombay* (Maniratnam, 1995), "Chaiyya chaiyya" from the film *Dil Se* (Maniratnam, 1998), "Mauja hi mauja," and "Nagada nagada" from the film *Jab We Met* (Ali, 2007), "Mayya mayya" from the film *Guru* (Maniratnam, 2007), and "Shava shava" from the film *Kabhi Khushi Kabhie Gham* (Johar, 2001) were woven with the iteration of hook words and used intensively for film publicity on television and FM stations.

It would be useful here to borrow the concept of redundancy (Fiske 1982) in interpersonal communication meant to ensure the flow of communication channels. In normal day-to-day conversation, phrases like, "you know," "I mean," "I am like," "What the hell!" and "you see" are redundant or low-information fillers that help sustain the flow of communication. More importantly, these words add layers of meaning to conversations, enabling the insertion of an individual style. In a similar vein, the repetitive use of hook words in songs like "Mayya mayya" or "Nach baliye" allowed style to seep in, creating spaces for the singer/performer to make the song her own. The hook lines in contemporary songs work through this enunciative capacity of redundancy, opening up the song to express a unique style of vocal performativity. The hook lines allowed the singer to create a spectacle in which the voice, orchestration, and a dancing body came together through heightened codes of visuality. Spectacle-driven singing contest shows allowed a large number of teenage women to actively intervene on reality television and play with the *recreation* of the musical mode. Having grown up listening to Lata Mangeshkar, on the one hand, and Shania Twain and Mariah Carey, on the other, teenage girls were able to project their voices in their own unique styles in conjunction with a performative body. The role models for these girls were no longer just Lata or Asha, and the songs they performed on the show were originally sung by a diverse range of singers, including Usha Uthup, Alisha Chinai, Ila Arun, and Maryam Tollar.

In *Indian Idol 5*, Bhoomi Trivedi performed "I Love You," a youthful, hippy-style duet performed by Usha Uthup and Asha Bhosle in the original version in the film *Hare Rama Hare Krishna* (Anand, 1971). Bhoomi incorporated the vocal style of both Asha Bhosle and Usha

Uthup, shifting her pitch to match the original song, and got rave reviews from the judges. Sunidhi Chauhan appreciated the way Bhoomi sang the low notes in the song. A quick replay of Bhoomi singing a part of the song in the low notes illustrated the comment. Sunidhi then advised Bhoomi to give more power to her higher notes, a comment that was followed by another short replay of Bhoomi singing the higher notes in Asha's style. This disassembling of the song in a format that combined "liveness" with edited flashbacks of recordings highlighted the performance of the voice and trained the audiences in close listening. Television shows brought together new amateur singers, singing stars, judges (as critics), and audiences on the same platform, becoming trained as better musicking bodies.

Voice and Body as Digital Data

The song that emerged out of digital studios was a porous, contingent, and malleable entity that permanently changed its relationship to cinema. Digital technologies and audio software brought seismic changes in production practices, blurring the distinctions between composing, arranging, and recording (Booth 2008, 84). It is important to emphasize, however, that the shift to digital sound practice was not a sudden, radical change in Bollywood's sonic landscape. As I have shown in chapter 4, the introduction of tracking systems in the music studios created the conditions for dubbing. As the number of tracks used for creating a song started multiplying, there was a fundamental shift in the way the voices of singers were selected, recorded, and made audible. Instead of singing along with a full orchestra, singers could get their voice recorded on a given track, a practice that fragmented the process of making the song. With the introduction of digital audio stations, sound engineers could "punch in" some sections of the song without disturbing the rest of the track, further fragmenting the process of production. In Asha Bhosle's (1993, 53) own words:

> In our times, recording studios had only two tracks—one for the music and one for the vocal. So, we knew we had to come back the next day to complete a song. But today studios have 16 tracks, 24 tracks! To top it all, the work pressure has

> increased three-fold, singers dash in and out of studios, they don't even know the complete song. After singing the *mukhda* they have to be reminded of the *antara*. I blame the dubbing system for this. Everything has become so mechanical.

Asha Bhosle's views show a deep dissatisfaction with a rapidly changing system in which the idea of the "complete song" remains permanently deferred. Interestingly, while recording technologies fragmented the production of the song, it was during live shows or televised music contests that one could experience the song in a single spatiotemporal zone, where the singers and the musicians came together for a "live" musical event.

Following Deleuze's understanding of the machinic assemblage, Drew Hemment (2004, 78) has argued that music needs to be seen as a dispersed category, a sonic event that is part of a new play with indeterminacy in which "music is set adrift in multiple, uncertain circumstances that can never be fully understood in advance." A. R. Rahman, the most celebrated composer of this phase, leveraged new technologies to foreground the sense of play and indeterminacy in the creation of songs. Artists in Rahman's studio in Chennai were invited to sing to a basic key with a freedom to improvise with as many variations as they wanted to. This sonic material was then used to digitally assemble a song through an intense editing process. The voice of the singer in the digital studio became just one more sound to be processed. Rahman's style of recording challenged the "naturalized" and conventional relationship between vocal and orchestral tracks, dispensing with the heavy reliance on string orchestra. Rahman managed to dramatically change the sound of the song to remain in step with contemporary global aesthetic norms. In Rahman's own words:

> By the 1990s, the younger generation in India had started listening to a wide range of international music and they wanted a new sound, music that would respect traditional Indian melody and yet offered something new and exciting to them. The approach we used for the *Rangeela* soundtrack had an international feel—the melodies and rhythms. It didn't sound like the soundtracks of Hindi or Tamil cinema of the

> time. *Rangeela* started a trend. And the film was a kind of rebirth for Asha Bhosle. (Cited in Kabir 2011, 35)

The opening song of *Rangeela* (Varma, 1995) remained on the top ten lists of various television and radio shows for months. "Yai re yai re" begins with a repetitive and bare tapping sound until we are introduced to Asha Bhosle's powerful singing of the *mukhda*. As the song builds up, the soundtrack becomes a dense amalgamation of melodies and rhythms. This intricate detailing and precision became a signature Rahman trait. Rahman's use of digital technology allowed sound to be manipulated "one note at a time," which led to a greater amount of "musical precision, intimacy and nuance" (Sarrazin 2014, 41).[15] "Mangta hai kya," another popular song, presented the unusual, androgynous voices of Shwetta Shetty and A. R Rahman. This was a continuation of his idea of using a greater range of voices from a pool of talent as diverse as the Tamil film industry, Indi-pop music, as well as new, unheard voices. As Rahman recalls, "We had multiple track recorders and I could spend time coaching and producing a new singer at my pace" (Kabir 2011, 63).[16]

How do we understand the production of the voice in a postdigital setup where musical improvisation (doing random things) is brought in step with the dynamic relationship between the voice, computer software, and the machinic assemblage, or, to borrow from Bill Brown (2010, 58), between different orders of materiality. In *Bunty Aur Babli* (Ali, 2005), Shankar-Ehsaan-Loy (SEL) created "Kajra re" as a fusion *qawwali* by drawing on a mélange of genres like folk music, Indi-pop, and *mujra*.[17] Jayson Beaster-Jones (2015, 164) has discussed the song as an instance of the cosmopolitanism of the Indian film song and SEL's innovative approach to music. Noted for its high production values through choreography, art direction, lighting, unusual lyrics, and a lineup of stars like Amitabh Bachchan, Abhishek Bachchan, and Aishwarya Rai, the song had a prolific presence on television, in nightclubs and at wedding celebrations.[18] SEL's decision to ask Alisha Chinai to provide the lead vocals for Aishwarya Rai merits some consideration. According to Chinai, the composers in the Bombay industry had always associated her with a westernized style of singing, and it was SEL who had the vision to perceive her beyond that (CU 2007). In an interview with First City, SEL share their experience of working with Chinai as follows:

> She came and got a shock when she heard the melody. She was like, "You guys mad? I can't sing this song . . . it's too high pitch this and that" . . . That song could have been easily sung like a Mahalaxmi Iyer, or a Shreya Ghoshal or an Alka Yagnik. In 20 minutes! But then this song would have just passed, gone, not so noticed! It was that girl's effort that it got so completely out of the bag, so wild, and that effort is seen. (Shankar Ehsaan Loy, 2006)

SEL's selection of the voice for "Kajra re" became critical for the aural attention that it received. Chinai's edgy voice not only militated against existing genre frameworks but also ensured that listeners would notice the random, wild quality of the song, giving it a cosmopolitan turn. The extended introduction, the cobbling together of genres, the use of chorus backed by whistling and clapping sounds, and the spatial setting of a nightclub imploding into the simulated space of a *kotha* further enhanced Alisha Chinai's vocal style through a form of "becoming" that subverted the musical form.

The changing relationship between voice, body, and sound production technologies is at the center of this destabilization. Writing about the discourse networks of 1900, Kittler (1999, 16) argued that noise produced by the larynx gets inscribed onto the phonograph before any semiotic order and linguistic meaning. What gets inscribed on the apparatus is the "real," the essence of man, which can be played back and analyzed by psychiatrists and detectives. However, the computer as an interface in the recording rooms has destabilized the notion of the real. The introduction of software like Pro Tools enabled pitch correction and auto-tuning of the voice, while the sound engineer as a key listener became an important figure in the studio. One can only speculate whether SEL used pitch-raising software, carefully moving between the real and the virtual to treat Alisha Chinai's voice. The song that we finally hear may have been entirely different from how the singer imagined her own voice.

According to Galloway (2012), the computer needs to be seen not as an ontological object but as a set of practices in relation to the world. Responding to the relationship between human subjectivity and digital technologies in the writings of scholars like Kittler and Manovich,

Mark B. N. Hansen (2010, 178–79) notes, "As distinct from phonography where the grooves of a record graphically reproduce the frequency ranges of humanly perceivable sound, and from film, where the inscription of light on a sensitive surface reproduces what is visible to the human eye, properly computational media involve no direct correlation between technical storage and human sense perception."

The use of voice-processing applications like Auto-Tune, or software applications like DeBreath, alerts us to digital recording's ability to create fissures between the subjective voice of the woman and its sonic presence in the public domain, just as the microphone did in an analogue system. Music creation in digital studios is not confined to just cleaning voices or pitch correction but also includes a dense layer of noise, gesturing toward the presence of nonhuman voices and media infrastructures. Drew Hemment (2004, 80) has used the term Edison *defect* while drawing attention to Edison's early phonographic recordings marked by "the surface of noise," which obscured the human voice. This "imperfection," according to Hemment (80), was a musical potential "that would come to be explored" in electronic music. In "Yeh ishq hai," a popular song from the film *Jab We Met* (Ali, 2007), the intercession between Shreya Ghoshal's voice and the computer incorporates these "defects." Interestingly, the song fetched Shreya Ghoshal a national award for playback singing. The song is performed by Geet (Kareena Kapoor) on her way to Manali, celebrating the anticipation of a new life. Enjoying her newfound freedom, Geet is in a liminal zone, driven by a desire to enjoy the visually spectacular expanse of the snow-capped mountains, while simultaneously presenting herself as part of this spectacle, dancing for the attention of the hero, Aditya (Shahid Kapoor), and the spectator. The sequence was shot in identifiable places like the Rohtang Pass and Naggar Fort near Kullu, and the sonic dimension of the song incorporates "folk" sounds of the region, integrating local music with global sounds. Ghoshal's voice, though prominent, is undergirded by sound processing techniques creating a sonic texture that brings out an embodied experience of freedom and enchantment. The refrain "Yeh ishq hai," repeated after each *antara*, is crowded with voices, creating a multivalent register of the voice. This effect is produced through a spillage of voice(s) with a slight delay or a lag, while in other segments of the song, double tracking of Ghoshal's voice with EQ effects creates yet another unique vocal effect. Rather than being a separate entity, as was the norm in the analogue era, the playback singer's voice is deeply embedded within the sonic structure of the song.

Focusing on the changing conditions of film exhibition and consumption in India's postglobalization era, Amit Rai (2009, 4) has drawn our attention to the affective body, fluctuating "across key thresholds, times, and technologies of digital control." Further, Rai argues that sound is central to this new media assemblage, engendering a range of bodily affectivities across exhibition spaces, digital audiovisual technologies, and consumer habituations of private as well as public spaces (99). The contours of the female voice in contemporary Bollywood songs need to be seen as part of a new media ecology where the human-computer interface is part of our everyday life. Technological mediations in voice production are intimately enmeshed in the wider landscape of aural consumption as we experience the spillage of songs through ever-fluctuating sonic registers across multiplex theaters, mobile phone ringtones, amplified sound systems in nightclubs, or DJ-dominated weddings. Our daily encounter with the city is mediated by digitally produced robotic female voices that we encounter through the General Packet Radio Service (GPRS) system or the elevators of the city's skyscrapers as part of our shifting acoustic landscape. In "Subah hone de," a dance track in *Desi Boyz* (Dhawan, 2011), sound-processing techniques are used to give a clubby feel to the song. However, in contrast to Mika Singh's robust voice, Shefali Alvares's electronically treated vocals remain subdued, mimicking the female robotic aural registers in our cityscape. In the "Break Up" song from *Ae Dil Hai Mushkil* (Johar, 2016), Jonita Gandhi's voice remains embedded in the track, with interlude sections switching to electronically treated voices singing a faster version of the refrain that sounds like gibberish. This connects with Steve Savage's (2013, 76) description of digital strategies such as the vari-speeding of vocals to create wild, unsingable effects. The amplification of digitally manipulated voices in Bollywood songs enables their easy circulation across diverse media platforms and screens, aiding their recall on the dance floor. Effects like double tracking of the voice with a slight delay in one track create an aural trace that flows through the media assemblage.[19]

The popularity of songs like "Kajra re" set the trend for another wave of "item girl" songs like "Munni badnaam hui," "Chikni chameli," "Sheela ki jawaani," and "Baby Doll," expanding the range of voices in Bollywood songs. The female performer's sexualized body was central to the item numbers, mounted as spectacles with high production values, even as these numbers carry the visual and aural registers of "B" genres and the flavors of regional music. The visualization of dance movements in item songs has depended on prerecorded music tracks, providing salience to the voice of the playback singer. However, the practice of lip sync in item girl songs has become increasingly casual, even as these songs work as important star vehicles for Bollywood celebrities. Tracing the links between the rise of digital sound technologies and item numbers, Silpa Mukherjee (2016, 66) underscores the loudness of the voice as "sonic eroticism," constructed through auto-tuning software to push the voice toward a high vocal range. The voice of the playback singer gets marginalized through digital production practices that are harnessed to create a hypersexual sound.

The dense soundtrack of "Kaisa jadoo dala re" (You have created a magic), from the film *Khakee* (Santoshi, 2004), is a mix of digitally created noise, glitches, and ominous low-pitched vocal effects. The sounds of sirens, blasts, screams, drops, and digitally modulated vocal tracks bring in the element of destruction in item songs. In "Shiela ki jawani" from the film *Tees Maar Khan* (Khan, 2010), the energy of the song is created by varying the levels of loudness. Sunidhi Chauhan's voice is double-tracked, giving it a powerful amplified presence in some sections while the blast of the fireballs, the whistling sounds, and the male chorus add to the layered soundtrack. In "Kamli kamli" from the film *Dhoom 3* (Acharya, 2013), we see Katrina Kaif dancing in a warehouse that is lined with metallic scaffolding with workers welding the metallic structure. Dressed in factory dungarees, Katrina starts dancing to Sunidhi Chauhan's powerful voice; we see sparks flying out of the background structure at regular intervals. The song has been created not only by EQ effects and double tracking of Chauhan's voice but also by the (non) musical sounds of clapping, gushing air, simulated sparking, and welding, and the aural traces of garbled singing. This unusual EQ effect given to the voice through the Digital Work Station (DAW) is used in "Sun saathiya" (Listen my friend), from the film *ABCD 2* (D'Souza, 2017), a slow and melodious track with piano and guitar riffs. The song shows Shraddha Kapoor rehearsing her dance movements with fellow dancers.

The jerky, volatile movements of the dancing body, combined with the artifice in the voice, offers a counterpoint to the soft, melodic track that opens with an alap in Priya Saraiya's voice. Musical creations in the digital studio need no longer emanate from musical notes but can originate from a reimaged sonic landscape that can amplify certain moods and sensations through an interface between the human and the nonhuman.

Voice as a Dispersed Object

The material practices involved in the sonic production of the voice in film songs are intimately connected to the new multiplex film form and existing listening practices. Background songs provide a unique sonic identity to multiplex films for their publicity. However, when songs recede into the background the most significant change is visible in song sequences. In her discussion of transformations in song and dance sequences and the couple form, Sangita Gopal (2011) traces the retreat of the song into the soundtrack. Gopal frames this new aesthetic practice in contrast to the older logic of romantic duets that worked as "adjunct modules" offering a space of autonomy and privacy to the couple denied to them by the narrative. Song sequences work as formal devices to fulfil the demands of the industry as a commercial enterprise, offering images of "proscribed forms of desire," which were not allowed to spill into the narrative (2011, 39). The retreat of the film song into the soundtrack, according to Gopal, is a sign of its attenuation, since the couple no longer depends on it. Further, borrowing on Prasad's formulation, Gopal links this phenomenon to the emergence of the sound-image, where sound is "disciplined" through "reading competence and is now perceived as an image" (46).

I offer my reading to the retreat of the song into the soundtrack by focusing on the fluctuating relationship between the singing and the listening body in the narrative framework. In an insightful analysis of a song from *Dil Se* (Mani Ratnam, 1998), Neepa Majumdar (2009, 321) argues that song in recent films no longer emanates "from a diegetic body." As Majumdar writes, "Listening as a disembodied practice is naturalized in the contemporary film, with no need to assert ownership over the song's sentiment through the act of singing. While the song still functions as a signifier of desire and a point of contact between lovers, here the voice exists in relation to listeners alone, rather than to singers and listeners."[20]

Indeed, in background songs, the singing voice is no longer attached to a particular on-screen performer or claimed by a specific listener. The song becomes a porous force moving through malleable acoustic territories, hybrid media, and digital networks. This dispersion of the song in the soundtrack needs to be seen not as a mark of its subordination to the image but as a new aesthetic form commensurate with the enmeshment of our bodies in digital technologies and expanded sonic terrains. Anahid Kassabian's (2013) concept of ubiquitous listening, part of our daily habitat, as we move into elevators and shopping arcades guided by AI voices, becomes relevant in this discussion. Though inattentive, this ambient form of listening draws affective responses (2013, xi). Background songs in film soundtracks become slippery objects of ubiquitous listening that stretch time and affective states, showing characters in a state of reflection or despair, or as fragmented from the environment. Bodies traverse across the screen, at times blending with and at other times extending or diverging from the aural registers of the song. Evoking stylized movements like slow-motion strobe effects, these songs isolate the lead characters from other on-screen bodies. This is in complete contrast to the way lip sync is presented on-screen in the visual field by highlighting the facial expressions of stars.

A dispersed form of singing becomes evident in *Fashion* (Bhandarkar, 2008), as the voice recedes into the background to allow for greater flexibility in the song's placement in the film. "Mar jawan," a background song, is yielded through an interface between machines, voices, and digital technologies. Created through a bricolage of sounds, musical sections, rhythmic grooves, and an ensemble of voices, "Mar jawan" (I will die) is presented with a lead female voice singing the lyrical sections. The song plays on the track when Kangana Ranaut and Priyanka Chopra walk the ramp for a fashion show, staged as a live event, heavily covered by the media. In a film with a strong female protagonist (Priyanka Chopra), "Mar jawan" is the only song in the film with a dominant female voice. A close analysis of "Mar jawan" demonstrates how non–lip synch songs function as dispersed objects not belonging to or claimed by any particular character in the narrative community of the film. This sets the tone for the attenuation of the voice in Bollywood songs, which has greater repercussions for the female voice. A key aspect of the new millennial song is the way it absorbs multiple sources and sonic registers. In the case of "Mar jawan," we are presented with a complex structure that combines diverse voices, tonalities, and languages (each language having its unique tonal register) as part of the musical edifice of the song track. "Mar jawan" opens with a piano track, followed by the first refrain of Arabic lyrics sung by Salim Merchant. The use of a percussive beat at regular intervals throughout the song is based on looping techniques, a common trope of electronic music. The female vocal section after the first Arabic refrain is almost unintelligible, since the voice is processed to create an edgy high sibilance effect. This is followed by a third vocal element, the voice of the lead female singer (Shruti Pathak) singing the line "Mar jawan" (I will die) in a much deeper register than Salim Merchant's voice. Deeply embedded in the soundtrack, the voice remains unattached to any specific body in the visual field. Moreover, it has to compete with other compelling sonic elements of the song. What gets distilled is the existence of the voice as part of an assemblage of sounds, rhythmic grooves, and designed sound patterns. Salim Merchant's voice with Arabic lyrics creates a lofty effect while the sonic in Shruti Pathak's voice, particularly its deeper tonality, gestures at the dark underbelly of the fashion industry. What is important to note here is that "Mar jawan" is not addressed to anyone in particular within the narrative community. The bodies of women on-screen walking the ramp remain mute and voiceless, while the disembodied voice unhinged from the body articulates the despondency and death wish of a fashion model.[21]

In "Mar jawan," the mimetic interaction between the playback singer and the on-screen actor is jettisoned, arguably to make way for a dispersed affect. What is missing is the point of contact that connects the voice of the playback singer with the on-screen star. This fundamentally changes the way the sound of the voice is aurally perceived: no one sings the song and therefore the voice is not directed at a specific listener in the narrative world. Hence, no one is specifically involved in the act of listening. The relationship between on-screen bodies and the song as an aural entity is contingent, often shifting across a diverse media landscape. Despite this, what is interesting is that songs like "Mar jawan" work to create a state of affective listening.

The depiction of bodies in slow motion in contemporary song sequences resonates with Mark Hansen's (2004, xi) views that in digital media, the image of the body becomes dynamic, capable of being modified at any moment. Like the voice that has gone through EQ effects and digital alteration, the bodies embodying technologies become active sources of meaning. Without lip sync, the body is freed from the demands of sound synchronization, demanding new modalities for producing its phantasm on the screen. However, this also raises questions about female aural stardom and its critical role in upholding the star body onscreen. For instance, in *No One Killed Jessica* (Gupta, 2011), the song "Yeh pal jo hain voh hadse hain" (These moments of eternal crisis) creates an unusual conjunction of image and sound that points to the attrition of the female voice. Shilpa Rao's voice in the song blurs the boundaries between the inner and the outer as it fades up in the track when Sabrina (Vidya Balan) is confronted with the reality that the key witness she had come to meet in Kolkata has turned hostile. The song opens with a flashback establishing the private moments that the two sisters shared with each other before Jessica is killed. The track is punctuated with Sabrina/Vidya Balan's speaking voice competing for attention with Shilpa Rao's singing voice. The song is used intermittently, its elastic structure allowing conversations and ambient sound to interrupt its cadence. The song retreats for a moment when Sabrina, in a fit of rage, informs her father that they are going to lose the case as their key witness has turned hostile. In the next segment of the song, we see Sabrina entering the frame on her terrace in slow motion. Framed against a city that has shown no empathy for her family, Sabrina starts screaming, letting out her anguish, but her scream remains inaudible (figure 5.3). The use of slow motion, while framing Vidya Balan's face, further widens the gap between her body and Shilpa Rao's singing voice in the background. By completely muting Sabrina's screams, the song foregrounds the anguished body as the source of the scream, a disconcerting image of the body without sound. This clever strategy in *No One Killed Jessica* critiques the overreliance on sound-image synchronization, and its failure to give women agency. Digital technologies work here toward abstracting time—the body in slow motion destabilizes the voice/body relationship to give a granular experience of the present.

Figure 5.3. The muted scream in *No One Killed Jessica* (Gupta, 2011). Screenshot by author.

The porosity of background songs, as they are presented in film texts, has fundamentally changed their formal properties: they appear as fragmented objects without a distinct beginning or end. As the film industry moved toward sync sound recording, since the early 2000s, soundtracks of Bollywood films have become attentive to the narrative's spatial setting and the actor's sensory engagement with the profilmic space. Pavitra Sundar's (2023, 10) use of the term "sound work" is extremely productive to engage with the way we listen to postdigital cinema, where boundaries between musical and nonmusical elements are getting increasingly blurred. Gautam Pemmaraju (2013, 65) notes the inauguration of a "radically different tone, texture, timbre and dynamics of contemporary sounds," making audible an unheard universe and "current modes of sonic bricolage." He cites Resul Pookutty's work in films like *Slumdog Millionaire* (Boyle, 2008), which became central to the film's composite, textured, and multidimensional soundtrack (Pemmaraju 2013, 74). An interesting example is Pookutty's crafting of "Ring ring ringa," with onomatopoeic words that allude to our sensory entanglement with the mobile phone. The song foregrounds the widespread use of mobile phones for music consumption that "coexists with the spawning of informal livelihoods clustered around electronic and digital media" (Deo and Duggal 2017, 42). The introductory music of "Ring ring ringa" grafted on the image and the rumbling sound of a fog machine in the city's underpass, where Jamal meets the blind alms-seeker, leads us to the song sung by Ila Arun and Alka Yagnik. In the next scene, when we see Jamal and Salim looking for Latika in the red-light area of Pila Street, the noise of traffic, mixed with the voices of sex workers and street hawkers, adds a crucial layer to the sound of the track. Unlike with the Choli song sung by the same singers, there is no female body deployed here to lip-synch or own these voices. The porous and layered soundtrack of the song resonates with David Beer's (2007) argument that mobile music devices allow the listener to remain connected with the aural ecology of the city to encounter dense sonic geographies and networked territories.[22]

In narratives located in metropolitan cities and small towns, the sonic is a crucial terrain to capture the energies of subaltern populations and the expanding informal networks of media (Sundaram 2015). With their ability to accommodate ambient sound and noise, along with the voice of the singer, songs become an important aesthetic device to record the sensory expansion of media infrastructures (2015, 5). Let me cite the example of the song "Yahi meri zindagi hai" (This is my life), from *Dev D* (Kashyap, 2009), which is played as a background track to introduce Lenny's character in the film. Lenny's story in *Dev D* was partly inspired by an incident of a sexually explicit video clip of two high school students that became viral as a multimedia message (MMS) in December 2004.[23] The song fades up in the background, mapping a day in Lenny's life. Lenny (Kalki Koechlin) steps out of her home, raises the hemlines of her skirt in her school uniform, and gets whistled at by a man on the street. The sound of the whistle, the street being swept by a broom, and the city traffic compete for aural attention with the song. While the lyrics remain unintelligible, the refrain, "Yehi meri zindagi hai" (This is my life) comes across prominently[24] As the song progresses, we see Lenny spending the afternoon with her boyfriend, framed by a voyeuristic camera. Lenny's return to the school is captured through the optics of her peers, who start heckling her. The sounds from the water sprinkler, the basketball in the playing field, and the distorted voice of the boys shouting "Lenny tu best hai" (Lenny you are the best) acquire an edge. A dense auditory experience is captured by the repetitive use of incoming notifications and ringtones, referencing the viral circulation of the MMS, as Lenny turns in the direction of a dark corridor (figure 5.4). The crafting of the sequence

Figure 5.4. Images from "Yehi meri zindagi hai," background song in *Dev D* (Kashyap, 2009). Screenshots by author.

with visuals in slow motion heightens the affective state of the body as the sniggering becomes more intrusive, alienating Lenny from the social and spatial context. More than the pervasive circulation of the image, it is the aural trace of the event that haunts Lenny. The song foregrounds the listening sentient body as part of a feedback loop in the contemporary media ecology. The sequence concludes with the singer's voice getting stretched to reach a stage of implosion. The image of Lenny's affected body and the singer's voice are digitally modulated. One of the important fallouts of digital media, as this song sequence demonstrates, is the ability of sound media to absorb and translate the everyday experience of the body into intelligible as well as volatile sounds.

Elsaesser and Hagener (2015, 147) note that the privileging of sound in postdigital cinema helps to tether it to the indexical, providing a "set of 'truth conditions' for the digital image." The body is central to this imagination, since the sonic terrain provides a productive link to the body's materiality. Presented as layered and dense soundtracks, thickened by memories and shifting temporalities, background songs capture bodies and objects caught in moments of shock/affect in layered sonic terrains. In these nuanced moments, even bystanders get caught, their bodies somehow expressing the flow of these moments. "Gustakh dil" (Audacious heart), a background song in *English Vinglish* (Shinde,

2012), maps the interaction of a body in shock within the spatial contours of New York City, comprising its habits, events, and objects. The city suddenly becomes strange and unpredictable when Shashi (Sridevi) rushes out of an awkward situation with Laurent, her admirer, who tries to become intimate with her. "Gustakh dil," sung by Shilpa Rao, describes the state of an errant, confused mind as Shashi starts walking toward the subway: she soon rams into another pedestrian, her papers flying away (figures 5.5 and 5.6). The visual effects, such as slow motion, render the people and the objects on the sidewalk distant and strange. While the singer's voice layered on the guitar riff remains prominent, all other ambient sounds remain muted. The song captures Shashi's body

Figures 5.5 and 5.6. Slow motion in "Gustakh dil" as a background song in *English Vinglish* (Shinde, 2012). Screenshots by author.

in shock, inattentive to her surroundings, except for the slivers of sound, a screeching car, the fluttering of paper, a baby crying on the sidewalk, and the rustling of leaves. This selective use of sound brings out the city as a place of collision and assault, with the mobile female body fluctuating across key thresholds, struggling to make sense of this space. The singer's voice occupies a neutral space, neither assimilated as an inner voice nor completely separated, thus complicating the "separation of first- and third-person perspective on bodily experience" (Wegenstein 2010, 21). What is striking about the song sequence is the way it foregrounds the affective experience of bodies in relation to the objects and infrastructures of the city.

Songs like "Gustakh dil" or "Yeh pal" do not demand focused aural attention, yet work to bring out an affective sensory response, as discussed by Kassabian (2013). Voice, lyrics, and music are joined to comment on the circumstances in which the protagonists find themselves in a larger spatial terrain. In *Pink* (Sircar, 2016), the song "Kaari kaari raina" (This intensely dark night), describes the experiences of three women protagonists who see a desolate city fettered by smog, fear, and darkness. Sung by Qurat-ul-Ain Balouch, the song is played in short snatches in two separate sections of the film, each time with the camera becoming distant, showing the cityscape of Delhi. The resonant voice of the singer works as a narrator, while the camera captures the night, with metro trains crisscrossing the city, forming an important part of its vista. These images of the city, intercut with shots of the three young women in their apartment, work to slow down the narrative, allowing characters to be themselves, free for a few moments from the tyranny of narrative events.

On the other hand, songs like "O womaniya" from the film *Gangs of Wasseypur* (Kashyap, 2012) rely on sonic excess and a dramatic shift in the way voices are selected and recorded for a distinct local flavor. Madhuja Mukherjee (2017, 188–89) has observed the thickening of the soundtrack of *Gangs of Wasseypur*, with layers of locals sounds, cries, and utterances bringing out a novel sensorial interaction between music, sound, and noise. "O womaniya" is crafted by using the voices of two women in a *sawal-jawab* taking control of the soundtrack with a female chorus adding to its dense quality. This hip rustic track was recorded in a small studio in Patna, with local women singers, in a live take with their "voices leaking into each other" (Jhingan 2015). The aural and the visual tracks move on two separate registers: the first offers a quirky comment on leery men, advising women on how to deal with them; the second shows Sardar Khan (Manoj Vajpayee) and Durga's playful dalliance with each other. The sound aesthetics here are a striking departure from earlier practices of recording the playback singer's voice with an emphasis on controlled breathing and the production of a voice that could convey purity and intimacy and an inner journey of the self. In "Dil chi cha lader," another background song in *Gangs of Wasseypur*, Khanwalkar invited twelve-year-old Durga, a migrant from Andhra Pradesh, who was spotted singing in Mumbai local trains while seeking alms to record her voice.[25]

Priya Jaikumar (2020, 237) has identified Bollywood's cinema's move toward sync sound recording and location-based filming as part of larger shift in production protocols of the industry, in tune with global practices. Jaikumar highlights the challenges that location-based filming poses, such as handling of noise and crowds at a time when the film industry is moving toward corporatization, coupled with its drive to show "images of extreme wealth, financial mobility" in a global cosmopolitan ethos (249).[26] Jaikumar has insightfully shown how the push toward shooting in actual locations with sync sound recording has been accompanied by a compelling zeal to uphold the appearance of "Brand India" tied to the commodification of land and spaces (285).[27] Jaikumar also signposts the rise of the alternative and multiplex films that depict "detail-rich images of India's cities, shantytowns, urban slums and rural locations" (285). What is common to both Bollywood blockbusters and alternative films is a "formal commitment to audio-visual realism," an aesthetic practice that turns sites of film production into a new kind of interface between corporate-driven professionalization and unskilled below-the-line film work (285–86). My investment in the auditory terrains of postdigital cinema relies on close listening to the density of soundtracks as expanded vocal timbres (such as the rough-and-ready voices of singers like Durga in *Gangs of Wasseypur*), dialects, local media devices, and the din of the crowded streets and bazaars, in conjunction with digitally produced noise, seep into the film song tracks. As malleable entities, background songs have expanded the sonic registers of contemporary films by absorbing the messiness of cities through the registers of raw voices, digitally modulated vocal tracks, and environmental sounds.

In the contemporary digital ecology, the voice, and its enmeshed quality in the track, demands a far more diffused kind of listening on mobile screens, television shows, YouTube videos, and other platforms. How do we read these transformations while remaining fully cognizant of the erosion of the female voice in song sequences? In the conclusion, I will turn to the reconfiguration of the "female" voice in the new platform economy.

Conclusion

Lata Mangeshkar passed away in February 2022, almost two decades after she had stopped singing for commercial recordings. Her exit from the recording studios marked the beginning of the decline of the female playback voice and lip-synched song in the formal industry. By the late 2000s, singers like Sukhwinder Singh, Rahat Fateh Ali Khan, and Mohit Chauhan started dominating the Indi-pop genre. Ironically, even in films where the narratives were driven by strong female characters (*The Dirty Picture* [Luthria, 2011], *Piku* [Sircar, 2015], and *Kahaani* [Ghosh, 2012]),[1] "big" voices of male singers started dominating the soundtracks. For instance, *Aashiqui 2* (Suri, 2013), a remake of Hollywood's *A Star Is Born* (Wellman, 1937), became a star vehicle for Arijit Singh, sidestepping the narrative drive of a female singer's rise to stardom.

However, the attenuation of the female playback singer's voice needs to be seen against a larger shift in the sound practices of Bollywood cinema, the rise of the multiplex film, transformations in listening practices, and attention economies in the post–digital media ecology. In these tectonic transformations, the film song itself has become a malleable, tenuous object, cut loose from the presence of a stable lip-synching body on-screen. *Kaminey* (Bhardwaj, 2009) introduced onomatopoeic sounds of action sequences of films from the 1970s through "Dhan te nan," sung by Sukhwinder Singh and Vishal Dadlani. Sudhir Mahadevan (2015, 10–11) notes that the "recycling" of familiar images and sounds in "Dhan te nan" was built on our experience of the everyday, intimately mediated through cinema. The song was filmed in a dark Bombay nightclub, capturing the exhilarating experience of crime and drugs with its subterranean routes in international syndicates of crime. What was striking about this nightclub sequence was the absence of women. However, its strong aural hook opened it up for a range of possibilities and assertions, as para-textual material. Thus, Priyanka Chopra, the female actor of *Kaminey*, who had been sidelined in the filmed sequence of the song, asserted her own star power by performing on a remixed track of "Dhan te nan" at the Indian Premier League (IPL) Awards night in 2010. In this heavily mediatized event, Chopra performed to Anoushka Manchanda's vocals in a reworking of the song. This claiming of the song by Chopra and Manchanda shows how sound as digital data offers new ways for women artists to stake their claim on songs and media platforms by challenging industry logic through creative interventions. Recently, Aswin Punathambekar and Sriram Mohan (2020, 20) have drawn our attention to the importance of cloud infrastructures in enabling new ways of listening and expressions of sonic citizenship. Women singers and actors are now performing genres of songs that were hitherto denied to them by the industry. In a film award show, for instance, Priyanka Chopra donned the attire of a male cop to perform songs like "Hud hud dabbangg," while imitating Salman Khan's hypermasculine bodily gestures, gait, and dancing style as a North Indian cop.

Discussions on postcinema remind us that digitization turns all images and sounds into data or information that can be disassembled and recirculated in startling ways (Shaviro 2016, 371). Background songs in films have created a unique space for recalibrating women's vocality in eclectic ways. In *Highway* (Ali, 2014) and *Tiger Zinda Hai* (Zafar, 2017), the androgynous voices of the Nooran sisters enable further mutation of the song. In the latter film, the Nooran sisters' voices in "Tera noor" are grafted onto a thrilling action sequence performed by Katrina Kaif as an undercover agent. While the lyrics of the Sufi song are dedicated to the praise of a spiritual God or a beloved, the soundtrack is created by incorporating electronic sounds of whirs, mild explosions, rumbles, gunshots, and police sirens associated with thrilling video games, as a counterpoint to the voice. In this heady mix, the Nooran sisters' voices become an ode to a new spectacle of female power, staged with quick camera movements, strobe effects, slow motion, and the use of CGI, as we see Kaif navigating her body in the air to attack her opponents. The intersections between techne and labor produce a hallucinatory effect.

In *Highway*, "Patakha guddi" (Bomb girl), sung by the Nooran sisters, occasions an important moment in the film where Veera (Alia Bhatt), the daughter of a rich industrialist and a victim of sexual abuse, declares her freedom from the stifling norms of her upper-class and caste upbringing, despite being held for ransom by a gang of criminals. The "Patakha guddi" sequence highlights a sense of liberation in an unbounded space, celebrating a "coming out" moment similar to a queer outing. Despite their powerful vocals, the Nooran sisters' musical journey shows how they have remained marginalized in the industry, performing boundary work for Bollywood. On the other hand, digital technologies enable stars like Alia Bhatt to sing for the characters that they are playing in films.

In *Highway*, director Imtiaz Ali deftly employs a song to build an intense relationship between Veera and Mahabir, one of her abductors. "Sooha saha" (Red rabbit) is first introduced when Mahabir hums its tune, and when prodded, he reluctantly tells Veera that it was a lullaby his mother used to sing for him. In the next scene, Veera begins humming the tune, slowly expanding it from the seams, while Mahabir listens in shock. The soothing tone of the song is sharply intercut with images of a child being slapped repeatedly and a man abusing his wife. The slow unfolding of the song prepares the audience for its deep association with Mahabir's life. Veera's voice singing the lullaby in the background yields splintered images and sounds from Mahabir's childhood, giving visual force to the trauma of witnessing his mother endure years of violence and sexual abuse. By introducing the mother's song through Veera, the film foregrounds an intimate connection between the two women, both victims of the oppressive silence around gender-based violence, despite the difference in class and social backgrounds.

The acoustic transference from Mahabir's voice to Veera's is given an extra textual force in a behind-the-scenes video of Alia Bhatt preparing herself to sing "Sooha saha" in a digital studio. The video shows Imtiaz Ali and A. R. Rahman in an intense discussion while Bhatt is seen practicing in the recording booth. After Rahman instructs her to emphasize a particular note by singing it himself, Bhatt turns toward the camera and whispers, "This is so difficult." By singing "Sooha saha," Bhatt presents an intense embodied engagement with the character of Veera. The video highlights how songs are crafted to make room for multiple readings in the post–digital media ecology and invites viewers to revisit the affective alliance forged between Bhatt, Veera, and Mahabir's mother.

As song sequences get disassembled, we also need to consider how the female body is presented on-screen with a greater emphasis on the speaking voice. Sync sound technologies have created new inventories of stardom through the actor's voice in film narratives. To recall, there had been a practice of replacing the female actor's voice with the voice of professional dubbing artists in the Bollywood industry, thus disconnecting the actor's voice from her body. Voices of female actors, in particular, were scrutinized in conjunction with their imagined connections with the body, as indicators for caste, class, or ethnic identity. A prominent example is Vikram Bhatt's decision to hire a dubbing artist for Rani Mukherjee, a relatively new entrant in the industry, for *Ghulam* (Bhatt, 1998).[2] Speaking about her role as a young, rebellious woman living in an elite high-rise apartment complex in *Ghulam*, Mukherjee has recalled her disappointment when the director told her that he found her voice rather too husky, which was not expected from the heroines of the time.[3] Mukherjee's voice finally got noticed through its spectral presence in *Kuch Kuch Hota Hai* (Johar, 1998), wherein in an extended sequence as a dead mother, we hear her reading letters to her daughter. In *Veer-Zaara*, (Chopra, 2004) in a lawyer's role, Mukherjee's declamatory speeches in the courtroom were appreciated by critics and fans.

With the expansion of digital infrastructures and mobile screens, we encounter the female voice as an unbridled sonic force. In *Ragini MMS* (Kripalani, 2011) released in 2011, the uncanny presence of the paranormal is created through a digitally created soundtrack with breathing sounds, suppressed screams, and voices of the "female" figure. This unidentifiable, digitally created voice is in sharp contrast to the familiar voice of the playback singer, presented as an acousmetre in haunting songs, that finally is synchronized with the body. On the other hand, films with women characters from small towns, vernacular backgrounds, and subaltern classes have expanded the tonalities of female voices in contemporary cinema. Trailers of Vidya Balan's films piggyback on her vocal performance, giving audiences a chance to connect to her voice before the film's release.[4] Balan played the role of an actor known for her oversexualized image on-screen in *The Dirty Picture* (Luthria, 2011). The role was loosely based on the biography of Silk Smitha, an actor in the Tamil film industry in the 1980s. The trailers of *The Dirty Picture* open with Vidya Balan's acousmatic voice on a black frame, before leading us to her erotic dancing body. In *Tumhari Sulu* (Triveni, 2017), Vidya Balan plays the role of a simple housewife who becomes a radio disc jockey for a late-evening phone-in show. This overstepping of spatial boundaries has startling consequences: Sulu's erotically charged voice starts circulating as a rogue object in public spaces, causing deep anxiety to her family. The film foregrounds the voice-body relationship in the digital ecosystem as the sensory charge in Sulu's voice invokes disciplinary frameworks for the female body. However, the film also captures Sulu's naive but passionate involvement in using her voice as an instrument of public performance on a phone-in show. In *Gangubai Kathiawadi* (Bhansali, 2022), an author-backed performance by Alia Bhatt was staged through her extended public speeches and calibrated tonal performance. Gangubai's husky, measured voice in the film became a symbol of her powerful embodied presence. Interestingly, all of these films draw attention to the way women use sound technologies to negotiate their precarious lives in the public domain. In *Gangubai Kathiawadi*, an extended sequence of her public speech is encoded with the subtle use of an unwanted noise of the public address system, the foregrounding of the microphone in the frame, and emphasis on the gestures of the listeners.

On the other hand, television contest shows and social media continue to drive the recirculation of songs sung by the erstwhile playback stars. Videos uploaded on social media of both men and women performing iconic female solo songs capture a playful engagement with the older practices of lip-synching and performing the song.[5] As I have shown, escaping spatial, mediatic, and infrastructural boundaries, the female playback singer's voice is rehearsed as digital data, regurgitating the dominance of the female voice in eclectic ways.[6] The analogue-digital cognate in the contemporary moment is also marked by an "in and out movement of media objects," resisting a clear shift to the digital economy (Sundaram 2021, 15). For instance, Pritha Malhotra presents herself in the garb of the heroines of the 1950s and the '60s while performing Lata's songs in perfect lip sync on Instagram.[7] These black-and-white videos focus on her physiognomy, drawing attention to her darting side glances, facial gestures, and subtle eyebrow movements, reanimating the feminine body of the Bombay film heroines, in an intimate confessional form.

The mobile phone camera's close contact with her face, neck, mouth, and eyes also nudges us to relisten to Lata's voice, with her impeccable breath control and smooth voice modulation. By focusing on how the voices were imagined, recorded, edited, and repurposed in the analogue phase and the postdigital ecology, this book has tried to create a longer arc of the female voice in Hindi film songs to its shifting presence in contemporary sonic cultures and the way they have become co-constitutive of on-screen multi-sited bodies. Both as a method and a site of inquiry, listening opens the field to not only on-screen bodies but also auditory terrains that animate radio listeners, copy singers, television performers, bots, and YouTube stars.

Glossary

Alap: A phrase of musical elaboration without the use of syllables or words. Usually, alap involves the use of vowel sounds, especially "a." For instance, see the opening of "Ab toh hai tumse" (Now my life is with you), from the film *Abhimaan* (Mukherjee, 1973). www.youtube.com/watch?v=emKJ5_cMEHk.

Antara: The stanza that follows the *mukhda*. A film song is generally composed with a *mukhda* and two or three stanzas.

Bandhish: Musical composition in a raga in Hindustani classical music that allows the musician to engage in musical elaboration.

Barahmasa: A semiclassical or folk form of music in which all of the twelve months are described. It is also described as a song of the twelve months.

Bazaar: A market.

Bhajan: A Hindu devotional song.

Biraha: Popular folk genre of songs in the region of Bihar, Uttar Pradesh and Jharkhand with themes of intense longing and pain of separation.

Chaiti: Traditional seasonal folk song sung during the month of Chaitra (March–April). It is identified as a woman's genre.

Dadra: A light classical vocal genre akin to thumri with a more pronounced rhythmic lilt.

Dholak: A barrel-shaped percussion instrument with skin on both sides commonly played in folk music in South Asia.

Gharana: Referring to a family or a clan of Hindustani music with a distinctive style of music. Usually, the legacy of a *gharana* was passed on to the sons, nephews, or sons-in-law. According to Kumar Mukherji

(2006, 349), the names of the *gharanas* come from the towns or cities where the originator of the style lived. *Gharana* is a school in Hindustani classical music representing a specific music tradition. According to Ranade (1997, 138), it is the formulation of the basic music philosophy or ideology, which influences the conception, teaching, learning, performance, and codification of music.

Ghazal: A primary genre of Urdu poetry, sung as a light musical form.

Ghoomar: A traditional dance from Rajasthan that involves twirling movements by women. The dance has been traditionally associated with the Bhil tribe but in its popular form has been appropriated by Rajputs and other communities of Rajasthan.

Ghungroo: A string of metallic bells worn on the ankles by dancers in South Asia to create a rhythmic sound. In dance-based film songs, the sound of Ghungroo is simulated and amplified during the process of recording.

Hori: Light classical genre sung during the period of Holi. Hori songs usually describe the pranks and romantic play between Radha and Krishna during the color festival.

Kajali or *kajari*: A Bhojpuri folk song sung during the rainy season. The *kajari* is also known as a genre of light classical Hindustani music, similar to *thumri*, typically describing the state of a heroine who is separated from her lover during the rainy season.

Khyal: Literally meaning an idea, khyal is a major musical form in Hindustani classical music that allows greater freedom for improvisation and elaboration.

Kotha: A salon where the courtesans lived and performed for their patrons, displaying their skill and proficiency in music, poetry, and dance. According to Bhaskar and Allen (2009, 335–36), *kotha* was also an economic unit, offering hospitality that thrived on the courtesans' art and the generosity of the patrons.

Lavani: An erotic song and dance performance genre from Maharashtra that is performed with *dholki*, a percussion instrument. *Lavani* is associated with *Tamasha*, a folk theater form performed by the lower castes such as the Kolhati.

Mehfil: A gathering where music and dance are performed before an invited audience.

Mudra: In Indian classical dance forms, a mudra is a symbolic and stylized hand gesture. The Natya Shastra has described twenty-four kinds of mudras.

Mujra: A form of dance performed by the courtesans in a *mehfil*.

Mukhda: The refrain or the first two lines of the song that work like an aural hook of the song.

Murki: A musical embellishment.

Nattuvanar: A key figure who directs the bharatnatyam performance by conducting the orchestra and providing vocal percussion. Often, the guru and the *nattuvanar* can be the same person.

Nautch: An anglicized version of the Hindi *nach*, meaning dance.

Nayika: The heroine or the addressee in a classical text in Indian performing arts. Bharata described *Ashta nayika*, or eight kinds of heroines, depicted in classical dance, music, sculptures, and miniature paintings.

Padam: A musical composition in Carnatic music based on *shringara rasa* and depicting romantic love, erotic desire, and beauty. *Padams* are an important part of the repertoire of bharatanatyam.

Pukar: A style of vocal intonation in singing that lays emphasis on bringing intensity of emotion.

Raga or *rag*: A melodic framework in Indian classical music, bound by rules about the principal note, and certain norms about using a set of notes and the order in which they can be combined. In popular terms, a raga is considered to evoke certain moods and emotions.

Sarangi: A bowed instrument used in North Indian classical and semiclassical music.

Tanpura: A drone instrument used as an accompaniment in Indian classical and semiclassical music.

Tarannum: A style of reciting Urdu poetry with voice modulation.

Tawaif: A woman accomplished in music and dance who entertained the men of nobility during the Mughal era.

Thumri: a semiclassical genre of Hindustani music. Imbued with sensuality, *thumri* is considered to be a feminine form because the text often represents a woman's emotional state. In comparison to *khyal* and *dhrupad*, *thumri* is considered to be a more flexible form because of its "loose adherence to the grammar of *rag*" (Perron 2002, 174).

Ustad: A title for a well-respected Muslim music teacher who carries a legacy of excellence in music. The *ustads* could also be master performers.

Viraha: The anguish caused by separation from the beloved, as described in music and dance.

Virahini: The woman in a state of *viraha*.

Notes

Introduction

1 This echoes Sudhir Mahadevan's argument that cinema in India needs to be seen as a "techno material infrastructure," with many origins and intermedial connections (2015, 5).

2 According to Chandavarkar, the standard rpm records with their restricted time duration had a flattening effect on all recordings (1980). For a history of the recording industry in India, see Michael Kinnear (1994).

3 Since the mid-thirties, songs have worked as aural hooks for audiences, even before the films were released. Stephen Putnam Hughes has noted the connections between cinema, theater and gramophone records in the formative years of sound cinema (2007). Several scholars have noted that the predominance of songs in Indian cinema can be traced to the cinema's strong links with musical folk drama and the urban theater of the nineteenth century (Skillman 1986; Beeman 1980; Barnow and Krishnaswamy 1963). Kathryn Hansen has elaborated on the emergence of Parsi theater as a dominant dramatic form that flourished in urban India between the 1860s and the 1930s (2003). "Songs," writes Hansen (2003, 393), were "necessary adjuncts to narratives in creating stage appeal," and their importance grew with time. Music has been considered as an integral part of cinema in India during the silent era (Booth, 2008; Arnold, 1991). The coming of sound, according to Arnold (1991, 161), created "an immediate need for musical composition integral to the sound film" as opposed to the use of incidental music in silent cinema. Beeman (1980, 82) has suggested that the "total integration of music with other performance elements" played a constitutive role in creating sound expression in India (1981, 82). What this implies is that the Indian spectator was already trained to draw

pleasure from a plurality of vocal expressions that ranged from speech, dialogue, poetic recitation, intoned speech, and song in a continuum, and "the artificial 'break' which is felt in the west when an actor bursts into a song is thus less apparent to the Indian viewer" (83). Anna Morcom (2019, 132) has described song and dance sequences as hyperperformative texts that seem to "protrude" or "ostend" from mundane life with style and action. Ashok Da Ranade (1980) has made an important intervention in the debate by arguing that songs became important elements of cinema not only because of their close association with regional and folk theater but also due to the overwhelming presence of mythological content in the first five years of the talkie era.

4 Songs acquire a special resonance during momentous events like the death of a star actor or a playback singer.

5 Scholars like Alison Arnold (1991), Gregory Booth (2008), and Teri Skillman (1986) have tracked the early history of playback with the coming of sound cinema, focusing on the period when playback was first introduced in Indian cinema around 1935. Anna Morcom's *Hindi Film Songs and the Cinema* (2007) is an important book-length study based on the textual analyses of film songs in their cinematic form.

6 Debashree Mukherjee (2020, 146) has unpacked the cine ecology of Bombay cinema of the 1930s and the '40s when sound came to Indian cinema, highlighting the broader phenomenology of the voice across "song, speech and vocal gestures." Neepa Majumdar's work draws attention to the unique ways that early sound cinema addresses the listener/spectator (2009). More recently (2020), she has written about the different modalities of the female voice in Bombay cinema of the 1930s, when female stars like Shanta Apte sang and performed the songs on-screen. Madhuja Mukherjee's (2007; 2012) scholarship has also played an important role in highlighting the intersections between the cultural and technological practices in early sound cinema.

7 According to Gregory Booth (2008, 40), by separating the production of songs, "(physically, chronologically, procedurally, etc.) from that of films," playback technology intensified the interconnections between the two industries. In addition, Alison Arnold's (1991) unpublished thesis is a detailed historical survey of the transformations in the Hindi film song, taking into account the introduction of the playback system, through an ethnomusicological lens. Focusing on the shift to the playback system,

Arnold charts the gradual transformation from the actor-singer phase to the era of the playback singers and the resultant shifts in vocal style by providing a detailed list of singers in each category, including those like Suraiyya who continued to perform as both actors and singers until the 1950s.

8 Kiranmayi Indraganti (2016) has given a detailed account of different stages in sound cinema in the Tamil and Telugu film industry, taking into account the marketing strategies of the record industry on the one hand and the demands of the film industry for voice casting of singers or singer actors on the other.

9 The song can be accessed on www.youtube.com/watch?v=2uA0MEteMeY.

10 Doane discusses a television commercial in which Ella Fitzgerald's voice is played on Memorex tape. The commercial asks viewers if they notice any difference between the voice of Ella Fitzgerald and the Memorex tape. Thus, the commercial tries to sell the idea that the owner of the Memorex tape can directly access Fitzgerald's authentic voice.

11 In another work, Eidsheim (2015, 41) analyzes Juliana Snapper's experiment at underwater singing to draw attention to the material and embodied nature of sound and its reception. Eidsheim argues that voice and music need to be seen as intermaterial practices, defying a fixed notion of sound and the sonic event (2015, 2).

12 *Tawaifs* were singers and dancers who performed to entertain upper-caste men in private gatherings. Scholars working on the history of the *tawaifs* have shown how their stigmatization first began during the rebellion of 1857 by the British as a political propaganda (Oldenburg 1990) and continued in the early twentieth century, when middle-class female artists started entering the public stage (Jha 2009).

13 "Playback technology encouraged the continued development of two symbiotic industries," writes Gregory Booth (2008, 40), referring to the film and music industries. The production of songs was separated from that of films, thus enabling the recording industry to introduce film songs into the market as standalone commodities (40).

14 Emphasis mine.

15 According to Lelyveld, Sardar Patel, a nationalist leader and the first home minister of the Indian independent State intervened to ensure that singers and musicians,' whose "private life was a matter of public scandal," were barred from singing on the radio.

16 As Majumdar (2010, 192) writes, Moral hierarchies were created between the voice and body, to aid the "*cultural* anchoring of the female body on display."

17 In a sharp response, in *Economic and Political Weekly*, Ashwini Deshpande (2004, 5182) contested Sanjay Srivastava's ideas about Lata's voice as a marker of a certain kind of female identity, or that her arrival came at a time when "the nationalist project was looking for a thin voice to suit a regressive representation of women." Deshpande has also queried how a singer's voice can be analyzed without citing her recordings or the heterogeneity of her songs (5179–84). In a response piece, Lakshmi Subramanian (2005, 1561) also noted a certain ossification of meanings and cultural values around the female voice in the late nineteenth and the twentieth centuries and asked, "can we find multiple meanings in the term 'the female voice'?"

18 Emphasis mine.

19 In an article on the playback system and the use of chorus in Hindi film songs, I have shown how the music directors were able to introduce overlapping tonalities of voices by using the softer crooning style of the trained singers to their advantage in the 1940s and the '50s. In "Ramaiya vasta vaiya" (*Shri 420* [Kapoor, 1955]), Lata's voice, as performed by Nargis, is introduced as an alap to create a separation in tonalities with other voices such as the chorus. Further, lyrics were distributed between the chorus and the lead singers to signify the importance of voice in creating an intimate register. While the chorus sings "Ramaiya vasta vaiya," or the hook line, the lead singers render the more personal lines, "Maine dil tujhko diya" (I have given my heart to you, only to you) (Jhingan 2009).

20 For instance, in *Adalat* (Kalidas, 1958), Nargis plays the role of Nirmal, a middle-class woman, trapped in a *kotha*. While performing a *ghazal* (in Lata's voice) to entertain the gathered community, Nirmal refuses to make eye contact with the listeners. The lyrics express the emotions of a tragic figure and her sense of entrapment, which have already been elaborated in the film's narrative. Thus, the sequence subtly distinguishes between the off-screen listeners/spectators who have been privy to the tragic life and the on-screen listeners in the *kotha* who are not invited to be part of this flow of knowledge (Jhingan 2022, 254).

21 Sudipto Kaviraj (2004) considers the dispersion of Hindi film songs beyond the spatial imaginaries of the exhibition theater. Referring to

blaring romantic Hindi film songs from the radio and Tannoy devices in Nabadwip during the 1960s, Kaviraj recalls the sensory quality of sound as a key component in the organization of public spaces (64). Moving out of the closed context of the film, the song becomes part of an entire repertoire of songs, with their "idiosyncratic sequencing of words . . . [and] internal economy of images," offering, according to Kaviraj, a collective experience and a certain "mood" of the modern city (66).

22 Rosie Thomas (2011), too, offers an important corrective to the visualist framework through her analysis of *Lal-e-Yaman* (Wadia, 1933), highlighting the innovative use of sound through disembodied singing, thus contributing to the film's popularity. Thomas alerts us not only to the way sound in early talkie cinema contested the power of visuality but also to the visceral appeal of the singing voice.

23 See, for example, Neepa Majumdar (2010), Pavitra Sundar (2023), Madhuja Mukherjee (2007; 2017), Budhaditya Chattopadhyay (2015), Samhita Sunya (2020), and Debashree Mukherjee (2020).

24 Inaugurating a historical framework in sound studies, Jonathan Sterne (2003) has critiqued the ocular centrism of Western philosophy, highlighting a range of listening practices grounded in rationality and modern ways of knowing.

25 Jonathan Sterne (2003) has discussed the telephone and telegraph as audile technologies that dramatically transformed the culture of listening.

26 In an earlier work I have drawn attention to how the spectator/listener is invited to respond to the sensuous qualities of the voice in film songs. See Jhingan (2011, 169).

27 Vasudevan draws attention to songs that involve a break from the diegetic setting, as characters resort to a direct mode of address, drawing sustenance from heterogeneous popular forms.

28 Aarti Wani (2016, 93) has argued that in the decade of the 1950s, songs gestured toward "a whole spectrum of feelings in the experiential universe of romantic love" that were denied expression in the narrative.

29 The concept of *darshan* or *darshana* draws on a Hindu religious practice where visiting a temple means to "take darshan," or to be able to see the deity, which involves invoking the deity's returned look at the devotee. In early scholarship on Indian cinema and popular film culture, the concept gained ascendancy as a marker of Indian cultural practices of iconization, as seen in mythological dramas, art practice, and folk rituals that got translated to the screen. The idea of *darshan* also involves a relation of

perception with figures like kings, powerful public figures, and stars. For an insightful discussion on *darshan* in Indian film studies, see Vasudevan (2000). Geeta Kapur (1987, 80) inaugurated a discussion on frontality as a mode of representation in multiple popular forms, including "word, the image, the design, the formative act," that has a bearing on the mode of address, such as in proscenium theater to foreground the way decorative scenes are mounted for iconic viewing. Madhava Prasad (1998, 19) has argued that because of its emphasis on the "image as an anchor, a resting point for the gaze," a frontal mode of address jeopardizes the frame's ability to apprehend the real. In her discussion on the modalities of film stardom in Indian cinema, Neepa Majumdar (2010, 143) has argued that frontality works to collapse the "metaphoric foreground and background, the surface and depth, of star identities," and reduce the gap between on-screen roles and off-screen information.

30 Anna Morcom's *Hindi Film Songs and the Cinema* (2007) is an important book-length study based on the textual analyses of film songs in their cinematic form. Drawing from ethnomusicology, Morcom insightfully discusses the production process, the industrial context, and the musical style of film songs, and their meaning in the narrative context of the film.

31 Iyer (2020) proposes the term "dance musicalization," instead of the commonly used "song picturization," to "address differences in production and reception modalities when a dancer-actor is featured in a film or a musical number" (28). Further, she remarks that in dance-driven production numbers, the "movement vocabulary planned for the [that] sequence influences the kind of song to be recorded" (47).

32 This echoes Brandon LaBelle's (2010, xvi) ideas on the special ability of sound to create a "geography of intimacy" that is inclusive of noise and intrusion.

33 Elaborating on his concept of acoustic territories, Brandon LaBelle has shown how sound opens up a field of interaction. See LaBelle (2010).

34 Aswin Punathambekar (2010, 844) notes the popularity of Bombay film songs on Radio Ceylon's innovative shows like *Binaca Geetmala* to highlight radio's role in making "films, songs and stars of Bombay cinema as part of the daily lives of listeners." Vebhuti Duggal (2018) has examined radio listening practices to highlight the way film songs formed the bedrock to create a dispersed terrain of film reception. Ravikant (2015) has mapped an intermedial history of Hindi cinema to discuss the film song's

intermeshed relationship with radio and print media. Radio, as Ravikant notes, became an affective aural network, connecting listeners to film music in the most intimate way. Neepa Majumdar (2009, 310) has shown how sound in Indian cinema privileged the listeners. In song sequences that featured singers performing on the radio, says Majumdar, sound fidelity was jettisoned to make way for a "multi-layered visualization of the sound source" that connected voices to bodies. The voice was given an independent status through a focus on the presence of the radio singer and the "mediations of audio technology through the image of the radio box and the listening face" (2009, 322).

35 Drawing on Deleuze and Guattari's concept of the assemblage, Francesco Casetti (2015, 81) notes that an "assemblage refers both to the connections between different elements and the new unity that is thus created."

36 Peter Manuel's (1993) work on the "cassette Revolution" highlights the emergence of diverse genres, an exponential growth in music production and listenership that began at the end of the 1970s.

37 Sangita Gopal and Sujata Moorti (2008, 24) have shown how the arrival of satellite television and digital technologies changed the production practices in the music industry that altered the relationship between song and film. Referring to their interactions with Javed Akhtar, they note how the film song has become "a kind of perk that is offered in the film," without having any organic relationship with the narrative. Anustup Basu (2010, 161) has suggested that with the greater presence of Bollywood films in the world market, song sequences have become an "eminently consumable eccentricity" in the transnational leisure economy. Basu further notes that as aural and visual spectacles, songs "remove bodies from the propositional flow of narratives," placing them in settings that lie outside the milieu of the story (162).

38 Michele Hilmes (2008) has insightfully argued that silence around television sound in media and sound studies scholarship is because television's multitextual form, with its wide range of genres, aesthetics, and modes of address, has not been given serious attention.

39 Though responses and performances by celebrity judges are scripted in advance, I contend that they bring out the sonic complexity of the televisual form, giving importance to sonority of diegetic music and its effect on the listener.

40 The Gramophone Company of India began its operations in 1901. Later, its name was changed to Gramophone Company (India) Limited. The records brought out by the Gramophone Company carried the trademark of HMV (His Master's Voice), which became a metonym for the company. In 2000, the name of the company was changed to Saregama India.

Chapter 1

1 "Nautch girls" was a term used by the British to describe the singing and dancing girls. The word "nautch" is corrupted from *nach*, which means dance.

2 In his work on the history of photography in India, Christopher Pinney has pointed to early photography's tendency to individuate owing to its techno-materiality. Pinney (2002, 110) argues that due to the slackening of exposure time, it was easier for the photographer to manage and shoot single persons rather than "marshalling collective bodies."

3 In early recordings, artists were asked to announce their names at the end of each recording. This was required because the wax masters were sent to Hanover to press the records, and this was considered the most foolproof method for identifying musicians. Secondly, the artists had to improvise and use their own ingenuity to present a *bandhish* within the stipulated time of three minutes.

4 Amlan Das Gupta (2005) has insightfully suggested that women artists used the neutral space of recordings to recast their musical identities.

5 Further, women, according to Chatterjee (1993, 126), were subjected to a new patriarchy that was based on creating "a marked *difference* in the degree and manner of westernization of women, as distinct from men, in the modern world of the nation."

6 See Sarah Niazi's (2011, 6) unpublished dissertation.

7 Saleem Kidwai (2004) has insightfully suggested that the arrival of cinema allowed the courtesans to renegotiate their identity. Many courtesans continued to perform in *mehfils*, even though they were regularly singing for gramophone companies and the film industry.

8 All India Radio also devised ways to bar women whose "respectability" was considered tainted. They were not allowed to sing for their music programs.

9 In her work on musicophilia in Mumbai, Tejaswini Niranjana (2020, 29) has elaborated on the women from the Devadasi tradition who moved

from Goa to Bombay and took training in Hindustani music from the Muslim *ustads*.

10 Bhirdikar (2007, 229) adds that Hirabai Barodekar could claim a *gharana* identity not only because of her music but also because she was able to mold her image as "both gharanedar and respectable in the larger context of the fashioning of respectable femininity on the Marathi stage and by extension in public concerts."

11 In chapter 3, I have focused on the writings of the music critics to highlight the easy connections they made between the emotional register of the songs and the singers' personal lives.

12 Analyzing some of the testimonies of women artists from early cinema, Reena Mohan and Dibya Choudhuri (1996, 4–14) have noted that "the logic was circular: respectable women did not join films, women who did were disreputable, therefore any woman who did join must be an outcaste in society."

13 In another interview on Doordarshan, Rajkumari recalls, "There were no microphones in *natak* (theatre). We had to amplify our voice and sing at the top of our voice. I used to work in *natak* and then I was chosen for films." www.youtube.com/watch?v=L5KPw3ulx3U.

14 As cited in C. S Lakshmi (2000).

15 There are several claims made about the origin of the use of playback singing. In an interview, Saraswati Devi (1983, 72), considered to be India's first female music composer, said that she introduced playback singing in *Jawani ki Hawa* (1934), when her sister Chandraprabha, the actor-singer, could not sing due to a bad throat. "I asked Chandraprabha to move her lips while I kept the mike in front of me." The other claim is that music composer Rai Chand Boral introduced the technique in *Dhoop Chaon* (1935), as suggested to him by the sound recordist Mukul Bose (Ranade 2006).

16 This allowed for the presence of larger orchestras and the introduction of chordal harmony.

17 In most of the songs, we see her directly engaging the camera, engaging as it were a live community of listeners. In this direct mode of address, the voice of the singer remains locked to her body. It is only in the interlude sections of the song that the camera reveals other characters or objects, thus expanding the visual field.

18 According to Ashraf Aziz (2003, 10), Noor Jahan translated vocalization to overt action.

19 In his work on the music arrangers of the Bombay film music industry, Bhaskar Chandavarkar (1987) has highlighted the importance of scoring or orchestration in transforming film music of the 1940s. The arrangers from Goa and Pondicherry were largely responsible for introducing chordal harmony in film music, adding color and richness to the basic composition of the music directors. The singers were now expected to sing live with a larger number of musicians, which accorded these musical entities greater complexity. Therefore, we can assume that this would have led to composers seeking trained singers, thus contributing to the separation between the actors and the singers.

20 In her discussion on the 1940s, Kiranmayi Indraganti (2016, xxvi) shows how women could make active professional and personal choices to sing for the industry.

21 As Raghunath Seth (1980, 55) has written, "With Lata Mangeshkar the new era of women's voices began."

22 In her account in *Film Sangeet* (1965) Mangeshkar writes that it was Biswas who taught her how to breathe with singing without breaking the *tala* and the *laya* of the song (cited from a translated reproduction of the article in *Cinema Vision*, Mangeshkar 1983b).

23 In popular print media, an oft-repeated remark, "if Asha's voice has body, Lata's has soul," has been attributed to Anil Biswas. See Bharatan, (1971c, 45). In his work on playback, Gregory Booth (2008, 46) has argued that Lata's projected a "nonphysical and nonsexualized public persona."

24 One of the singers who had to quit the industry after 1947 was Zohrabai Ambalewali. She gave her reasons in an interview in 1972: "I quit singing because I was no longer asked to sing the heroine's songs and after singing for the leading stars for so many years, I was not willing to become a chorus girl." As quoted in *Madhuri*, February 1, 1971, 21.

25 Sundar reframes Michel Chion's audiovisual contract specifically to discuss it in the context of gendered discourse of playback singing in Hindi cinema and to theorize that Lata Mangeshkar's vocal dominance in playback singing was based on certain anxieties about the body being a site of vice.

26 Another instance is Manek Premchand's biographical account in which he writes about the struggle that the Mangeshkar family faced when Dina

Nath Mangeshkar died in 1942. Singing for films, according to Premchand (2003, 275), was not an option at that time, as Lata's voice was "too thin for the heavy-type heroines of the time." The emphasis here is not on Mangeshkar's age but the physicality of her voice in relation to the "heavy-type" heroines.

27 In a conversation with Nasreen Munni Kabir (2009, 162), Lata shares, "I actually don't change my voice, but when I sing for Saira Banu or any other star, I think to myself, 'if I sing like this it will look right for her.' So I add some touch to add to her personality."

28 Broadcasting in India was totally in the control of the postcolonial nationalist state until the opening of the economy in the early 1990s. This applied to both radio and television.

29 Majumdar (2009, 304–5) makes a distinction between technical and cultural noise. The former involves the aural training of listeners in their negotiation of the machine element of radio or gramophone. At the same time, both the gramophone and radio regulated and standardized cultural noise, associated with the timbre of the female voice.

30 *Dal-bhaat* is a simple meal of rice and lentils.

31 In an interview by Gangadhar Gadgil (1967, 37), Mangeshkar shared that she had to overcome prejudices as "it used to be said disparagingly in those days that songs sung by Maharashtrians smelt of dal and rice! I had to disprove it and cultivate a Hindustani accent as well. There was so much else to learn, too, and I had to do it mostly by myself." And in her conversation with Kabir (2009, 67). In a biographical piece Sumit Mitra (1983a, 42) wrote, "One day, Naushad introduced her to Dilip Kumar, the actor, in a third-class compartment of a local train. Dilip Kumar was amused by her Marathified Hindi, and teased her till 'my ears tingled in shame.' Over three decades later, Dilip Kumar himself recalls the incident and says his own ears tingle when he hears Lata pronouncing each Hindi and Urdu word with a rare eclat."

32 In an interview, Lata acknowledged that she had picked up the pronunciation of Urdu words like *beqaraar* or *paighaam* by listening to Noor Jahan's songs carefully (1983a, 45).

33 As Girija Rajendran (1983, 42) has noted, Lata Mangeshkar had to struggle to "render songs in a pitch that was not hers."

34 Alison Arnold (1991, 145) suggests that Lata followed Noor Jahan in "terms of her own narrow vocal sound, and also introduced to the Hindi

film song a higher vocal register, pushing to the upper extreme of her wide vocal range."

35 In the same interview with Ashok Ranade, Rajkumari (1983, 17) notes, "Today, I will have to sing the way I am told to sing. The way another sings."

36 For example in songs like "Chup chup khade ho zaroor koi baat hai" from the film *Badi Behen* (Kashyap) and "Uthaye ja unke sitam" from the film *Andaz* (Khan), both released in 1949, the scale is much lower than in "Jab se balam ghar aaye" from the film *Awaara* (Kapoor, 1951).

37 However, this shift needs to be seen both musically as well as via the new codes of femininity being presented on-screen by female stars. In terms of musicality, the singers' ability to sing at a higher pitch gave composers greater room for tonal complexity in the melodic development of the song. Ashok Da Ranade (2006, 409) has noted that "wide pitch-range, quickness of movement in all directions, [and] considerable timbral variety" were the virtues of Lata's voice. On the other hand, technology has also been seen to play a hand, with preference being given to higher pitches. According to Sanjeev Kohli (2007), Laxmikant Pyarelal, or LP, introduced high-pitched singing because they used to record in Mehboob Studios, where the machines were "bad and the quality [of sound] was distorted." Given the fact that the popularity of songs depended on the sale of records and their proliferation on radio, composers preferred to work with singers who could sing at higher pitches.

38 The vocal range of male singers is considered naturally higher than that of female singers. Male singers sang at a lower pitch in duet songs to accommodate the female vocal range. With Lata Mangeshkar singing at a relatively higher pitch, even the duet songs were recorded at a higher pitch. Shankar Jaikishan, Madan Mohan, and Lakshmi Kant Pyarelal are known to have recorded songs at higher pitches.

39 It is in the third line of both of the *antaras* that the voice hits a very high note, in excess of the star's performance on-screen. See 1.59 seconds and 3.31 seconds on www.youtube.com/watch?v=Fvi7bfgWsK4.

40 Lata Mangeshkar won the first "Best Playback Singer" award by *Filmfare* for "Aaja re pardesi" from the film *Madhumati* (Roy) in 1958.

41 Unlike the earlier example of "Rasik balma," in which Mangeshkar's voice touched a very high note in only one line of the *antara*, creating a gap between the performance of the actor and that of the singer, here

the entire song was recorded at a pitch with which Mangeshkar was not comfortable.

42 Though Mangeshkar was able to forge a new identity distinct from that of the earlier singers through the use of her high pitch, we cannot overlook her struggle to sing at a vocal range in which she was comfortable.

43 Bhaskar (2012, 174) elaborates on the Indian melodramatic form during the period of incipient modernity, where human desires of both men and women are articulated but their "full bodies consummation and realization are denied."

44 Since Lata sang so many songs with the alap, several fans have assembled these alaps and uploaded the videos.

45 The Five-Year Plans were inaugurated by the Nehruvian state in postcolonial India to execute a planned development in the country through an accent toward greater role of the state in accord with socialist principals.

46 The use of the "double" here is different from the "double role," in which the same star plays two look-alike characters. Yet, in this sequence there is a distinct similarity in the hairstyle and persona of the dancing girl and those of Rita. Though Rita is wearing a gown and the actor who is dancing to the song is wearing a sari, both have similar body structures and are depicted as westernized, modern women.

47 Kavita is married to an overworked but upright lawyer who is unable to devote much time to his family. Realizing Kavita's feeling of loneliness, Nirmal encourages her to pursue her taste in music.

48 All of the songs performed by Nargis in *Lajwanti* were sung by Asha Bhosle. According to off-screen discussions, S. D. Burman had stopped inviting Lata to sing for his compositions after a misunderstanding in the latter half of the 1950s. It was in 1961 that the partnership was resumed. During this intervening phase, it was Asha Bhosle who became the preferred voice for S. D. Burman. In films like *Lajwanti* (Suri, 1958), *Nau Do Gyarah* (Anand 1957), *Sujata* (Roy, 1959), and *Bombai Ka Babu* (Khosla, 1960), Asha Bhosle became the dominant voice. In these songs, Asha tries to match the tonalities of her older sister, Lata Mangeshkar.

49 Beyond the confines of the courtesan-based films, *mujras* have been an integral part of Bombay social films, with *tawaifs* represented as antiheroines (*Bazooband* [Sagar, 1954], *Anhonee* [Abbas, 1952]) or as side heroines (*Devdas* [Roy, 1955], *Kala Pani* [Khosla, 1958]) or appearing in a parallel narrative (*Chaudvin Ka Chand* [Dutt, 1960]). In several films, these songs

bring to life the social milieu inhabited by the protagonists (*Sahib Bibi aur Ghulam* [Alvi, 1962], *Bahu Begum* [Sadiq, 1967], *Dharmputra* [Chopra, 1961]), or the antihero (*Zindagi aur Khwab* [Banerji, 1961]).

50 For instance, in "O jaanewale ruk ja koi dam," Chandramukhi performs for only the hero and his friend. Instead of the harmonium and the sarangi, the song gives prominence to the sound of the flute and the sarod, but the source of the sound of these instruments is not a part of the visual field.

51 See Mubarak Begum's interview by Sheila Vesuna (Begum 1992, 56–57). In this interview Mubarak Begum describes how composers stopped giving her singing assignments. When she asked them why she was being sidelined, they said, "You can only sing ghazals, not geets. Was the Hamrahi number a ghazal, I'd like to ask them. Then they said my voice was too different to be accepted. But the masses liked my voice."

52 For instance, in *Madhumati* (Roy, 1958), Mubarak Begum sings "Hum hale dil sunayenge, suniye ke na suniye" (I will tell you my woeful tales, though you may not even care to listen). In the film this song is performed by a *tawaif* for the villain (Pran) at his *haveli* (mansion). The song is cut off abruptly with the entry of the hero. Not a single shot of the actor who performs the *mujra* is shown in a close-up or with lip sync, pointing toward the marginal status of the song, the actor, and the playback singer. Despite this, "Hum hale dil sunayenge" drew an enthusiastic response, being a great favorite of Mubarak's fans as its complete version circulated through LPs and cassettes.

53 In duet songs of Hindi films, two characters sing the same composition of a song while interacting with each other.

54 This is a clear departure from the norm. In Bombay films it was common practice to have two versions of a song, one sad and the other happy but set to the same tune.

55 In his autobiography on Lata Mangeshkar, Raju Bharatan (1995, 225) has referred to this song to suggest how Madan Mohan erred in trying to follow O. P. Nayyar by using Asha Bhosle's voice to please the "trade." As he wrote, "That such Ashaised Nayyarising" should have intruded on the silver screen—though not on the rpm record—into an "Adalat' Lata-Madan classic like *Jaa re jaa saajna kaahe sapnon mein aaye*—was something that hurt the ear." The 78 RPM record of the song (N52795) was brought out as a solo san Asha Bhosle's voice.

56 For instance, Raju Bharatan (1971c) quotes this in "Ghost Voice Goes a Haunting," in *Filmfare*, attributing it to Anil Biswas.

57 Kiranmayi Indraganti (2016, 92) has argued that an important factor in playback stardom is the hierarchy between lead singers and secondary singers, where the latter were deployed to sing for minor characters and for young starlets and debutants in the industry.

58 In his biography of Lata Mangeshkar, Raju Bharatan (1995, 40) has referred to Mangeshkar's voice in "Aayega aanewala" as "the ghost voice that haunts."

59 The term *pukar* refers to a high-pitched intonation in North Indian classical vocal music that is used to create a heightened effect.

60 The sequence shows an exchange between Dai Maa (Lalita Pawar) and Poonam as she is getting ready to leave the mansion. Dai Maa warns Poonam not to cross moral boundaries by going out at night and meeting people when her husband is away.

61 In an interview by Yatindra Mishra (2016, 333), Lata has recalled that she was well aware of the situation of the song in *Kohraa*. Because the woman's gestures and facial expressions were not made visible on-screen, she got a free hand to push the song in the direction that she wanted. She adds that she tried to bring in the expression of an intoxicated woman who is slowly becoming distant in her vocal performance (translated by the author).

62 In the opening sequence of *Rebecca* (Hitchcock, 1940), we hear the acousmatic voice of Joan Fontaine, who plays the role of the second wife. Fontaine's voice-over mentions the presence of a supernatural power, pointing toward Rebecca as a ghostly figure.

63 In the sequence that follows the song, Poonam's whispering voice almost leads Rajeshwari to her death.

64 This resonates with Mary Anne Doane's (1987, 174) analysis of *Rebecca* as a film that chronicles the emergence and disappearance of female subjectivity.

65 *Mangalsutra* is a particular kind of necklace made with black beads that is a sign of marriage worn by a married woman.

66 Interestingly, the music director for both the films *Mera Saaya* and *Sanjog* was Madan Mohan. In a way, through this sequence with the gramophone player, the film was acknowledging the popularity of Lata Mangeshkar's songs composed by Madan Mohan.

67 What follows is a flashback sequence, where we are introduced to Geeta singing the song at a party while Dutt is playing the piano looking lovingly at his wife. This is the moment in the film when the voice is finally assigned to the body.

68 Several of these songs have been included in Lata Mangeshkar's list of top ten or top twenty-five songs. For instance, in a list of Lata's twenty-five favorite songs, both "Aayega aanewala" from the film *Mahal* (Amrohi, 1949) and "Lag ja gale" from the film *Woh Kaun Thi?* (Khosla, 1964) are included. See *Filmfare*, March 12, 1971, 27.

69 Lata Mangeshkar herself has acknowledged that "Aayega aanewala" played a crucial role in her meteoric rise in the industry (cited in Bharatan 1995, 40).

70 In "Aaja re pardesi," Salil Chowdhury used the seventh chord or the "chord of incompletion" to express unfulfilled desires.

71 Text credited to A. Virendra Luthra on the album cover.

Chapter 2

1 Another category is that of shape-shifting snakes, which turned into female bodies. For instance, in films like *Nagin* (Jaswantlal, 1976) and *Nagina* (Malhotra, 1986), Reena Roy and Sri Devi performed a "snake dance" to popular songs by Lata Mangeshkar.

2 *Bazaare-husn* literally means a market where beautiful women can be bought and sold. In *Pakeezah* (1972), Amrohi created a grand setting for the *Bazaare-husn* sequence that was expensively mounted to show a vibrant bazaar with several *kothas* where courtesans can be seen entertaining men with music and dance.

3 While the songs of *Pakeezah* (Amrohi, 1972) were composed by Ghulam Mohammed, the background score was composed by Naushad Ali. In an interview, Naushad Ali (1992, 23) confirmed that he had composed the music for the *Bazaare-husn* sequence.

4 This is similar to Mubarak Begum's song in *Devdas* (Roy, 1955) presented in a disembodied voice to create an aural milieu for the exterior spaces of the bazaar area. See chapter 1.

5 In his work on early cinema, Noel Burch has alerted us to film's spatial illusion in providing the spectator access to deep space. Cited in Bruno (2002, 250).

6 When Meena Kumari dances to the song, we can see the deep space of the bazaar framed by the camera, with several dancers dancing in the background. What adds drama to the visual field is the camera showing the outbreak of a scuffle in the street in the background. While the visual field is dense and multilayered, the sonic field remains monophonic, with only the sound of "Inhi logon ne" playing on the soundtrack.

7 The background score for *Pakeezah* (Amrohi, 1972), a dense sonic space with voices of singers, tabla beats, sarangi strains, and murmurs, was recorded in a studio by Naushad. For an interesting discussion on the aesthetics of sound of Indian cinema, see Ashish Rajadhyaksha (2007), who has insightfully argued that there was a gradual tendency to replace sounds captured during the shooting stage with postproduction effects generated in the studio.

8 As in a typical fast-paced *dadra*, the rhythmic beats of the percussion instruments play a dominant role in "Inhi logon ne." But what is noticeable here is the amplified use of the sound of *ghungroo*, or dancing bells, as part of the percussion elements of the song.

9 A story describing Meena Kumari's return to the set of *Pakeezah* (Amrohi, 1972) with photographs was prominently carried by *Filmfare* in its April 1964 issue.

10 For example, "Chalte chalte" is performed by a younger-looking Meena Kumari. But the next time she performs the same song for the Nawab on his houseboat, we see a much older star. This is followed by a sequence in the forest where a much younger-looking Meena Kumari sings "Mausam hai ashkana."

11 See Roshmila Mukherjee (1994).

12 Padma Khanna played marginal roles like the westernized vamp or the villain's sidekick. In an interview, Padma Khanna recalled that Meena Kumari asked her to copy her gait closely during the dance (R. Mukherjee 1994).

13 "Hari bin kaise jioon ri," sung by Vani and available on the *Guddi* record album, was never used in the film.

14 In *Parichay*, Jaya plays the role of Rama, who imbibes classical music from her talented father, Nilesh (Sanjeev Kumar). The song "Beeti na bitai raina," sung by Bhupinder Singh and Mangeshkar, based on a classical raga, depicts Rama clad in a simple white sari, listening to and practicing with her father. The song poignantly foregrounds the father-daughter relationship, with Rama seen as the bearer of her father's musical legacy,

similar to Lata taking forward the legacy of her father, Dina Nath Mangeshkar.

15 Kanha is another name for Krishna, a revered deity of the Hindus. This is part of the Vaishnava mythology that describes Krishna's dalliance with Radha and other *gopis* from Vrindavan.

16 Raghu is hired by the family, desperate to find domestic help who will stick around and meet the demands of its eccentric and large household. But the climax of the film reveals that Raghu, armed with a reformist agenda, has a secret mission.

17 Though Jaya's dance is never explicitly framed as bharata natyam, the mudras and the costume gesture to a broad appropriation of the form. Moreover, after the performance is over, Raghu informs the family that he had worked as a cook for Kancheevaram Guru Ellappa Pillai and was therefore able to help Krishna prepare for her performance.

18 I would like to thank Krishna Menon, a trained bharata natyam dancer and professor at AUD, for pointing this out to me.

19 Jaya performs the song wearing an ankle-length sari similar to the way Balasaraswati wore her costume. This is a clear departure, since in Hindi cinema a bharata natyam dancer was usually shown wearing the traditional costume. Guru Ellappa Pillai is mentioned by Raghu (Rajesh Khanna) as his previous employer. He was Balasaraswati's *nattuvanar*. I would like to thank Krishna Mennon for pointing this out to me.

20 In her work on gender and the politics of voice in Karnatik music, Amanda Weidman analyzes Rukmini Devi Arundale's writings. According to Weidman (2006, 129), "although she (Devi) could not completely efface the physicality or eroticism of dance, her writings point to the necessity, in her view, of putting physicality to some higher use. Music was, for her the divine influence that would insure this."

21 Raj Kapoor is also known to have been miffed by Lata's attempt to ensure part of the royalty payment from songs for singers.

22 Lata includes Jaya's name in the list of actresses who did full justice to her songs on-screen.

23 For instance, in another piece in 1970, Bharatan mentions the monopoly of a few playback singers in the industry, while adding that music directors had been gripped by "fear psychosis" and had bartered their self-respect for "the patronage of certain singers and filmmakers" (35).

24 Lata Mangeshkar won two National Awards for playback singing for songs that were performed by Jaya in the 1970s. They were "Beeti na bitai" from *Parichay* (Gulzar, 1972) and "Roothe roothe piya" from *Kora Kaagaz* (Ganguly, 1974).

25 *Sitara* means "star" in Hindi and Hindustani.

26 This aural strategy is unusual for films of that time, since the usual practice was to privilege the sonic quality of the song over all other sounds. Though this strategy was not repeated in other songs, the soundtracks of the nightclub songs acquired a distinct aural style.

27 Asha Kasbekar (2001, 289), for instance, notes the vamp figure, while providing an antidote to the heroine's traditional image, became a locus of voyeuristic pleasure through her erotically staged presence in the nightclub.

28 In a detailed discussion on song sequences performed by nightclub singers and office girls with Anglo-Indian names and fluid religious identity, Wani (2016, 102–3) shows how these urban cosmopolitan women offered a "route to modern selfhood" by singing songs about love and its fragile pleasures.

29 Bradley Shope (2014) has highlighted the popularity of Latin American rhythms and their inclusion in the repertoire of live bands.

30 Some of these films are *12 O'Clock* (Chakravorty, 1958); *China Town* (Samanta, 1962); *Anari* (Mukherjee, 1959); *Jaali Note* (Samanta, 1960); *Dil Apna Aur Preet Parai* (Sahu, 1960); *Kala Bazaar* (Anand, 1960); and *Chhote Nawab* (Akbar, 1961).

31 Helen plays the role of Suzie, who is in love with Mike, a Chinatown gangster who turns out to be the long lost brother of Shekhar (Shammi Kapoor).

32 An interesting example is "Jab nain mile nainon se," sung by Shamshad Begum (*Jadoo* [Kardar, 1951]), where the sound of castanets and the piano dominate along with the use of energetic chorus voices. The song was performed by Nalini Jaiwant, a "deviant" who falls in love with a police constable.

33 See www.youtube.com/watch?v=_oW6tZ-2REs.

34 In *Jaali Note* (Samanta, 1960), Helen's lighthearted nightclub song with Bhosle's vocals in "O mister dil, badi mushkil" (O mister romantic, what trouble you have put me in) includes Dev Anand and a male chorus singing "Ae chiki chiki" in the interlude sections with Rafi taking over

the song. In another song from *China Town* (Samanta, 1962) Helen sings "Yamma yamma, tu parwana main shama" (Yamma yamma you are moth, and I am fire).

35 Ranjani Mazumdar (2007, 90) describes the *Kati Patang* cabaret as an instance of a "dichotomized narrative of sexuality presented through a tableau framing the 'westernized vamp' and the 'Indian woman' as a recurring trope."

36 The *Kati Patang* song sharpens moral boundaries through the edgy use of attire, color, hairdo, body language, and lyrics. Asha Parekh is playing the role of a young widow dressed in a white sari, while Shabnam is dressed in a provocative orange jumpsuit with slits on the thighs. The choreography deployed slithering movement on the floor by both the female dancer and her male accompanists.

37 In an interview with Arbaaz Khan, Helen has shared that this song was inspired from a show at the Crazy Horse club of Paris. www.youtube.com/watch?v=lz0fohkOXzo. Accessed on January 5, 2024.

38 The opening scream was also included in the LP record released by Polydor in which "Kaanp rahi main" was listed on side one of the record.

39 The theme of rape, distilled through the woman's dancing (and singing) body, was never really explored in the film.

40 According to Aniruddha Bhattacharjee and Balaji Vittal (2011), Uthup introduced not only Western bass but also the correct intonation of English words without the fake accent.

41 However, Usha Uthup, who started her professional life with singing in Trincas in Calcutta, soon realized that she could sing for only the "bad girls" of popular cinema.

42 In fact, the popular songs of *Qurbani* were reintroduced in the market with English lyrics, a trend that was repeated during the audio boom of the 1990s.

43 Biddu composed *Disco Deewane*, a pop album with Nazia and her brother Zoheb, in 1981, and it became a massive hit.

44 For example, in "Mere naseeb mein," Lata stressed on "re" in "mere" to suggest an anglicized accent.

45 The three songs mentioned here are "Ab to ji hone laga" from the film *Mr. and Mrs. 55* (Dutt, 1955), "Kabhi aar kabhi paar" from *Aar Paar* (Dutt, 1954), and "Leke pehla pehla pyar" from the film *CID* (Khosla, 1956).

46 Sundar takes forward Martha Seifert's (2017, 70) observation "that the technological separation of the song from the singer meant that the image of singing did not have to reflect the physicality of the bodily production."

47 See "Ab ke baras bhej bhaiya ko babul" (This year, dear father, ask my brother to visit me), sung by Asha Bhosle. www.youtube.com/watch?v=e-UlyMrUzjc.

48 Though there is never a direct reference to caste, folk performers or street singers are usually referred to as *Bhands* or *Mirasis* or *nachne wali*, which marks them as women from marginalized castes.

49 Hema Malini performed the role of a working-class woman with a shrill voice, a sharp tongue, and a mobile body in films like *Raja Jani* (Segal, 1972) and *Sholay* (Sippy, 1975).

50 Another notable song is "Dilbar" (My beloved), from *Caravan* (Hussain, 1971), where we see Aruna Irani playing the role of an itinerant singer/dancer performing to Lata's voice. The choreography, the dance movements, and Irani's bodily gestures perfectly match Mangeshkar's erotically charged staccato voice.

51 Lata sang songs for other heroines as well who pretended to be drunk in a public soiree, especially in the films of the late '60s and early '70s. For instance, "Sharabi, sharabi, mera naam ho gaya" (Drunkard, that is my name now) for Meena Kumari in the film *Chandan Ka Palna* (Memon, 1967) and "Haan ji haan maine sharab pi hai" (Yes, yes, I have been drinking alcohol) for Hema Malini in *Seeta Aur Geeta* (Sippy, 1972).

52 Shamshad Begum sings for Biswajeet as a "woman," while Asha Bhosle lends her voice to Babita, who is dressed as a man.

53 Chhaya Ganguly won the National Award for the "Best Female Playback Singer" the song.

54 In an interview, Rekha (1993) has described the evening when Muzzaffar Ali offered her the role of Umrao Jaan. "He invited me to listen to the story. When I went to his house Khayyamsaab was waiting for me. They kept playing Begum Akhtar's *ghazals* to give me the 'feel of the subject.' That's the kind of music the film would have, Khayyamsaab explained."

55 Personal communication with Khayyam.

56 In *Alaap* (Mukherjee, 1977), a film based on the life of a classical musician, Kumari Faiyyaz and Dilraj Kaur broadened the range of female voices, while Runa Laila's "Do deewane is sheher mein," (two crazy lovers in the

city) from the film *Gharonda* (Bhimsain, 1977), made it to the top ten popular songs on the Geetmala list.

57 The erotic content of women's songs describing amorous encounters with men or the lascivious relationship between a woman and her *devar* (brother-in-law), usually sung in private gatherings of women during weddings, was now getting mass marketed through cassettes (Manuel, 1993).

58 In *Batwara* (Datta, 1989), for instance, "Yeh ishq dank bichua ka" (This love is like a scorpion bite) opens with Ila Arun's voice accompanying a high-angle shot of a group of women dancing in black *lehengas*. At the end of the first line of the *mukhda*, a chorus takes over and the rest of the song is then performed by Amrita Singh using Lata Mangeshkar's voice.

59 Pallavi is shown dancing and playing with water in sheer joy with her friends. The song "Megha re megha" (Rain-filled clouds) is sung by Lata Mangeshkar with accompanying vocals by Ila Arun and a female chorus.

60 Viren learns that Pallavi is the daughter of his father's close friend, a well-respected elder from the Rajput clan.

61 *Registan* is the Hindi word for desert. In contrast Rajasthan is a geo-political territory.

62 The reference to "choodiyan" (bangles) in the lyrics of "Morni baga ma" is introduced by Pallavi and resonates with Sridevi's popular performance of "Mere hathon mein nau nau choodiyan hai" (My hands are adorned with nine bangles) in *Chandni* (Chopra, 1989) with Lata Mangeshkar's voice.

63 In her early days in the industry, Sunidhi Chauhan dazzled her listeners and music composers in the industry by singing "Morni," by incorporating the style of both Ila Arun and Lata Mangeshkar. See www.youtube.com/watch?v=KaQcwxvRk7Q.

64 A duet song's conventional structure involves the opening of the *mukhda* or refrain by one singer, followed by its repetition by the co-singer. The *mukhda* is followed by an interlude created by instrumental music. The *antara* or stanzas are divided between the two singers with an interlude between the two stanzas. Both singers sing the same tune and follow a single rhythmic structure. In "Morni," however, Ila Arun's sections are sung in a slow tempo and at a lower scale, when compared to Lata's sections. Secondly, after the first *antara*, Ila Arun intrudes into the instrumental section, performing in an improvisatory style, invoking a secondary layer to the song that carries a residual trace but does not get picked up

by Lata. This layering, which is very common in the contemporary song with digital software, was unusual for the time in "Morni."

65 "Choli Ke Peeche" got involved in a debate on obscenity and vulgarity in film songs due to its lyrics. In an interview, Ila Arun (1993), defended the song, arguing that it hails from the "rich and vibrant" folk tradition that often contains "naughty" lyrics. Arun mentions the folk tradition of *Naqtora* in Uttra Pradesh where some women get into role play and "exchange comments and verses. Often the verses are naughty, pointing to funny relationships between brothers-in-law, sisters-in-law, etcetera. And often the emphasis is on female anatomy and other details."

66 Subhash Ghai cast Neena Gupta to perform the role of the ethnic woman, miming Ila Arun's already established rustic voice, while Alka Yagnik, who had trained herself to sound like Lata, sang for Madhuri Dixit as Ganga. In this song sequence, Dixit is impersonating a dancing girl.

67 The "Choli" song was preceded by Dixit's sensual performance in the "Ek do teen" number from *Tezaab* (Chandra, 1988) and "Dhak dhak karne laga," from *Beta* (Kumar, 1992). It was followed by dancing numbers from films like *Hum Apke Hain Kaun* (Barjatya, 1994), *Anjaam* (Rawail, 1994), *Raja* (Kumar, 1995), and *Dil To Pagal Hai* (Chopra, 1997) Most of these numbers were choreographed by Saroj Khan. For a detailed discussion of the Dixit-Khan partnership, see Usha Iyer's *Dancing Women* (2020).

Chapter 3

1 These nine *rasas* or affective states are the erotic (*shringara*), comic (*hasya*), pathetic (*karuna*), furious (*raudra*), heroic (*vira*), terrible (*bhayanaka*), disgusting (*bibhatsa*), marvelous (*adbhuta*), and tranquil (*shanta*).

2 As I discuss later, Raju Bharatan wrote reviews of record albums of films published by HMV in his regular column titled "On Record." His discussions of radio broadcasts of film music were limited. However, he did respond in a general way to the popularity of some songs or singers based on radio shows.

3 In a column on completing two years of writing "On Record," Raju Bharatan (1968, 35) wrote that his column "has fulfilled a long felt need for a critical analytical evaluation of our film music."

4 In the mid-eighties, Bharatan started writing a regular column in the form of a quiz, in which he would ask readers to answer questions about various composers, varying from identifying the singers or the raga on which film

songs were based. Many of these quiz entries gave substantial information to readers about the tunes of these songs or anecdotes circulating about film music. These worked as clues, but also allowed Bharatan to give his opinions or general information about singers or a rivalry between composers and singers.

5 "Who's Afraid of the Mangeshkars?" appeared in the December 13, 1974, issue in which Bharatan reiterated his claim that the Mangeshkar sisters were blocking younger women singers. "Has Asha Forgotten O.P.?" appeared in the August 9, 1974, issue of *Filmfare*. Interestingly, the cover page prominently displayed the title of the article in bold text.

6 For instance, he writes, "It is this gift of melody that has fetched Vani Jairam the Mian Tansen award for her Mian Malhar melody of Bole re papihara. Young and well-schooled in her art, Vani has Lata for her model—even as Lata had Mallika-e-tarannum Noorjehan for her ideal. However as soon as Lata found her niche, she broke away to assert her individuality and how! Vani Jairam—who like Asha is endowed with a voice of her own—needs to develop a similar individuality if she hopes to build on the windfall of Bole re papihara. Unless she does so, moving in the shadow of the melody queen, she will end up as just another Suman—the poor man's Lata" (1972b, 33). Bharatan does not bother to explain why he thinks Lata is a role model for Vani Jairam.

7 Highmore is referring to the work of Alexander Baumgarten, a philosopher for whom "aesthetics was the field of sensate perception" and concerned with creaturely life. Baumgarten's work, according to Highmore (2010, 121), "recognized that philosophy's traditional occupation with logical and conceptual thinking simply remaindered whole territories of life."

8 For instance, see Bharatan (1974a). "Has Asha Forgotten O.P.?" carried a photograph of Asha with O. P. Nayyar. Similarly, see Bharatan (1977).

9 K. M. Nanavati, a naval commander, faced trial for the murder of Prem Ahuja, his wife's lover, in 1959. This sensational story received a lot of attention in the print media. Several films have been made inspired by this event.

10 See Bhosle (1964). The photograph has been credited to Jitendra Arya.

11 See also Manek Premchand (2003, 123–24).

12 The captions accompanying these photographs usually gave information to the readers about the recording of a song by the singing star for a particular film.

13 I am borrowing John Ellis's (2002, 93) argument that star images are "composed of clues rather than complete meanings."

14 "O mere lal aja" was performed by Nargis and sung by Lata in *Mother India* (Mehboob, 1957).

15 For instance, *Madhuri* carried a piece by Harish Tiwari (January 8, 1971) where the monopoly of a few playback singers dominating the industry was highlighted. Tiwari added that the music directors, in their zeal to grab more and more films, were not ready to invest in training new and upcoming singers.

16 For instance, in writing about Vani Jairam's success in films like *Guddi* (Mukherjee, 1971), Bharatan (1971d) wrote, "Now that Guddi has demonstrated that a new face looks so much sweeter with a new voice, will our overbusy music directors pause to give our jaded music a voice-lift? After all, Lata is 42, and Asha, though at her peak, is already 38." In "Has Asha Forgotten O.P.?," Bharatan's bias against the two sisters could be gauged by the tone of the entire piece, in particular in the way he quotes O. P. Nayyar, "They may block her (Vani Jairam) but for how long?" alluding to the domination of the two sisters of the industry (Bharatan 1974a).

17 I find it interesting that *Filmfare* chose Surinder Singh, a well-known vocalist in Hindustani classical music, for this response.

18 As shown earlier, Bharatan wrote several pieces criticizing Vividh Bharti for its countdown shows and request programs for either catering to the masses or being controlled by a few producers and music directors. For instance, he wrote that Vividh Bharti has "debased our taste" through "catchpenny commercialism" (Bharatan 1971a).

19 In his biography on Gauhar Jaan, Vikram Sampath (2010, 150) describes the celebrated courtesan's individualized performance style which made every single member of the audience feel she had sung exclusively for them.

20 As in the text of *thumris*, the beloved in film songs is often referred to as *shyam*, *saanvra*, or the dark one (all names for Krishna), with the female narrator addressing herself as *Radha* or *Meera*, drawing on the Vaishnava bhakti tradition of poetry (Booth 2008).

21 This process continued until the late mid-nineties, until directors like A. R. Rahman, Viju Shah, and Sandeep Chowta began to experiment with heavier reliance on electronic sounds.

22 The sound of musical instruments was raised during the interludes or the musical sections of the song and faded down when the singer started to sing in front of the microphone.
23 This is related to the production economies of film songs in the Bombay industry. If the singer or the musicians made mistakes, it meant re-recording the entire song, which could lead to delays and giving overtime payment to the musicians.
24 Responding to Dhurandhar's piece, Vishakhadutt D. Patil (1988, 9) from Bombay wrote a letter to the editor: "Dhurandhar crosses the limit when he states that it is his conviction that C. Ramachandra was head over heels in love with Lata Mangeshkar. Agreed there existed a special relationship between the great singer and the maestro which resulted in priceless songs like Yeh Zindagi Usiki hai . . . But to make such a statement is not only audacious but utterly laughable. Even Raju Bharatan in his forty years of writing has never made such a statement."
25 A three-part series carried out in *Madhuri* in the April 22, May 3, and May 20, 1988 issues.
26 Song from the film *Mohabbat Zindagi Hai* (Nirula, 1966).
27 In this article, Khushwant Singh, the author and editor of *Illustrated Weekly of India*, describes his meeting with Lata Mangeshkar, in the presence of Raju Bharatan. Singh (1970) quotes Bharatan, who credits Lata with "some" sixteen thousand discs. Bharatan claims his source to be a quote by J. G Stanford, deputy chief executive of EMI, as listing Lata among their top ten sellers in the world. Later, Raju Bharatan repeated this claim in an article in *Filmfare* (Bharatan 1971 c).
28 In 1987, Punita Bhatt carried a cover story on Lata in which she lashed out at Bharatan for being responsible for the Guinness mistake in the first place.
29 I am aware that Freud's understanding of fetish is located in the sense of sight.
30 As cited by Georgina Born (2011, 377–78).
31 *Dekh Kabira Roya* (Chakravarty, 1957), a farcical comedy involving three couples, is known for its classical-based music that was not attuned to the genre of the film. The songs that Bharatan mentions, "Tu pyar kare ya thukraye" (You love or reject me), "Ashqon se teri humne" (With my tears), and "Meri veena tum bin roye" (My lute cries for you), appear one after the other with the female actors lip-synching them in the film.

Chapter 4

1 The British-owned Gramophone Company of India (GCI) established a record-pressing factory in Calcutta in 1908. It started marketing its records under the label name "His Master's Voice," or HMV. According to Peter Manuel (1993, 37–38), GCI was able to maintain its dominance because of its well-established network with retailers, and by owning the only record-pressing factory in the country. In 1931, HMV was acquired by EMI, which became the largest recording company in the world. The RPG group took over the company in the latter half of the 1980s. Despite this takeover, it continued to use the HMV label. In this chapter, I have used HMV synonymously with GCI, since it has remained a popular and stable label for the company.

2 This view has been contested by others who claim that film songs need to be seen as commodities that have their independent status and routes of circulation.

3 The term "cover version" has a controversial history and has always been associated with the "inauthentic." In the 1950s and the '60s in America, music publishing companies decided to exploit the marketing potential of rhythm and blues music. Instead of simply marketing the recordings of black artists themselves, they introduced these songs by getting them re-recorded by white artists. This gave birth to rock and roll music. This also meant that the original black artists were deprived of their royalties. With the rise of the black rights movement, these cover versions received scathing criticism. According to Nicholas Cook (1998, 6–7), the discourse around rock music has, as a result, pushed the idea that "there was something dishonest about playing music that wasn't your own."

4 According to Kohli-Khandekar (2010, 183), Gulshan Kumar's T-Series pushed its revenues from Rs. 200 million in 1985 to Rs. 1.3 billion by 1989.

5 According to Ajit Kohli, the A&R Manager of SCI, *Karma* (Ghai, 1986) was the first film whose songs were brought out by SCI as cover versions. Kohli, 2007.

6 *Antakshari* is a musical game played in South Asia where the contestants sing popular film songs. Each contestant sings the refrain of a song, and the next team has to quickly pick a song that begins with the letter (in Hindi) on which the previous team ended its singing.

7 For instance, Raju Bharatan (1975) wrote, "After all, didn't it take even Lata a good four years to overcome the Noor Jahan fixation? And for how long Asha tried to be Lata. And to be Geeta when she was not Lata."

8 As Mukta Kodikal (1961b) wrote in *Filmfare*, "the playback singers seem content, even complacent, to be copies of existing top-notchers. Perhaps they may cry in self-defence that they hold these few top-ranking singers merely as their ideal. Why then the endeavour to turn themselves into facsimiles? Why no individuality? For, even in the era of actor-singers, a song made history because of the individuality of the singer."

9 In his biography on Lata, Raju Bharatan (1995, 366) has suggested that that singers like Alka, Kavita, Anuradha, and Poornima were rendering a song for Rs. 500, "on the express understanding that there was no guarantee the number would be retained."

10 The practice of dubbing had been deployed by the industry even in the "golden period" of the playback era, in some unusual circumstances when playback singers like Lata Mangeshkar were not available due to some illness.

11 Though the practice of dubbing was used for both female and male voices, it attracted more attention for female singers, as it got tied with the larger issue of the hegemonic control of the Mangeshkar sisters over the industry.

12 This resonates with the way journalists writing on Lata's early career noted that she was forced to sing songs that had been "composed in Noor Jahan's range," (see chapter 1).

13 Music composers like Kalyanji Anandji and Lakshmikant Pyarelal especially trained upcoming singers to prepare them for the music industry.

14 In another work, I have drawn attention to the "phenomenological experience of bodies that can 'hear' as well as be 'heard,' bodies that get immersed in the affective force field of musicality" (Jhingan 2011, 173).

15 In her insightful work on remixes, Vebhuti Duggal (2010, 51) has shown how singers were getting their names listed in business directories as replicas of particular playback singers like Mukesh or Rafi, getting their identity completely submerged in this practice of replication.

16 I want to thank an anonymous reviewer for pointing this out.

17 Quoted in Friedrich Kittler (1999, 45).

18 Quoted from a catalog released by HMV.

19 Quoted from a catalog released by HMV.

20 Quoted in Ashish Rajadhyaksha (2007). In pronouncing its judgment on September 9, 2003, on a case of copyright violation involving Super Cassette Industries Limited (T-series) and Bathla Cassette Industries, the Delhi High Court pronounced that "The voice is the soul and essence of a vocal rendering in a sound recording."

21 "*Time* on Lata Mangeshkar" (August 31, 1959) as cited in a box item in *Illustrated Weekly of India* (May 14, 1969, 16).

22 As reported in *Madhuri* by Suman Sarin (1987, 45). According to Sarin, a film on Lata Mangeshkar was shown at this event held in Oberoi Towers. In his speech at the event, Mr. R. P. Goenka, the chairman of HMV, reportedly said, "if HMV has survived in the last forty years, it is only because of Lata Mangeshkar."

23 Further, it was during the recording of songs from *Majboor* (Ajmeri, 1948) that music directors like Naushad and Khem Chand Prakash heard Lata's voice.

24 "Sun sahiba sun" (Listen, sir, listen) became a huge sensation and was performed by several copy artists.

25 HMV PMLP 1170-1173 and TPH 41316-41319.

26 Prominent among these were her photographs with Jawaharlal Nehru and Indira Gandhi.

27 *My Favourites* Volume II PMLP 1121-1122.

28 The other two objects that Stewart discusses are the miniature and the gigantic.

29 This advertisement appeared in *Screen* on October 2, 1989. *Lekin* was produced by Lata Mangeshkar and her brother Hridayanath.

30 See Siraj Syed (1989). According to Syed, HMV was finding it difficult to meet the demand for this album due to its growing popularity.

31 By the end of the 1980s compact discs had entered the market, further expanding the scale of the audio business.

32 CD PSLP 5590.

33 According to a report, at the release function of *Shraddhanjali: My Tribute to the Immortals* (1992), held at Leela Kempinski Hotel in Bombay, Lata Mangeshkar lit ceremonial lamps under the portraits of all of the six immortal artists. An audiovisual presentation on the making of *Shraddhanjali* was also shown. *Film Information*, October 3, 1992.

34 During the Kargil crisis, Lata Mangeshkar was flooded with offers to sing in Delhi in memory of the *jawans* who had died at Kargil. "Ae mere watan

ke logo" was constantly played by news channels when the bodies of *jawans* were brought back from Kargil. The song resurfaced on television channels after the Mumbai terror attacks in November 2008. See Lata Mangeshkar (1999, 118–19).

35 Noor Jahan passed away in 2000 and Suraiya passed away in 2004.

36 Version singers like Vandana Vajpayee were reported by magazines to be peeved that "their versions were frowned upon, while what Lata ji does, doesn't raise an eyebrow" (S. Mukherjee, 1994).

37 Many singers felt victimized by the T-series' partnership with Anuradha Paudwal. For instance, when Indra Kumar sold the music rights of *Dil* (Kumar, 1990), to SCI, two of Alka Yagnik's songs were re-recorded by Anuradha Paudwal. The voice tracks by Alka Yagnik were "scrapped" to make way for Paudwal's voice. See Praveena Bhardwaj (1990).

38 According to Gauri Warudi (1991), each company was promoting a female singer. Anupama Deshpande was promoted by Venus while Poornima was called a Tips girl.

39 Anuradha Paudwal, author's interview, January 24, 2010.

40 Anuradha Paudwal, author's interview, January 24, 2010

41 Quoted from the HMV catalog.

Chapter 5

1 For an insightful discussion on global flows of Hindi Film Songs, see Gopal and Moorti (2008).

2 Punathambekar (2013, 6–7) draws on Henry Jenkins's concept of media convergence to trace the emergence of Bollywood as a global media industry.

3 The prepublicity posters of *Aashiqui* (Bhatt, 1990) foregrounded the sonic elements of the film with an image of a young couple locked in an embrace with a jacket covering their faces. This was a departure from the standard practice of introducing a film to spectators through the iconic images of the stars.

4 In an interview with the author, Richa Sharma recalls: "When I started out it was difficult for me. I wanted to make a place for my voice. They used to think that *koi banjaran ja rahi hai to uske upar apki awaz use hogi ya phir koi* [my voice could only be used for a gypsy woman or] background song . . . or some folk situation, but not on any heroine. Not on any actress will your voice be used, because of the thickness of the voice, the power

of the voice. So, it was difficult and it took me three years or so in that phase. I needed some reason to be here [Bombay]. T series was making a remix of Ila Arun songs which she was supposed to sing. But she had some differences with the company and they were looking for singers who could match that voice, and I mimic Reshma ji, Noorjehan and Ila Arun's voice. I used to sing Ila Arun songs and they felt that I sing in the same genre. That album became a big hit and then the problem was that I got more offers to sing those kinds of songs. But that was not me" (Sharma 2010).

5 The show was named *Close-Up Antakshari* because it was sponsored by Close-Up toothpaste

6 Some of the contestants who made their mark were given an opportunity to record a few songs for *Mohabbatein* (2000), a film by Yash Chopra.

7 Kohli worked with Polydor and HMV for many years, and was instrumental in expanding the content of both music publishing companies. In the 1990s, he joined Yash Raj Chopra and set up Metavision, the company that produced *Meri Awaz Suno*. He is also the son of Madan Mohan, one of the key music composers in the industry. Interview on December 28, 2007.

8 This again underscores the importance of the acoustic memory of Lata Mangeshkar's voice. While Akhtar sings the same words and the same tune running parallel to the clip of the song playing on the projected screen, there is a distinct gap between Akhtar's vocal performance and the sonic trace of Lata's voice.

9 Originally based on the British television series Pop Idol, this format was introduced by Fremantle Media in South Africa, the United States, and Malaysia before it made its way into India.

10 There has been a considerable amount of scholarly interest in the entry of Hindi film songs in "various spaces of globalization" (Gopal and Moorti 2008, 7). Sharmishtha Gooptu (2007, 20) has gestured toward the harvesting of sound technology as "an innovative resource for globalizing Bollywood." Ranjani Mazumdar (2007, 94) has described song sequences of the 1990s as vehicles for global travel, marked by an "increasing fragmentation of the narrative."

11 Although the judges on the show always praised her performance, they often asked Ankita to concentrate on her singing.

12 See Ankita Mishra's performance, www.youtube.com/watch?v=aERlb-zOQlk. Accessed on December 7, 2021.

13 Blog by Poonam Sharma, September 1, 2007, alchemistpoonam.wordpress.com/.

14 saregamapashow.com/2007/05/participants-intro-mauli-dave-from.html (URL unavailable).

15 As Madan Gopal Singh (1998, 4–9) notes, "Rahman begins with either a bare human voice or a single musical instrument and gradually builds the orchestral movement, drawing in various musical strands, one by one, until it becomes fully choreographed. The movement is almost visual."

16 Even as we acknowledge Rahman's unique style, criticism of his musical practices also exists. Sarrazin (2014, 41) notes how sampling and synthesizers have given music directors greater control and room to exploit the talent of individual artists. Singers were expected to sing at odd hours in the night in his studio in Chennai, attuning themselves to both his spatial and temporal style of working (Jhingan 2015). The vocal and musical tracks stored on his computer are treated as raw materials that he plays around with. Citing the experience of an oboe player, Booth (2008, 290) has drawn attention to the way sampling as practiced by Rahman consolidates a process that makes musicians dispensable.

17 See Nikhil Taneja (2009).

18 It has been reported that "Kajra re" was voted to be the most popular song in South Africa. According to Nikhat Kazmi (2006), this shows how the song "transcended spatial, national, territorial boundaries to become the new age anthem."

19 There is software that allows the flanging of effects and doubling of vocals. The latter are referred to as Fix Doublers. In the analogue system, doubling of voices was produced through ADT, or Artificial Double Tracking, which was achieved through tape delay. With digital workstations ADT has been replaced by techniques like digital delay. But many recordists still prefer to use analogue methods to produce desired effects through ADT.

20 Majumdar (2009, 322) also notes the use of noise and diegetic voices on the soundtrack while the song "Ae ajnabi" is played as a radio song.

21 The use of low notes in the song complements the lyrics that articulate the desire for death. Though "Mar jawan" is an idiomatic expression in Punjabi that stands for intense and almost unbearable affect, it also alludes to a desire for death. The camera constantly focuses on Sonali (Kangana Ranaut), the leading model of the show, who commits suicide later in the film.

22 David Beer (2007) offers a critique of Michael Bull's argument that mobile music reproduction devices shut out the listener from the urban soundscape, arguing instead that the listener, even while strapped to mobile music technologies, remains connected to porous sonic terrains, to foreground an integrated, yet distracted engagement with the information structures of the city.

23 *Dev D* is inspired by Devdas, a novel written by Sarat Chandra in 1917. Several films with the same title have been made, inspired by this Bangla novel.

24 Interestingly, Aditi Singh Sharma, who sang the song, revealed in an interview that at the time of recording the song she had no idea "what the song was for—who, where, what characters, what actor. The Urdu words were so difficult. I had no idea what the lyrics meant!" See Sawhney (2013).

25 See Durga's interview on Youtube, www.youtube.com/watch?v=0N5WGPDMkjw.

26 The audiovisual realism in the postglobalization films turns toward models rather than junior artists to "populate upscale locations" in spectacle-driven blockbuster films. In this bifurcated universe of the industry, the alternative films catering to multiplex audiences too draw on realist aesthetics by mining the shantytowns, urban slums, and rural location (Jaikumar 2020, 285).

27 This is a clear departure from an earlier practice of postshoot dubbing, when actors had to dub their voices while watching the filmed sequences. The practice of sync sound recording emerged in the early 2000s.

Conclusion

1 This observation is also based on how a certain process of selection and erasure is involved in the prepublicity and post-publicity of the films under discussion. In *The Dirty Picture* (Lutharia, 2011), "Ooh la la," with Bappi Lahiri and Shreya Ghoshal's voices, became an aural hook for the film before its release. The film's soundtrack also included "Ishq sufiyana" in two versions. It was the male version in Kamal Khan's voice that was given greater prominence than Sunidhi Chauhan's version. In the film only Kamal Khan's version was used.

2 In the song "Aati kya khandala," Alka Yagnik sang for Rani Mukherjee, while Amir Khan's own voice was used through the playback system.

3 See “When Aamir Khan Admitted That He Made a ‘Huge Mistake’ by Dubbing Rani Mukerji’s Voice in Ghulam,” *Indian Express*, March 21, 2022. indianexpress.com/article/entertainment/bollywood/when-aamir-khan-admitted-huge-mistake-dubbing-rani-mukerji-voice-ghulam-7823843/. Also see “Now My Voice Is My Identity,” Rani Mukherjee, YouTube, www.youtube.com/watch?v=VvCXNNizPbA. Accessed on March 21, 2023.

4 Vidya Balan has played the role of a radio disc jockey in two films and became a star voice for Draupadi in *Mahabharat* (Khan, 2013).

5 Titles of programs like “Bhule Bisre Geet” (Forgotten and Faded Songs) on the radio are presented by matching the tonalities and voice modulation of the radio anchors of the analog era.

6 In a way similar to HMV’s attempt at creating an aura around its own archive that I discussed in chapter 4, Yash Raj Films has tried to strengthen its brand image by foregrounding its role as a custodian of Lata’s voice.

7 See Pritha Malhotra’s Instagram account. For instance, www.instagram.com/p/DFyerq7zANo/ where she performs to “Bahon mein chale aao,” originally sung by Lata Mangeshkar in *Anamika* (Jalani, 1973).

Works Cited

Adorno, Theodore. 1988. *An Introduction to the Sociology of Music*. Continuum.

Ali, Naushad. 1992. "Rewind to Melody." *Cinema Vision* 2 (2): 21–26.

Ambalewali, Zohrabai. 1971. "I Was Not Willing to Sing in Chorus." Interview in *Madhuri*, February 1, 21.

Anantharaman, Ganesh. 2008. *Bollywood Melodies: A History of Hindi Film Songs*. Penguin Books.

Arnold, Alison. 1991. "Hindi Filmi Git: On the History of Indian Popular Music." PhD diss., University of Illinois at Urbana-Champaign.

Arun, Ila. 1993. "The Song Is Being Deliberately Misunderstood." Interview with Sriprakash Menon. *Metropolis*, August 31.

Aziz, Ashraf. 2003. *Light of the Universe: Essays on Hindustani Film Music*. Three Essays Collective.

Bakhle, Janaki. 2005. *Two Men and Music: Nationalism in the Making of Indian Classical Tradition*. Oxford University Press.

Barnow, Erik, and S. Krishnaswamy. 1963 *Indian Film*. Columbia University Press.

Basu, Anustup. 2010. *Bollywood in the Age of New Media: The Geo-Televisual Aesthetic*. Edinburgh University Press.

Barthes, Roland. 1977. *Roland Barthes: Image Music Text*. Translated and selected by Stephen Heath. Fontana Press.

Baudrillard, J. 1983. *Simulations*. Translated by Paul Foss, Paul Patton, and Philip Beitchman. Semiotext(e).

Beeman, William O. 1980. "The Use of Music in Popular Film: East and West." *Indian International Quarterly* 8 (1): 77–88.

Beer, David. 2007. "Tune Out: Music, Soundscapes and the Urban Mise-en-Scène." *Information, Communication, and Society* 10 (6): 846–66.

Begum, Mubarak. 1992. "They Would Bring Out My Cassette Only If I Bought 5000 Copies." Interview by Shiela Vesuna. *Filmfare*, July 1992, 56–57.

Benjamin, Walter. 1969. "The Work of Art in the Age of Mechanical Reproduction." In *Illuminations: Essays and Reflections*. Schocken Books.

Bharatan, Raju. 1968. "On Record." *Filmfare*, October 10, 35.

Bharatan, Raju. 1970. "Ghosts that Haunt Composers." *Filmfare*, March 13, 35.

Bharatan, Raju. 1971a. "On the Threshold." *Filmfare*, January 1, 46.

Bharatan, Raju. 1971b. "The Transistor Revolution." *Filmfare*, February 12, 37.

Bharatan, Raju. 1971c. "Ghost Voice Goes a Haunting." *Filmfare*, March 12, 44–46.

Bharatan, Raju. 1971d. "Jaya Vani: New Voices for Old." *Filmfare*, November 19, 43.

Bharatan Raju. 1972a. "Pakeezah: Meena Kumari's Supreme Test." *Illustrated Weekly of India*, January 30, 52–53.

Bharatan, Raju. 1972b. "On Record: Not So Mod World." *Filmfare*, May 5, 33.

Bharatan, Raju. 1974a. "Has Asha Forgotten O.P.?" *Filmfare*, August 9, 29.

Bharatan, Raju. 1974b. "Who's Afraid of the Mangeshkars?" *Filmfare*, December 13, 37, 45.

Bharatan Raju. 1975. "Is the Asha-RD Duet Over?" *Filmfare*, May 30, 39.

Bharatan Raju. 1976. "Vasant Desai: His Music Belonged to the Court—Not the Pit." *Filmfare*, January 9, 46–47.

Bharatan, Raju. 1977. "The Composer Is Supreme." *Filmfare*, March 4, 50–51.

Bharatan, Raju. 1984. "I Remember Madan Mohan." *Filmfare*, December, 84–85.

Bharatan, Raju. 1985a. "She Stopped Singing to Save Her Marriage." *Filmfare*, February 1, 89.

Bharatan, Raju. 1985b. "The Listener Needs Variety." *Filmfare*, March 1, 88–89.

Bharatan, Raju. 1995. *Lata Mangeshkar: A Biography*. UBS Publishers.

Bhardwaj, Praveena. 1990. "Dil: Double Trouble." *Filmfare*, July, 48–49.

Bhaskar, Ira. 2012. "Emotion, Subjectivity, and the Limits of Desire: Melodrama and Modernity in Bombay Cinema, 1940s–'50s." In *Gender Meets Genre in Postwar Cinemas*, edited by Christine Gledhill. Illinois University Press.

Bhaskar, Ira. 2018 "Expressionist Aurality: The Stylized Aesthetic of Bhava in Indian Melodrama." In *Melodrama Unbound Across History, Media, and National Cultures*, edited by Christine Gledhill and Linda Williams. Columbia University Press.

Bhaskar, Ira, and Richard Allen. 2009. *Islamicate Cultures of Bombay Cinema* Tulika Books.

Bhatt, Punita. 1987. "The Lata Legend." *Filmfare*, June 1, 21–31.

Bhattacharjee, A., and Balaji Vittal. 2011. *R. D. Burman: The Man, the Music*. Harper Collins.

Bhattacharya, Indranil. 2021. "Sound." *BioScope: South Asian Screen Studies* 12 (1–2): 178–81.

Bhaumik, Kaushik. 2004. "A Brief History of Cinema from Bombay to Bollywood." *History Compass* 2 (1): 1–4.

Bhimani, Harish. 1995. *In Search of Lata Mangeshkar*. Harper Collins.

Bhirdikar, Urmila. 2007. "The Spread of North Indian Music in Maharashtra in the Late Nineteenth and Early Twentieth Century: Sociocultural Traditions of Production and Reception." In *Music and Modernity: North Indian Classical Music in an Age of Mechanical Reproducibility*, edited by Amlan Das Gupta. Thema.

Bhirdikar, Urmila. 2009. "The Heroine's Song in the Marathi Theatre between 1910 and 1920: Its Code and Its Public." In *Playhouse of Power: Theatre in Colonial India*, edited by Lata Singh. Oxford University Press.

Bhosle, Asha. 1964. "Star Focus: Asha Bhosle." *Filmfare*, December 11, 14–17.

Bhosle Asha. 1990. Interview by Subhash K. Jha. *Filmfare*, June, 49–53.

Bhosle, Asha. 1993. "Her Golden Voice" Interview with Praveena Bhardwaj. *Filmfare*, September. 52–57.

Biddu. 2010. *Made in India: Adventures of a Lifetime*. Harper Collins.

Bishnoi, Indu. 1993. "Portrait of a Melody Queen." *Cinema Vision* 2 (2): 48–50.

Booth, Gregory. 2008. *Behind the Curtain: Making Music in Mumbai's Film Studios*. Oxford University Press.

Born, Georgina. 2011. "Music and the Materialization of Identities." *Journal of Material Culture*, 16 (4): 376–88.

Bourdieu, Pierre. 1984. *Distinction: A Social Critique of the Judgment of Taste*. Harvard University Press.

Brooks, Peter. (1976) 1995. *The Melodramatic Imagination: Balzac, Henry James, Melodrama, and the Mode of Excess*. Yale University Press.

Brown, Bill. 2010. "Materiality." *Critical Terms for Media Studies*, edited by W. J. T. Mitchell and Mark B. N. Hansen. University of Chicago Press.

Bruno, Giuliana. 2002. *Atlas of Emotion: Journeys in Art, Architecture, and Film*. Verso.

Butler, Judith. 1990. *Gender Trouble: Feminism and the Subversion of Identity*. Routledge.

Casetti, Fransesco. 2015. *The Lumière Galaxy: Seven Key Words for Cinema to Come*. Columbia University Press.

Chakravorty, Pallabi. 2017. *This Is How We Dance Now! Performance in the Age of Bollywood and Reality Shows*. Oxford University Press.

Chandavarkar, Bhaskar. 1980. "The Great Film Song Controversy." *Cinema Vision* 1 (4): 66–75.

Chandavarkar, Bhaskar. 1987. "Birth of the Film Song." *Cinema in India*, April, 7–11.

Chatterjee, Partha. 1993. *The Nation and Its Fragments: Colonial and Postcolonial Histories*. Vol. 11. Princeton University Press.

Chattopadhyay, B., 2015. "The Auditory Spectacle: Designing Sound for the 'Dubbing Era' of Indian Cinema." *New Soundtrack* 5 (1): 55–68.

Chion, Michel. 1994. Audio-Vision: Sound on Screen. Translated by Claudia Gorbman, Columbia University Press.

Chion, Michel. 1999. *The Voice in Cinema*. Translated by Claudia Gorbman. Columbia University Press.

Chow, Rey. 1989. "Walter Benjamin's Love Affair with Death." *New German Critique* 48:63–86. http://www.jstor.org/stable/488233.

Conway, Kelley. 2001. "Flower of the Asphalt: The Chanteuse Realiste in 1930s French Cinema." In *Soundtrack Available: Essays on Film and Popular Music*, edited by Pamela Robertson Wojcik and Arthur Knight. Duke University Press.

Cook, Nicholas. 1998. *Music: A Very Short Introduction*. Oxford University Press. (Indian Edition, 2005).

CU. 2007. "I Am Re-Living My Journey with Some of My Contestants." Interview with Alisha Chinai. *Screen*, April 6, 23.

Das Gupta, Amlan. 2005. "Women and Music: The Case of North India." In *Women of India: Colonial and Post-Colonial Periods*, edited by Bharti Ray. Sage.

Daughtry, Martin. 2017. "Acoustic Palimpsests." In *Theorizing Sound Writing*, edited by Deborah Kapchan. Wesleyan University Press.

Deo, Aditi, and Vebhuti Duggal. 2017. "Radio, Ringtones, or Memory Cards, or How the Mobile Phone Became Our Favourite Music Playback Device." *South Asian Popular Culture* 15 (1): 41–56.

Deleuze, Gilles. 2005. *Difference and Repetition*. South Asia Edition. Continuum.

Deleuze, Gilles, and F. A. Guattari. 1987. *A Thousand Plateaus: Capitalism and Schizophrenia*. Vol. II. University of Minnesota Press.

Deshpande, Ashwini. 2004. "Lata Mangeshkar: The Singer and the Voice." *Economic and Political Weekly* 39 (48): 5179–84. www.jstor.org/stable/4415842.

Devi, Saraswati. 1983. "Lasting Lady, Khurshid Saraswati." Interview by Shashikant Kinikar. *Cinema Vision* 2 (2): 7–72.

Dhurandhar, Arvind. 1976. "Vintage Songs from Pakistan." *Filmfare*, March 4, 18.

Dhurandhar, Arvind. 1983. "Unbeaten because Unbeatable." *Filmfare*, February 1, 25–27.

Dhurandhar, Arvind. 1988. "Lata Plays Favourites." *Filmfare*, February 16, 14–17.

Doane, Mary Anne. 1985. "The Voice in Cinema: The Articulation of Body and Space." In *Movies and Methods*, volume 2, edited by Bill Nichols. University of California Press.

Doane, Mary Anne. 1987. *The Desire to Desire: The Woman's Film of the 1940s*. Indiana University Press.

Duggal, Vebhuti. 2010. "The Hindi Film Song Remix: Memory, History, Affect." PhD diss., Department of Cinema Studies, School of Arts and Aesthetics, Jawaharlal Nehru University.

Duggal, Vebhuti. 2018. "Imagining Sound through the Pharmaish: Radios and Request Post-Cards in North India, c. 1955–1975." *BioScope: South Asian Screen Studies* 9 (1): 1–23.

Dutt, Geeta. 1971. "All My Songs Are Special to Me." *Madhuri*, January 8. (Special issue on playback singers.)

Dwyer, Rachel, and Divia Patel. 2002. *Cinema India: The Visual Culture of Hindi Film*. Rutgers University Press.

Eidsheim, Nina S. 2011. "Sensing Voice: Materiality and the Lived Body in Singing and Listening." *The Senses and Society* 6 (2): 133-55.

Eidsheim, Nina S. 2015. *Sensing Sound: Singing and Listening as Vibrational Practice*. Duke University Press.

Eidsheim, Nina S. 2019. *Race of Sound: Listening, Timbre, and Vocality in African American Music*. Duke University Press.

Ellis, John. 2002. *Visible Fictions: Cinema Television Video*. Routledge.

Elsaesser, Thomas, and Malte Hagener. 2015. *Film Theory: An Introduction Through the Senses*. Routledge.

Feld, Steven. 2003. "A Rainforest Acoustemology." In *The Auditory Culture Reader*, edited by Michael Bull and Les Back. Berg.

Fernandes, Naresh. 2012. *Tajmahal Foxtrot: The Story of Bombay's Jazz Age*. Roli Books.

Felski, Rita. 1995. *The Gender of Modernity*. Harvard University Press.

Fiske, John. 1982. *Introduction to Communication Studies*. 2nd ed. Routledge.

Frith, Simon. 1989. "Towards an Aesthetic of Popular Music." In *Music and Society: The Politics of Composition, Performance, and Reception*, edited by Richard Leppert and Susan McClary. Cambridge University Press.

Frith, Simon. 1998. *Performing Rites: On the Value of Popular Music*. Harvard University Press.

Gadgil, Gangdhar. 1967. "Meet Lata Mangeshkar." *Illustrated Weekly of India*, April 30, 36–37.

Gadihoke, Sabeena. 2011. "Sensational Love Scandals and their After-Lives: The Epic Tale of Nanavati." *BioScope: South Asian Screen Studies* 2 (2): 103–28.

Galloway, Alexander. 2012. *The Interface Effect*. Polity.

Gandhy, Behroze, and Rosie Thomas. 1991. "Three Indian Film Stars." In *Stardom: Industry of Desire*, edited by Christine Gledhill. Routledge.

Gehlawat, Ajay. 2023. "Disco Nazia: Disarticulating Female Playback and the Heroine in Early '80s Hindi Cinema." *South Asian History and Culture* 14 (3): 285–97.

Ghosh, Shohini. 2002. "Queer Pleasures for Queer People: Film Television, and Queer Sexuality in India." In *Same-Sex Love and Eroticism in Indian Culture and Society*, edited by Ruth Vanita. Routledge.

Ghosh, Shohini. 2004. "Bollywood Cinema and Queer Sexualities." In *Queer Theory: Law, Culture, Empire*, edited by Robert Leckey and Kim Brooks. Routledge.

Gibbs, Anna. 2010. "After Affect." In *The Affect Theory Reader*, edited by Melissa Gregg and Gregory Seigworth. Duke University Press.

Gledhill, Christine. 1991. "Signs of Melodrama." In *Stardom: Industry of Desire*, edited by Christine Gledhill. Psychology Press.

Gold, Tim. 2012. "Towards an Ecology of Materials." *Annual Review of Anthropology* 41:427–44.

Gooptu, Sharmishtha. 2007. "The Talkie Revolution: Indian Cinema c. 1931 and Thereafter." *Biblio* 12 (1 & 2): 20.

Gopal, Sangita. 2011. *Conjugations: Marriage and Form in New Bollywood Cinema*. University of Chicago Press.

Gopal, Sangita, and Sujata Moorti. 2008. Introduction to *Global Bollywood: Travels of Hindi Song and Dance*. University of Minnesota Press.

Gopalan, Lalitha. 2002. *Cinema of Interruptions: Action Genres in Contemporary Indian Cinema*. BFI Publishing.

Gregg, Melissa, and Gregory Seigworth, eds. 2010. Introduction to *The Affect Theory Reader*. Duke University Press.

Grosz, Elizabeth. 1994. *Volatile Bodies: Towards a Corporeal Feminism*. Indiana University Press.

Hansen, Kathryn. 1999. "Making Women Visible: Gender and Race Cross-Dressing in the Parsi Theatre." *Theatre Journal* 51:127–47.

Hansen, Kathryn. 2003. "Linguistic Pluralism and Community Formation in the Nineteenth Century Parsi Theatre." *Modern Asian Studies* 37 (2): 381–405.

Hansen, Mark B. N. 2004. *New Philosophy for New Media*. Foreword by Tim Lenoir. MIT Press.

Hansen, Mark B. N. 2010. "New Media." In *Critical Terms for Media Studies*, edited by W. J. T. Mitchell and Mark B. N. Hansen. University of Chicago Press.

Hansen, Miriam Bratu. 2000. "The Mass Production of the Senses: Classical Cinema as Vernacular Modernism." In *Reinventing Film Studies*, edited by C. Gledhill and L. Williams. Arnold.

Hassam, Andrew. 2012. "'It Was Filmed in My Home Town': Diasporic Audiences and Foreign Locations in Indian Popular Cinema." In *Travels of Bollywood Cinema: From Bombay to LA*, edited by Anjali Gera Roy and Chua Beng Huat. Oxford University Press.

Hemment, Drew. 2004. "Affect and Individuation in Popular Electronic Music." In *Deleuze and Music*, edited by Ian Buchanan and M. Swiboda. Edinburgh University Press.

Hennion, A. 2003. "Music and Mediation: Toward a New Sociology of Music." In *The Cultural Study of Music*, edited by M. Clayton, T. Herberts, and R. Middleton. Routledge.

Hennion, A. 2004. "Pragmatics of Taste." In *The Blackwell Companion to the Sociology of Culture*, edited by Mark Jacobs and Nancy Hanrahan. Blackwell.

Highmore, Ben. 2010. “Bitter after Taste: Affect, Food, and Social Aesthetics.” In *The Affect Theory Reader*, edited by Melissa Gregg and Gregory Seigworth. Duke University Press.

Hilmes, Michele. 2008. “Television Sound: Why This Silence?” *Music, Sound, and the Moving Image* 2 (2):153–61.

Hughes, Stephen. P. 2007. “Music in the Age of Mechanical Reproduction: Drama, Gramophone, and the Beginnings of Tamil Cinema.” *Journal of Asian Studies* 66 (1): 3–34.

Indraganti, Kiranmayi. 2016. *Her Majestic Voice: South Indian Female Playback Singers and Stardom, 1945–1955*. Oxford University Press.

Iyer, Mahalakshmi. 2010. Interview conducted by the author. May 18.

Iyer, Usha. 2020. *Dancing Women: Choreographing Corporeal Histories of Hindi Cinema*. Oxford University Press.

Jaikumar, Priya. 2020. *Where Histories Reside: India’s Filmed Space*. Orient Blackswan.

Jha, Shweta. 2009. “Eurasian Women as Tawa’ifs Singers and Recording Artists: Entertainment and Identity-Making in Colonial India.” *African and Asian Studies* 8 (3): 268–87.

Jha, Subhash, K. 1988. “The Cover Version Craze.” *Filmfare*, 1, 36.

Jha, Subhash K. 1998. “Musical Notes.” *Filmfare*, July, 138.

Jhingan, Shikha. 2001. *Born to Sing* (a documentary on the Mirasans of Punjab), IGNCA.

Jhingan, Shikha. 2009. “The Singer, the Star and the Chorus.” *Seminar*, Special Issue on Circuits of Cinema, 598.

Jhingan, Shikha. 2011. “Re-Embodying the ‘Classical’: The Bombay Film Song in the 1950s.” *BioScope: South Asian Screen Studies* 2 (2): 157–79.

Jhingan, Shikha. 2015. “Backpacking Sounds: Sneha Khanwalkar and the ‘New’ Soundtrack of Bombay Cinema.” *Feminist Media Histories* 1 (4): 71–88.

Jhingan, S. 2016. “Sonic Ruptures: Music Mobility and the Media.” In *Media and Utopia: History, Imagination, and Technology*, edited by Arvind Rajagopal and Anupama Rao. Routledge India.

Jhingan, Shikha. 2022. “The Textual, Musical and Sonic Journey of the Ghazal in Bombay Cinema.” In *Bombay Cinema’s Islamicate Histories*, edited by Ira Bhaskar and Richard Allen. Orient Blackswan.

Jhunjhunwala, Udita. 2009. *Jaya Bachchan: Women in Indian Film*. Zubaan.

Joshi, G. N. 1980. “The Phonograph Comes to India.” *Cinema Vision* 1 (4): 41–47.

Beaster-Jones, Jayson. 2015. *Bollywood Sounds: The Cosmopolitan Mediations of Hindi Film Song*. Oxford University Press.

Kabir, Nasreen. 2009. *Lata Mangeshkar . . . in Her Own Voice: Conversations with Nasreen Munni Kabir*. Niyogi Books.

Kabir, Nasreen. 2011. *A. R. Rahman: The Spirit of Music; Biographical Conversations with Nasreen Munni Kabir*. Om Books International.

Karamblekar, Deepak. 1997. "Singing Sensation." *TV Today*, February 1, 82–83.

Kasbekar, Asha. 2001. "Hidden Pleasures: Negotiating the Myth of the Female Ideal in Popular Hindi Cinema." In *Pleasure and the Nation: The History, Politics, and Consumption of Public Culture in India*, edited by Rachel Dwyer and Christopher Pinney. Oxford University Press.

Kassabian, Anahid. 2013. *Ubiquitous Listening: Affect Attention and Distributed Subjectivity*. University of California Press.

Katz, Mark. 2004. *Capturing Sound: How Technology Has Changed Music*. University of California Press.

Kaviraj, Sudipta. 2004. "Reading a Song on the City: Images of the City in Literature and Films." In *City Flicks: Indian Cinema and the Urban Experience*, edited by Preben Kaarsholm. Seagull Books.

Kazmi, Nikhat. 2006. OPED, *Times of India*, January 14.

Khayyam. 1992. "A Music Odyssey." Interview with Sathya Saran. *Cinema in India*, April, 20–24.

Kidwai, Saleem. 2004. "The Singing Ladies Find a Voice." *Seminar*, 540. Seminar Magazine on CD-ROM, 1988–99.

Kinnear, Michael. 1994. *The Gramophone Company's First Indian Recordings: 1899–1908*. Bombay Popular Prakashan.

Kittler, A. Friedrich. 1999. *Gramophone, Film, Typewriter*. Stanford University Press.

Knapczyk, Peter. 2022. "Reflections from Padmini's Palace: Women's Voices of Longing and Lament in Sufi Romance and Shi'i Elegy." In *Bombay Cinema's Islamicate Histories*, edited by Ira Bhaskar and Richard Allen. Orient BlackSwan.

Kodikal, Mukta. 1961a. "Ghost Voices of the Indian Screen, Part I." *Filmfare*, November 17, 25–28.

Kodikal, Mukta. 1961b. "Ghost Voices of the Indian Screen, Part II." *Filmfare*, December 1, 19–21.

Kohli, Ajit. 2007. Interview conducted by the author, May 23.

Kohli, Sanjeev. 2007. Interview by the author, December 28.

Kohli-Khandekar, Vanita. 2010. *The Indian Media Business*. Response Books.

Kopytoff, Igor. 1986. "The Cultural Biography of Things: Commoditization as a Process." *The Social Life of Things: Commodities in Cultural Perspective*, edited by Arjun Appadurai. Cambridge University Press.

Krishnamurthy, Kavita. 1987. "Who's That Girl?" Interview by Aplana Chaudhary. *Playback, Play Forward*, February, 12–16.

Krishnamurthy, Kavita. 1996. "Crooning Glory." Interview by Jitesh Pillai. *Filmfare*, June, 80–83.

Kumar, Gulshan. 1990. "Is Gulshan Kumar Striking a False Note?" Interview by Praveena Bhardwaj. *Filmfare*, September.

Kumatkar, R. M. 1992. "Audio Reviews: Shraddhanjali, Inspiring Tributes." *Screen*, October 16, 23.

LaBelle, Brandon. 2010. Introduction to *Acoustic Territories: Sound Culture and Everyday Life*. Continuum.

Lakshmi, C. S. 2000. "Interview with Naina Devi." In *The Singer and the Song: Conversation with Women Musicians*. Kali for Women.

Lastra, J. 1992. "Reading, Writing and Representing Sound." In *Sound Theory, Sound Practice*, edited by Rick Altman. Routledge.

Lawrence, Amy. 1988. "The Pleasures of the Echo: The Listener and the Voice." *Journal of Film and Video*, no. 4 (Fall): 3–15.

Lelyveld, David. 1994. "Upon the Subdominant: Administering Music on All-India Radio." *Social Text* 39:111–27.

Leppert, Richard. 1993. *The Sight of Sound: Music, Representation, and the History of the Body*. University of California Press.

Liang, Lawrence. 2005. "Porous Legalities and Avenues of Participation." In *Bare Acts, Sarai Reader 05*. CSDS.

Liang, Lawrence. 2015. "Cinematic Justice: The Law in/and of Films in India." PhD diss. Department of Cinema Studies, School of Arts and Aesthetics, Jawaharlal Nehru University.

Lutgendorf, Philip. 2006. "Is There an Indian Way of Filmmaking?" *International Journal of Hindu Studies* 10 (3): 227–56.

Mahadevan, Sudhir. 2015. *A Very Old Machine: The Many Origins of Cinema in India*. State University of New York Press.

Majumdar Neepa. 2001. "The Embodied Voice: Song Sequences and Stardom in Popular Hindi Cinema." In *Soundtrack Available: Essays on Film and Popular Music*, edited by Pamela Robertson Wojcik and Arthur Knight. Duke University Press.

Majumdar, Neepa. 2009. "Beyond Song Sequences: Theorizing Sound in Indian Cinema." In *Sound and Music in Film and Visual Media: A Critical Overview*, edited by G. Harper, R. Doughty, and J. Eisentraut. Continuum.

Majumdar Neepa. 2010. *Wanted Cultured Ladies Only! Female Stardom and Cinema in India, 1930s–1950s*. University of Illinois Press.

Majumdar, Neepa. 2020. "Between Rage and Song: Voice, Performance and Instrumentation in Shanta Apte's Films of the 1930s." In *Indian Sound Cultures, Indian Sound Citizenship*, edited by Laura Brueck, Jacob Smith, and Neil Verma. University of Michigan Press.

Mangeshkar, Lata. 1958. "Indian Film and Music Directors." *Filmfare*, January 3, 42–43.

Mangeshkar, Lata. 1964. "Star Focus: My Colleagues in the Profession." *Filmfare*, October 2, 20–23.

Mangeshkar, Lata. 1983a. Interview by Sumit Mitra. *Cinema Vision* 2 (2): 44–45.

Mangeshkar, Lata. 1983b. "Lata on Others." *Cinema Vision* 2 (2): 46–47.

Mangeshkar, Lata. 1999. "Lata Plays Favourites." Interview by Subhash K. Jha. *Filmfare*, October, 118–23.

Manovich, Lev. 2013. *Software Takes Command*. Bloomsbury Academic.

Mankekar, Purnima. 1999b. *Screening Culture, Viewing Politics: An Ethnography of Television, Womanhood, and Nation in Postcolonial India*. Duke University Press.

Manuel, Peter. 1993. *Cassette Culture: Popular Music and Technology in North India*. Oxford University Press.

Marks, Laura. 2000. *The Skin of the Film: Intercultural Cinema, Embodiment, and the Senses*. Duke University Press.

Mazumdar, Ranjani. 2007. *Bombay Cinema: An Archive of the City*. University of Minnesota Press.

Mazumdar, Ranjani. 2009. "Cosmopolitan Dreams." *Seminar*, Circuits of Cinema, 598, 14–20.

Mazumdar, Ranjani, and Shikha Jhingan. 1998. *The Power of the Image*. Twelve-part series on Bombay Cinema. BITV.

Mazzarella, William. 2003. *Shoveling Smoke: Advertising and Globalization in Contemporary India*. Duke University Press.

Miller, Daniel. 2005. "Materiality: An Introduction." In *Materiality*. Duke University Press.

Mini, Darshana Shreedhar. 2021. "Body." *BioScope: South Asian Screen Studies* 12 (1–2): 39–42.

Mishra, Ankita. 2008. Interview by author, December 9, Delhi NCR.

Mishra, Yatindra. 2009. "The Bai and the Dawn of Hindi Film Music (1925–1945)." Translated by Anamika and Madhu B. Joshi. *Book Review*, 33(2): 46–47.

Mishra, Yatindra. 2016. *Lata: Sur-Gatha; Musical Journey of Lata Mangeshkar*. Vani Prakashan.

Mitra, Sumit. 1983. "O Undisputable and Indispensable Queen." *Cinema Vision* 2 (2): 38–43.

Mohan, Reena, and Dibya Choudhuri. 1996. "Of Wayward Girls and Wicked Women." *Deep Focus* 6:4–14.

Mohan, Shanti. 1983. "Unbeaten. . . ." Letters to the editor. *Filmfare*, March 16, 6–7.

Morcom, Anna. 2007. *Hindi Film Songs and the Cinema*. Ashgate.

Morcom, Anna. 2016. *Courtesans, Bar Girls, and Dancing Boys: The Illicit World of Indian Dance*. Hachette India.

Morcom, Anna. 2019. "Performing, Performativity and Melodrama as Dramatic Substance in Hindi Film Songs." *Studies in South Asian Film and Media* 10 (2): 129–47.

Mukherjee, Debashree. 2020. *Bombay Hustle: Making Movies in a Colonial City*. Columbia University Press.

Mukherjee, Madhuja. 2007. "Early Indian Talkies: Voice, Performance and Aura." *Journal of the Moving Image* 6:39–61.

Mukherjee, Madhuja. 2012. *Aural Films, Oral Cultures: Essays on Cinema from the Early Sound Era*. Jadavpur University Press.

Mukherjee, Madhuja. 2017. "Music, Sound Noise: Interposition of the Local and the Global in Anurag Kashyap's Gangs of Wasseypur." In *Music in Contemporary Film: Memory, Voice, Identity*, edited by Jayson Beaster-Jones and Natalie Sarrazin. Routledge.

Mukherjee, Roshmila. 1994. "Nights in White Satin: Mujra, Men, Meena Kumari . . . the Pakeezah Tale Retold." *Filmfare*, September, 97–100.

Mukherjee, Silpa. 2016. "High-Octave Soprano to Auto-Tuned Rapper: Item Numbers and Technologies of Sonic Eroticism." *Soundtrack* 9 (1–2): 59–71.

Mukherjee, Subhendu. 1994. "Meet the Originals in the Version Business." *Times of India*, December 16.

Mukherji, Kumar. 2006. *The Lost World of Hindustani Music*. Penguin.

Muzavar, Ishaq. 1988. "Dastaan adhure pyaar ki." *Madhuri*, April 22, 46–47.

Nancy, Jean-Luc. 2007. *Listening*. Translated by Charlotte Mandell. Fordham University Press.

Nandy, Ashis. 2001. *An Ambiguous Journey to the City: The Village and the Other Odd Ruins of the Self in the Indian Imagination*. Oxford University Press.

Niazi, Sarah Rahman. 2011. "Cinema and the Reinvention of the Self: Women Performers in the Bombay Film Industry 1925–47." Master's thesis, Department of Cinema Studies, School of Arts and Aesthetics, Jawahar Lal Nehru University.

Niranjana Tejaswini. (2020). *Musicophilia in Mumbai: Performing Subjects and the Metropolitan Unconscious*. New Delhi, Tulika.

Oldernburg, Veena. 1990. "Lifestyle as Resistance: The Case of the Courtesans of Lucknow India." *Feminist Studies* 16 (2): 259–87.

Orsini, Francesca. 2009. *The Hindi Public Sphere 1920–1940: Language and Literature in the Age of Nationalism*. Oxford University Press.

Pandit, Sulakshana. 1980. "Mike or Camera—The Involvement Is the Same." Interview by Shyam Hardikar. *Filmfare*, June 16, 25–27.

Patil, Vishakhadutt. 1988. "Letters to the Editor." *Filmfare*, April 16, 9.

Paudwal, Anuradha. 1994. "Remains of the Day." Interview by Roshmila Mukherjee. *Filmfare*, May, 70–74.

Paudwal, Anuradha. 2010. Interview by the author, January, 24.

Pemmaraju, Gautam. 2013. "Soundbaazi: Space, Place and Meaning in the Hindi Film Soundtrack." *Art Connect* 7 (1): 60–81.

Perron, Lalita du. 2002. "Thumri: A Discussion of the Female Voice of Hindustani Music." *Modern Asian Studies* 36 (1): 173–93.

Pinney, Christopher. 2002. "The Indian Work of Art in the Age of Mechanical Reproduction." In *Media Worlds: Anthropology on New Terrain*, edited by Faye Ginsberg, L. Abu-Lughod, and Brian Larkin. University of California Press.

Prasad, Madhava. 1998. *The Ideology of the Hindi Film: A Historical Construction*. Oxford University Press.

Prasad, Madhava. 2013. "Diverting Diseases." In *Figurations in Indian Film*, edited by Meheli Sen and Anustup Basu. Palgrave Macmillan.

Premchand, Manek. 2003. *Yesterday's Melodies Today's Memories*. Jharna Books.

Punathambekar, Aswin. 2010. "From Indiafm.com to Radio Ceylon: New Media and the Making of the Bombay Film Industry." *Media and Society* 32 (5): 841–57.

Punathambekar, Aswin. 2013. *From Bombay to Bollywood: The Making of a Global Media Industry*. New York University Press.

Punathambekar, Aswin, and Sriram Mohan. 2020. "Sound Clouds: Listening and Citizenship in Indian Public Culture." In *Indian Sound Cultures, Indian Sound Citizenship*. University of Michigan Press.

Purushottam, A. 1998. "Music for the Uninitiated." September 1, 16.

Rag, Pankaj. 2006. *Dhunon ki yatra*. Rajkamal.

Rahaim, Matt. 2008. "Gesture and Melody in Indian Vocal Music." *Gesture* 8 (3): 325–47.

Rahaim, Matt. 2012. *Musicking Bodies: Gesture and Voice in Hindustani Music*. Wesleyan University Press.

Rai, Amit S. 2009. *Untimely Bollywood: Globalization and India's New Media Assemblage*. Oxford University Press.

Rajadhyaksha, Ashish. 1987. "The Phalke Era: Conflict of Traditional Form and Modern Technology." *Journal of Arts and Ideas* 14 (15): 47–78.

Rajadhyaksha, Ashish. 2007. "An Aesthetic for Film Sound in India." *Journal of the Moving Image*, 6.

Rajendran, Girija. 1973. "Why the Voice Famine." *Star and Style*, August 17.

Rajendran, Girija. 1983. "In Search of Self." *Cinema Vision* 2 (2): 42.

Rajendran, Girija. 1986. "Khayyam: Karoge Yaad Toh." *Filmfare*, September, 47–49.

Rajkumari. 1983. "When a Song Paid Fifty and Petrol was Six Annas a Dozen." Interview by Ashok Da Ranade. *Cinema Vision* 2 (2): 16–19.

Ram, Kalpana. 2011. "The Affective Pleasures of Music and Dance Spectatorship and Nationhood in Indian Middle-Class Modernity." *Journal of the Royal Anthropological Institute* 17:S159–S175.

Ramamurthy, Priti. 2008. "All-Consuming Nationalism: The Indian Modern Girl in the 1920s and 30s." In *The Modern Girl Around the World: Consumption, Modernity, and Globalization*, edited by Weinbaum, Alys Eve, Lynn M. Thomas, Priti Ramamurthy, Uta G. Poiger, Madeleine Yue Dong, and Tani Barlow. Duke University Press.

Ranade, Ashok Da. 1980. "The Extraordinary Importance of the Indian Film Song." *Cinema Vision* 1 (4): 4–11.

Ranade, Ashok Da. 1997. *Hindustani Music*. National Book Trust.

Ranade, Ashok Da. 2006. *Hindi Film Song: Music Beyond Boundaries*. Bibliophile South Asia.

Rao, Vidya. 1990. "*Thumri* as Feminine Voice." *Economic and Political Weekly* 25 (17): WS 31–39.

Ravikant. 2015. "Words in Motion: A Social History of the Language of 'Hindi' Cinema (c. 1931 till the Present)." PhD diss., University of Delhi.

Ravikant. 2021. "Language." *BioScope: South Asian Screen Studies* 12 (1–2): 121–24.

Rekha. 1993. "Rekha's Favourite Ten." Interview with Rauf Ahmed. *Filmfare*, March 11–15.

Sampath, Vikram. 2010. *My Name Is Gauhar Jaan*. Rupa.

Sangari, Kumkum. 2011. "Viraha: A Trajectory in the Nehruvian Era." In *Poetics and Politics of Sufism and Bhakti in South Asia: Love, Loss, and Liberation*, edited by Kavita Panjabi. Orient BlackSwan.

Sarin, Suman. 1987. "Swarangan." *Madhuri*, April 24, 45.

Sargam, Sadhana. 2011. Interview with the author, February 5.

Sarrazin, Natalie. 2009. "Songs from the Heart: Musical Coding, Emotional Sentiment, and Transnational Sonic Identity in India's Popular Film Music." In *Global Bollywood*, edited by Anandam P. Kavoori and Aswin Punathambekar. Oxford University Press.

Sarrazin, Natalie. 2014. "Global Masala: Digital Identities and Aesthetic Trajectories in Post-Liberalization Indian Film Music." In *More Than Bollywood: Studies in Indian Popular Music*, edited by Gregory D. Booth and Bradley Slope. Oxford University Press.

Savage, Steve. 2013. *Bytes and Backbeats: Repurposing Music in the Digital Age*. University of Michigan Press.

Sawhney, Isha Singh. 2013. "The Ladies Sing the Blues." *Caravan*, February, 92–101.

Schofield, Katherine Butler. 2015. "Learning to Taste the Emotions: The Mughal Rasika." In *Music, Literature, and Performance in North India*, edited by Francesca Orsini and Katherine Butler Schofield. Open Book Publishers.

Schreffler, G. 2011. "Music and Musicians in Punjab: An Introduction to the Special Issue." *Journal of Punjab Studies*, 18:1–48.

Sen, Biswarup. 2008. "The Sounds of Indian Modernity: The Evolution of Bollywood Film Song." In *Global Bollywood: Travels of Hindi Cinema*, edited by S. Gopal and S. Moorti.

Sen, Meheli. 2017. *Haunted Bollywood: Gender, Genre, and the Supernatural in Hindi Commercial Cinema*. Texas University Press.

Seth, Raghunath. 1980. "The Sound of Magic." *Cinema Vision* 1, no. 4 (October): 51–55.

Shankar, Ehsaan Loy. 2006. "Music Makers." *First City*, November, 31–37.

Sharma, Poonam. 2007. "Light Has Gone Out of Indian Idol." September 1. alchemistpoonam.wordpress.com/.

Sharma, Richa. 2010. Interview by the author, June 7.

Shaviro, S., 2016. "Splitting the Atom: Post-Cinematic Articulations of Sound and Vision." In *Post-Cinema: Theorizing 21st Century Film*, edited by Shane Denson and Julia Leyda. Reframe Books.

Shope, Bradley. 2014. "Latin American Music in Moving Pictures and Jazzy Cabarets in Mumbai, 1930s to 1950s." In *More Than Bollywood: Studies in Indian Popular Music*, edited by Gregory Booth and Bradley Shope. Oxford University Press.

Silverman, Kaja. 1988. *The Acoustic Mirror: The Female Voice in Psychoanalysis and Cinema*. Indiana University Press.

Singh, Khushwant. 1970. "The Editor's Page: Mangeshkar's Story for the Weekly." *Illustrated Weekly of India*, April 12, 39.

Singh, Madan Gopal. 1998. "Jottings on the Indian Film Song." *Cinemaya* 39–40:4–9.

Singh, Surinder. 1974. "The Maharanis Are No Witches." *Filmfare*, November 1, 30–31.

Skillman, T. 1986. "The Bombay Hindi Film Song Genre: A Historical Survey." *Yearbook for Traditional Music* 18:133–44.

Small, Christopher. 1998. *Musicking: The Meanings of Performing and Listening*. Wesleyan University Press.

Srivastava, Sanjay. 2004. "Voice, Gender and Space in Time of Five-Year Plans: The Idea of Lata Mangeshkar." *Economic and Political Weekly*, 39 (20): 2018–28.

Srivastava, Sanjay. 2006. "The Voice of the Nation and the Five Year Plan Hero: Speculations on Gender, Space and Popular Culture." In *Fingerprinting Popular Culture: The Mythic and the Iconic in Indian Cinema*, edited by Vinay Lal and Ashis Nandy. Oxford University Press.

Star and Style. 1973. "As Real as They May Have It." August 31, 15.

Sterne, Jonathan. 2003. *The Audible Past: Cultural Origins of Sound Reproduction*. Duke University Press.

Stewart, Susan. 1984. *On Longing: Narratives of the Miniature, the Gigantic, the Souvenir, and the Collection*. Duke University Press.

Stiegler, Bernard. 2010. "Memory." In *Critical Terms for Media Studies*, edited by W. J. T. Mitchell and Mark B. N. Hansen. University of Chicago Press.

Straw, Will. 2012. "Music and Material Culture." In *The Cultural Study of Music: A Critical Introduction*, edited by Martin Clayton, Trevor Herbert, and Richard Middleton. Routledge.

Subramanian, Lakshmi. 2005. "The Voice in Colonial and Post-Colonial India." *Economic and Political Weekly* 40(15): 1561–62.

Subramanian, Lakshmi. 2008. *New Mansions for Music: Performance, Pedagogy, and Criticism*. Social Science Press.

Sulakhe, Bela. 2011. Interview conducted by the author, February 3.

Sundar, Pavitra. 2017. "Gender, Bawdiness and Bodily Voices: Bombay Cinema's Audio-Visual Contract and the 'Ethnic' Woman." In *Locating the Voice in Film: Critical Approaches and Global Practices*, edited by Tom Whittaker and Sarah Wright. Oxford University Press.

Sundar, Pavitra. 2023. *Listening with a Feminist Ear: Soundwork in Bombay Cinema*. University of Michigan Press.

Sundaram, Ravi. 2010. *Pirate Modernity*. Routledge, India.

Sundaram, Ravi, ed. 2013. Introduction to *No Limits: Media Studies from India*. Oxford University Press.

Sundaram, Ravi. 2015. "Post-Postcolonial Sensory Infrastructures." *E-Flux*, number 64.

Sundaram, Ravi. 2021. "Analogue and Digital." *BioScope: South Asian Screen Studies* 12 (1–2): 14–17.

Sunya, Samhita. 2020. "High Fidelity Ecologies: India Versus Noise Pollution in the Contemporary Public Sphere." In *Indian Sound Cultures, Indian Sound Citizenship*, edited by Laura Brueck, Jacob Smith, and Neil Verma. University of Michigan Press.

Syed, Siraj. 1989. "Audio Reviews: Diamonds Forever." *Screen*, January 12.

Syed, Siraj. 1994. "Nostalgia Rules the Waves." *Times of India*, May 16.

Taneja, Nikhil. 2009. "From Melody to Dev D." *Hindustan Times*, December 31. web.archive.org/web/20101204160308/http://www.hindustantimes.com/From-Melody-to-Dev-D/Article1-492354.aspx.

Taussig, Michael. 1993. *Mimesis and Alterity: A Particular History of the Senses*. Psychology Press.

Thomas, Rosie. 2011. "Distant Voices, Magic Knives: Lal-e-Yaman and the Transition to Sound in Bombay Cinema." In *Beyond the Boundaries of*

Bollywood: The Many Forms of Hindi Cinema, edited by R. Dwyer and J. Pinto. Oxford University Press.

Tiwari, Harish. 1971. "Ubharte swar, samasyain aur hal." *Madhuri*, January 8, 43.

Vasudevan, Ravi. 2000. "The Politics of Cultural Address in Transitional Cinema." In *Reinventing Film Studies*, edited by Christine Gledhill and Linda Williams. Arnold.

Vasudevan, Ravi. 2010. *The Melodramatic Public: Film Form and Spectatorship in Indian Cinema*. Permanent Black.

Warudi, Gauri. 1991. "Striking the High Notes." *Sunday Observer*, June 2–8.

Wani, Aarti. 2016. *Fantasy of Modernity: Romantic Love in Bombay Cinema of the 1950s*. Cambridge University Press.

Wegenstein, Bernadette. 2010. "Body." In *Critical Terms for Media Studies*, edited by W. J. T. Mitchell and Mark B. N. Hansen. Chicago University Press.

Weidman, Amanda. 2006. *Singing the Classical, Voicing the Modern: The Post-colonial Politics of Music in South India*. Seagull.

Weidman, Amanda. 2021. *Brought to Life by the Voice: Playback Singing and Cultural Politics in South India*. California University Press.

Williams, Raymond. 1977. *Marxism and Literature*. Oxford University Press.

Williams, Raymond. 1994. "Selections from Marxism and Literature." In *Culture/Power/History: A Reader in Contemporary Social Theory*, edited by Nicholas Dirks, Geoff Eleye, and Sherry B. Ortner. Princeton University Press.

Yagnik, Alka. 1990. "Everyone Wants Us to Sound Like Lata Ji." Interview by Punita Bhatt. *Filmfare*, December, 34–37.

Yagnik, Alka. 2000. "The Natural: Alka Takes Centre Stage." Interview by Sub-hash K. Jha. *Filmfare*, September, 92–96.

Index

Note: Page numbers appearing in italics refer to photographs.